Queer Diplomacy: A Transgender Journey in the Foreign Service

ADST MEMOIRS AND OCCASIONAL PAPERS SERIES
Series Editors: LISA TERRY & MARGERY THOMPSON

In 2003, the Association for Diplomatic Studies and Training (ADST), a nonprofit organization founded in 1986, created the Memoirs and Occasional Papers Series to preserve firsthand accounts and other informed observations on foreign affairs for scholars, journalists, and the general public. Through its book series, its Foreign Affairs Oral History program, and its support for the training of foreign affairs personnel at the State Department's Foreign Service Institute, ADST seeks to promote understanding of American diplomacy and those who conduct it. In this compelling memoir, Robyn McCutcheon, a proud transgender woman, shares her remarkable journey as a diplomat with the U.S. Department of State.

RELATED TITLES FROM ADST SERIES

THOMPSON BUCHANAN, *Mossy Memoir of a Rolling Stone*

CHARLES T. CROSS, *Born a Foreigner: A Memoir of the American Presence in Asia*

JOHN GUNTHER DEAN, *Danger Zones: A Diplomat's Fight for America's Interests*

PETER D. EICHER, *Raising the Flag: Adventures of America's First Envoys in Faraway Lands*

BRANDON GROVE, *Behind Embassy Walls: The Life and Times of an American Diplomat*

DONALD P. GREGG, *Pot Shards: Fragments of a Life Lived in CIA, the White House, and the Two Koreas*

CAMERON R. HUME, *Mission to Algiers: Diplomacy by Engagement*

DENNIS JETT, *American Ambassadors: The Past, Present, and Future of America's Diplomats*

WILLIAM MORGAN and CHARLES STUART KENNEDY, eds., *American Diplomats: The Foreign Service at Work*

DAVID D. NEWSOM, *Witness to a Changing World*

RAYMOND F. SMITH, *The Craft of Political Analysis for Diplomats*

For a complete list of series titles, visit <adst.org/publications>

QUEER DIPLOMACY

A Transgender Journey in the Foreign Service

Robyn McCutcheon

Westphalia Press
An Imprint of the Policy Studies Organization
Washington, DC
2024

Westphalia Press
An imprint of Policy Studies Organization
1367 Connecticut Avenue NW
Washington, D.C. 20036
info@ipsonet.org

ISBN: 978-1-63723-639-0

Cover art by by Найк Волков (Nike Volkov)

Daniel Gutierrez-Sandoval, Executive Director
PSO and Westphalia Press

Updated material and comments on this edition
can be found at the Westphalia Press website:
www.westphaliapress.org

Table of Contents

For Dima

На малом огне, на огне памяти ничего не сгорает,
не полыхает, не гибнет, не пропадает навсегда.[1]

---

1   Tat'iana Tolstaya, "На малом огне [Na malom ogne – On a low flame]," in the collection Лёгкие миры [Aetherial Worlds] (Moscow: Izd. ACT, 2019). "On a low flame, the flame of memory, nothing burns away, nothing disappears in the blaze, nothing crumbles, nothing vanishes for all time."

Preface

The reader may also question why this volume should be published at all. As a matter of fact, I had not intended writing a book, but times have changed.[2]

The date is October 19, 2019. The sun and its last rays slipped below the horizon a half hour ago. Twilight is deepening. A light show of different shades of pink, orange, and red fills the western sky, and I sit on my porch in northern Maine watching. I'm not one of those well-off Washington, D.C., retirees on the coast. Like most transgender Americans, I am not wealthy. Even here in rural Penobscot County, I could not afford property on a lake, but I would not trade a waterfront sunset for the magnificent one I see from my porch. The front part of my thirty-five acres is planted in Norwegian pine, thickening to a denser second growth forest in the rear. If I sit still, the patterns of red between tree leaves and branches, marking the end of another day, suggest Japanese lanterns. A light breeze heightens the illusion, causing the lanterns to swing and shimmer. They are the lanterns that illuminate my life.

So why this book? Ambassador Joseph Davies's words in the epigraph to this preface refer to the 1930s and 1940s in the context of U.S.-Soviet relations, but they also describe the circumstances that motivate me. In the polarized politics and culture wars that swirl around us today, continuing to enjoy my sunset is a luxury. I am writing this memoir for a simple reason: I am a transgender American who served her country openly as a commissioned Foreign Service Officer (FSO) for the U.S. Department of State. I retired in August 2019. For over fifteen years I served in Moscow, Bucharest, and throughout Central Asia, not to mention in Washington, D.C.

Let that sink in. In July 2017, when Donald Trump announced he would not permit transgender Americans to serve in the military, I had just landed in Almaty, Kazakhstan. Amanda Simpson, former Deputy Assistant Secretary of Defense for Operational Energy, sat next to me. Amanda had been one of the first high level transgender appointees to the U.S. government under President Obama, and as such she outranked me by several

---

2   From the Foreword to Joseph E. Davies, *Mission to Moscow* (London: Victor Gollancz Ltd., 1945). Davies served as the second U.S. Ambassador to the Soviet Union in 1937–38. For the record, George F. Kennan detested Davies.

steps. An FS-02 mid-level FSO, a first secretary in the diplomatic rankings, I was roughly the equivalent of a lieutenant colonel in the military. My role with Amanda was that of a control officer to guide her through her visit and meetings in Kazakhstan.

That's the point. Amanda Simpson is rightfully an icon to many of us, but she served at the pleasure of the President and was gone from the government as soon as Trump took office. I, on the other hand, was a tenured, career FSO who had already served under both Republican and Democratic administrations. I had achieved my FS-02 rank despite taking what we call a *down-stretch* break to transition gender while at the U.S. Embassy in Bucharest in 2010–11. I then went on to ever more responsible positions until reaching the mandatory 65-year-old retirement age in 2019.[3]

I offer this thought to other transgender Americans who want to serve the U.S. government, the Constitution, and the American people. Military service is not the only option. I reassert the old adage that *the pen is mightier than the sword*. Diplomacy, in the words of Ambassador Bill Burns, is America's foreign policy tool of first resort.[4] Those with an interest in languages, cultures, and international relations should consider the Foreign Service. Being transgender is no obstacle.

That is why I am writing this book—to inspire other transgender Americans who wish to serve their country in diplomacy. That is the purpose and justification. If not for this, my life story would be of interest only to close friends and family.

So how does a transgender woman represent the U.S. government in the countries where she is posted? Is a gender non-conforming person able to influence U.S. policy in ways that a cisgender person is not? How does being a diplomat affect the personal life of someone who is gender non-conforming?

---

3   According to Sect. 812 of the Foreign Service Act of 1980, FSOs must retire at the end of the month when they turn 65. This mandatory retirement for age has been challenged in court several times, but the Supreme Court has ruled that mandatory retirement age is constitutional (Vance v. Bradley 440 U.S. 93 (1979)). A recent challenge in 2012 was unsuccessful. The Supreme Court having spoken, this is settled law.

4   William J. Burns, "The Lost Art of American Diplomacy," *Foreign Affairs*, May/June 2019; William J. Burns, *The Back Channel: A Memoir of American Diplomacy and the Case for Its Renewal* (Random House, 2019).

How does one become an FSO? It may be the most democratic, open hiring procedure in the United States today. Simply sign up for and take the Foreign Service Officer Test.[5] It's free to take. It is highly competitive, but it's not a specialized exam. Those who do well are people with broad educations and life experience. Those who pass are invited for an oral assessment in a group role-playing setting. Part of the beauty of the process is that it's anonymous until its later stages.

I could stop right there. For some, what I have written in these opening paragraphs may be all they need to know. Others, however, may want to know more, and that is what the bulk of this book is about. The structure is that of a memoir broken into parts by life and career phases. Diary entries in the appendices go into further detail on my day-to-day life in Moscow in 2005–07. The reader should view this work as a smorgasbord and feel free to sample what is of interest and leave the rest.

I should also state what this book is not. Anyone hoping for a soul-searching transgender or diplomatic memoir, a work of literature, or a study of gender theory should look elsewhere. There are numerous transgender memoirs dating back to Jan Morris's *Conundrum* in 1974,[6] and both Kate Bornstein and Julia Serano have published classic books on gender and transgender theory. There are excellent Foreign Service memoirs dating back to George Kennan.[7] There are academic studies on gender and on international relations. The works of many of these authors, academics, and pioneers figured prominently in my life. I look up to and admire their careers and literary achievements.

Still, imagine what it was like in the 1950s and 1960s to have never seen, met, be inspired by, or known the path of someone like myself—to have had no role models while being inundated with messages from society telling me I should be ashamed, that I was different in a way that was bad.

---

5   See https://careers.state.gov/work/foreign-service/officer/test-process/.

6   Jan Morris, *Conundrum* (Harcourt Brace, 1974).

7   Books and articles abound about life as an FSO. Bill Burns' already referenced *The Back Channel* is one of them. Another is George F. Kennan, *Memoirs 1925–1950* (Pantheon, 1983). For a real page-turner, I recommend Elizabeth Shackelford, *The Dissent Channel* (New York: Public Affairs Hachette Book Group, 2020). I have included selections from my personal diary in the appendixes to give a sense of what that day-to-day experience was like for me. *Diplopundit* (https://diplopundit.net) is a blog widely read by FSOs for the latest inside-the-Beltway news, rumors, and gossip of Foreign Service life.

My life has been one of perseverance, of overcoming. My purpose here is to communicate this life to others who may want to follow in my path. If I succeed in this, I will have accomplished my goal.

That said—a phrase FSOs, including this one, are wont to overuse—let the story begin.[8]

---

8   Where required by circumstance or by the need for anonymity, I have changed the names of several of the key actors in this memoir.

PART 1
Containment Policy (1954 – 2002)

In 1946, George F. Kennan wrote the most famous report in all of U.S. diplomatic history. Kennan's *long telegram* outlined what would become known as the policy of *containment,* the policy that would guide our relations with the Soviet Union for forty years. According to Kennan, the Western World War II allies had nothing in common with a Soviet government that under Stalin aimed to expand its territory and influence at every opportunity. To counter that expansion, the West must be ready with a credible threat of force. That force did not necessarily have to be used, but the threat must be credible and used if necessary.

As I delved into my family background and what it was like to grow up in 1950s and '60s America, I came to see my repeated denials of a transgender identity as a personal, purposeful form of *containment.* That will sound familiar to other transgender Americans of my generation. We kept our identities deep within us, rarely if ever showing our true selves to the outside world. The risk was too great. Disclosing our identities in the era of *I like Ike!* and even *Great Society* would mean loss of job, loss of career, loss of everything. No one needed to tell us that a transgender identity was not acceptable. We just *knew* it, sensing it from the culture surrounding us.

Containment policy describes my own path in those years, my repeated attempts to assert my identity followed by retreat and denial. What we didn't know in the days before the Internet was that we were not alone, that our paths had many similarities even if we didn't have the words to describe ourselves to ourselves.

1. How Scot-Irish Can You Get?

That's another way of saying I come from a family in which self-control and achievement were prized while emotions were suppressed. I think that will ring familiar to anyone with a Scot-Irish heritage. Throw in some German and English blood to boot, and the effect is magnified. Ours was a family in which the deepest of human emotions were expressed by meaningful looks from opposite corners of the room.

Ma was born Margaret Cecelia Geoghegan in Haverstraw, NY, in 1915. It was an Irish town then, as census records from the time readily show. The town industry was the mining of clay for brick making, a mining pursued to such abandon that a portion of the town collapsed into the Hudson River in 1906 when the ground under it subsided.

We don't know much about the Geoghegans. My grandfather Christopher Geoghegan may have been born in Haverstraw, or perhaps it was Lodi, NJ. Ma did not seem to know much about his origins even as she loved and revered him more than anyone in her life. She wasn't alone in this admiration. Christopher ran a general store in Haverstraw and kept extending credit to his customers after the onset of the Great Depression. When he went bankrupt himself, both the Democratic and Republican parties rallied around to elect him town clerk so that he could continue to provide for his family. Christopher was active in New York State progressive politics, and I still have a copy of James Farley's *Behind the Ballots* with a personalized inscription from him.[9] He died in the late 1930s, long before I appeared on the scene, but the stories and the look in Ma's eyes made him real to me. However it happened, I'm the one who inherited the silver-plated dinner service with his initials.

I know more about Ma's maternal line. My grandmother Mary Chapman brought mixed English and Irish blood. Even though she was our grandmother, my sisters and I called her Mom. Her father William Chapman had been a river boat captain on the Hudson in the late nineteenth century and was known as one of the *Five Bills of the Hudson*. I loved to look through the faded newspaper clippings about him in my grandmother's scrapbook. From what I could tell, the Chapmans had lived in the Hudson River Valley going back to the second half of the eighteenth century if not longer. William Chapman's wife, Cecelia Barrett, came directly from Ireland as a teenager during the potato famine. Her mother and father were turned away at Ellis Island, and she entered into America on her own.

Mom lived to see her ninety-eighth birthday, typical of the long-lived women in the Chapman line, but I remember her as *old* from first memory in my child's eyes. She lived alone in Haverstraw where we would visit on weekends and where she would always have ginger snaps waiting for me.

---

9   James A. Farley, *Behind the Ballots* (Harcourt Brace, 1938). Farley served as Postmaster General in the first two Roosevelt administrations in the 1930s.

She had once lived under the same roof with Ma and Dad, but my older sisters tell me there was always mother-daughter tension in the air. It didn't work, and Dad was the one charged with enacting gentle Scot-Irish eviction or removal more than once.

Dad's family was the mystery. His mother Agnes Traeder brought the German blood into the family as a first-generation immigrant, but she died in the influenza epidemic of 1918 when Dad was only five years old. Our grandfather Austin Allen McCutcheon was born in Shelburne, ON, a town that seems to have been the center for an extended McCutcheon family that emigrated from Northern Ireland to Canada in the early nineteenth century. He met and married Agnes after crossing from Canada to the greener pastures of Detroit in the early 1900s. Dad was born Allen Robert McCutcheon in 1913.

Now for the mystery: not long after Agnes' death, Austin went to work one day in Detroit—and never came home. According to Dad, the police conducted a search but found no trace. Austin had been a bookkeeper and looks rather dapper in the one photo we have. Dad said later in life that he thought Austin had ended up at the bottom of the Detroit River for knowing something he wasn't supposed to. Dad and his younger sister and brother lived for a time with their grandmother Ann Jane Allen before she, too, passed. After that the children were separated and sent to live with distant relatives. Dad spent his teenage years living in a parish rectory in Detroit, and it was the photo of his mentor Father Hayes that hung in our home when I was growing up. Father Hayes had become the father figure in Dad's eyes.[10]

Only long after Dad's passing did we learn that Austin had not sunk to the Detroit River bottom. Far from it, he had pulled up stakes and moved to Pennsylvania, where he remarried and had a second family. It was our previously unknown cousins from that second family who searched us out in 2020. Mystery solved.

Dad became a star student in high school under the tutelage of Father Hayes, but the onset of the Great Depression forced him to abandon college at Notre Dame after his first year. His goal had been to become a priest

---

10   Another mystery is how we came to be Roman Catholic whereas the McCutcheons in Shelburne, ON, are almost exclusively Presbyterian. One theory holds that Austin converted to Catholicism when he married Agnes.

like his mentor, and he also dreamed of becoming a doctor. Instead, he found himself in the Civilian Conservation Corps in northern Michigan. Then luck intervened. The district commander came through in search of someone who knew how to type. Dad was the only one who did, and the commander took him to work in the district office.

The Depression had dashed Dad's dreams of priesthood and medicine, but then he heard of an all-expenses-paid nursing program at St. Vincent's Hospital in New York City. He applied, packed his bag, and went. That's where he met Ma, who also had seen her one year at Barnard College cut short by the Depression. Strict rules barred nurse trainees from entering into relationships, but that's what happened. The open upper platforms of double-deck city buses were the venue for a budding romance. They married in secret in May 1937. To be precise, they eloped. Their wedding reception consisted of tuna fish sandwiches with a few close friends at Tavern on the Green in New York's Central Park. They spent one honeymoon night at the swanky Pennsylvania Hotel, but Dad came up short when it was time to pay the bill in the morning. A friend had to bail him out. Ma's family threw the two of them out when they took the train to Haverstraw to announce their marriage.

Ma was soon pregnant, and Dad abandoned the nursing program to find whatever work he could. They found an apartment, the first of several, in Brooklyn. My oldest sister Gail came into the world in 1938, and Irene followed in 1940. Ma was alone in the hospital when Irene was born, incredulous and hurt that no one came to visit and that Dad for some reason had become scarce. By tragic coincidence, Ma's father Christopher Geoghegan died a few days after she gave birth to Irene. Keeping the news from Ma, Dad had gone to Haverstraw to attend to funeral arrangements and to comfort the mother-in-law who had rejected him three years earlier.

By now Ma and Dad's constant changing of jobs and abodes becomes so complex that I am not able to untangle it. I do know that when the attack on Pearl Harbor happened on December 7, 1941, they were living in Takoma Park, MD. Apparently with the help of James Farley, Dad had found a job working in the fingerprint division of the FBI. That patronage, although vital to his family's survival, is something that I think rankled Dad. He wanted to make his own way.

Soon Ma and Dad picked up and moved to Michigan where Dad had found a job at Pontiac Motors. For a year they lived on a remote lake in a house with no indoor plumbing while Dad spent most of his time in Pontiac, rising before sunrise and returning after dark, dependent as he was on a friend for a ride to and from work. Later they moved up to a rental home in Pontiac, where Chris became my one sister to claim a Michigan birth in 1944.

I sometimes wondered why Dad had not fought in World War II. Later in life he said he thought there had been a clerical error, that a deferment he had while at the FBI stayed on the books throughout the war. Dad did nothing to correct that error. With a growing family, it's hard to blame him. In spring 1945, Dad heard of an opening for a bookkeeper in General Motors' Overseas Operations (GMOO) headquarters in New York City. Ma wanted to go back to New York, and this provided the chance. Dad later told the story how, as the train pulled into an upstate New York station, newsboys ran up and down the platform proclaiming VE Day.

Dad got the job. The family moved back to New York. For a time they lived in our grandmother's home in Haverstraw, but post-war prosperity had come. In 1947, they bought a small house on what had been a farm in Orangeburg. Mom moved in with them for a time until Dad enacted the gentle Scot-Irish eviction. My youngest sister Mary added herself to the household in 1947.

Dad bought an 8mm movie camera, and I have the movies he took of my sisters in Orangeburg in the late 1940s and early '50s. The property boasted a barn-turned-garage and the remnants of an orchard that included a dozen apple trees, two cherry trees, and a pear tree. It was childhood heaven for this family of four growing girls. The railroad tracks of the *Weary Erie* passed behind the property, and the engineer of the afternoon train threw candy to the children who waited eagerly each day.

My sisters recall how funny and playful Dad could be when they were little, but then something happened. I don't think any of us know what precisely, but Dad became more distant as my sisters grew. Perhaps it was the pressure of a career ladder that he had finally started to climb? From bookkeeper, Dad began to rise in GMOO's purchasing department. He became an assistant purchasing agent and later a general purchasing agent. By the time he retired in 1977, he had become Director of Purchasing for GM Overseas Operations.

Allen McCutcheon, furthest to the left in the back row, in 1948

If there is a legend we children share, it is awe over what Dad accomplished. Without a nurturing family in his own childhood, he pulled himself up from nothing to become a captain of industry. That awe and respect is colored by our memories of Dad as distant, demanding, severe, a perfectionist. Usually calm and controlled, he could sometimes explode verbally and become red in the face if things did not go according to plan. Given where he came from and what he accomplished, we have long ago forgiven him that distance. He had not known a mother and father's love except in his earliest childhood. He softened in his final years, however, and we saw how loving he could be with his grandchildren. Still, his demanding distance left its imprint on all of us.

Ma? She, too, fell into the shadow of Dad's perfectionism. Dad liked to pontificate and demonstrate his erudition at dinnertime. When *proved* wrong in the discussion of the day, Ma would sometimes exclaim, "It's a tragedy to have been born stupid."

Alcohol became a problem. I don't know that Ma became an alcoholic, but two of my sisters are in Alcoholics Anonymous and think Ma most definitely had an alcohol issue. It may have run in the family, as Ma frequently reminded us of our *Irish blood*. Her brother died under mysterious, perhaps alcohol-related circumstances at an early age. Ma would withdraw to her room after dinnertime altercations with Dad, sometimes remaining there for a day or more behind a locked door. Meanwhile, Dad enjoyed his role as cocktail hour enabler.

Margaret Geoghegan in 1953

Still, Ma and Dad loved each other as only couples who live together for sixty or more years can. At their sixtieth wedding anniversary, Dad still talked of Ma as the beautiful Irish lass who stole his heart. When Dad passed away before her in 1999, Ma never fully recovered from the emptiness left in her life.

Did I mention that we are all short? We thought of Dad, at five feet, eight inches, as tall. Ma was all of four feet, ten inches, and we the children ended up somewhere in between. There is hope for future generations, however, if our four feet, ten-inch grandniece continues to date her nearly six-foot tall British boyfriend.

But I get ahead of myself. For now, just know that ours was a very Scot-Irish-English-German family. We loved each other in our way even if we expressed the deepest of human emotions only through meaningful looks from opposite corners of the room. That the emotions were so expressed does not make them any less genuine.

2. Enter the Hero?

And so, the stranger wagged his finger at Ivan and whispered, "Shh!"[11]

I arrived on the scene on August 15, 1954. After giving birth to four daughters, Ma and Dad had given up hope for a boy. Seven years younger than Mary, I was the surprise child and the answer to their prayers.

I must have had a quiet mischievous streak even in the womb, as my arrival disrupted Gail's sweet sixteen party. Gail was born on August 26, and Ma had to turn over preparations to Dad whose strengths did not extend to parties for teenage girls. My *purposeful* disruption of my oldest sister's birthday party became a family legend.

What do I remember from the first five to six years of my life? Not much in detail, but there are feelings and scenes and shadows that have stuck.

For a small child, our property on the remnants of a farm seemed an immense universe. I remember walking through grass and bushes taller than me following our family dog on adventures. I remember an eternity of afternoons on the family swing set with its wooden seats or in the blow-up wading pool. I remember workmen on a road crew asking to use our hand well pump. I remember the deep snows of winter and crying when a hurricane blew down our cherry tree. When the entire family pitched in to shovel snow out of the driveway, I joined with my toy shovel to shovel the snow back in. I remember standing with Dad in our yard as he gazed at the sky to spy one of the first Sputniks when the Soviet Union seemed unbeatable in space. Irene took me on walks through Camp Shanks, an abandoned World War II transit camp, where she taught me vandalism by throwing rocks through windows. My sisters would take me with them on walks to a set of railroad tunnels not far away to which they had given names.

The political conventions of 1960 must have made an imprint on my child's mind. One night when Irene came into my bedroom to give me a goodnight kiss, I exclaimed, "Nixon will be our next president!" Irene corrected me that no, it would be Kennedy. When JFK gave his inaugural address in 1961, we sat huddled in coats and hats in front of our bulky B&W TV on a frigid day when our heat had gone out. When the Cuban

---

11 The Master to Ivan, in Mikhail Bulgakov's *The Master and Margarita,* in the chapter "Enter the Hero."

Missile crisis unfolded in 1962, I was old enough to understand that the grownups were scared.

I really did have a mischievous streak in those first years. I destroyed the family car by playing *gas station attendant* at age four or five, spooning gravel into the gas tank. Another time I reached over and released the emergency brake when Ma left me alone *for only a moment* in my car seat to run into the house for something she had forgotten. Our driveway being on an incline, the car rolled backward and knocked the *barn-turned-garage* off its foundation. Spankings were the rule for such mischief, and Dad, the giver of discipline, delivered his share.

Not understanding how hard my sisters worked on their hairdos, I delighted in turning the knob in our bathtub so that the shower head would unleash a torrent that destroyed their hard work. I got many a tongue-lashing in return. In those days of permanents and nights of sleeping with hair curlers, I was the lucky one who got the naturally curly hair, a fact that my sisters considered the height of injustice. Not infrequently I was the "chaperon" taken along for a ride in a new boyfriend's car. After all, what could happen with the little brother along for the ride? I would watch intently as Chris and her boyfriend practiced ballroom dancing in the living room.

One Year Old (Gail on the left, Mary on the right)

I *invented* things. Chris endured the *nut soup* that Ma would let me make in the kitchen by putting one peanut in boiling water. I took an interest in household efficiency by stretching strings between doorknobs that would let hangers be moved from one room to another without having to be carried. Well, at least that was the intention.

Both gender clueless and gender sensitive, I was surrounded by a life that was decidedly female. Dad was away at work from early until late, and I have little memory of him from the first years. The life and interests of Ma and my big sisters permeated the house. I played with their dolls as much as I did with the firetrucks and boy toys that were showered on me at Christmas. The other neighborhood children of my own age were all girls.

At age five or six I had a powerful dream of being lost in the woods and coming to a brightly lit, warm house. Only girls were allowed inside, and so I continued to wander. Again and again, I came upon the same house. Finally, exhausted and crying, I knocked at the door. The girl who opened the door looked at me, and I begged to be let in. "Of course!" she said. "You're one of us." I immediately woke up, elated but upset to find it was only a dream.

No one had to tell me that little boys aged five or six don't have dreams of being a girl. This was still the America of *I like Ike!* where behavior norms were understood by all without words. Strict Roman Catholic by-the-book morality ruled in our home, and even a child knew the Baltimore catechism would have nothing positive to say about sexual and gender minorities if, in fact, it had anything to say at all. Neither the catechism nor the six-year-old me had the needed vocabulary.

My dream elated me, and I prayed at bedtime each night to have the dream again. More than that, I would pray to wake up in the morning and find that the dream had become real. Then, in the light of day, I would run the other way. When a friend of Ma's addressed me with female pronouns after church one day, I screamed back, "I'm a boy!" When my sisters decorated my bedroom with ribbons and bows, I threw a tantrum, but when they dressed me up in their clothes and paraded me in front of Ma and Dad as their little sister, I made only a show of protest and loved every moment. Ma and Dad, in strict conformance to our Scot-Irish ways, said nothing.

My oldest sister Gail was so much my senior that I never knew her as a sibling at home. She was already away in college when I first had awareness, but I remember well how I *crashed* her wedding shower in 1960. As a boy, I had been sent to spend the day with our neighbors, but I wanted to be with my sisters. The home movies show me there with them, the one boy in a circle of women.

Kennedy's *New Frontier* brought a new frontier into my own life. In the fall of 1960, we moved from the old farmhouse to a brand new, modern, larger house in Monsey, NY. Dad was making his mark at GM, and we were moving up.

For me, the move was traumatic. I had started first grade in Orangeburg and now found myself with a new teacher in a classroom where I knew no one. I wet my pants in school not once but frequently, and I became a bedwetter at night. This passed, but I had retreated into a shell that would not be broken for several years. I regularly spent recess with the girls until, in the third grade, the teachers would pull me away and push me onto the sports field. I knew I was not wanted there, and I didn't want to be there either. Instead, I would go to the far end of the field to be by myself.

My inner fantasy life blossomed. In second grade and on the school bus I came to idealize one of my classmates. Her name was Robyn. She had pigtails and was smart while my grades were no better than C. In the bathtub I hid my penis between my legs under the water and willed it to disappear. Continuing with my *inventions*, I hooked a funnel to the family vacuum cleaner to see if I could somehow encourage my breasts to grow. I watched women on TV with an eye to what they were wearing. When the school offered a summer typing course after fifth grade, I joined most of the girls from my class to take it.

With Irene in 1961

11

By age eleven or twelve my breasts in fact did bud. I don't know why or how. It could be only that I had put on weight. Or could it have been that I delighted in riding my bicycle in the DDT cloud emitted by the fumigation truck that came through in the summers to control the mosquito population? Whatever the reason, could my dream become reality after all? I prayed even harder.

The year 1963 brought the national trauma of the JFK assassination and a second trauma in my own life: Irene left to join a convent, the Daughters of Charity in Maryland. Irene had become my second mom, the one who would hug me and give me comfort, even teaching me how to fight with my fists because yes, the neighborhood bully gave me his attention on a regular basis. Now she was gone, to be seen by us only on scheduled visiting days two or three times a year.

Irene's decision surprised everyone. Of all my sisters, she had been the rabble-rouser, the one who instigated practical jokes at school and showed me the fun of throwing rocks through windows of abandoned houses. Later she had boyfriends with sports cars and friends with whom she caroused at night, coming home late and so intoxicated that she knocked things over. By 1963, however, she had settled on Rudy, a PhD candidate in physics. The two of them were engaged, and wedding plans were in the works.

Chris was the super-religious one who had imbibed every drop of Catholic theology and morality. Quiet, studious, and hard-working, she observed every holy day and novena and went to mass daily. Rosaries and religious statues decorated her bedroom. She, not Irene, was the one destined for a convent. When the Daughters of Charity invited her for an interview, she didn't want to go by herself and took Irene along for company. After the interview, the Daughters contacted Irene and told her she was the one they wanted. Theirs was a teaching order, and Irene had gotten a BA in education from the Dominican College of Blauvelt, NY.

In this unexpected way, Irene and Chris exchanged places. Irene broke off her engagement with Rudy and joined the Daughters. Chris, in turn, started dating and married Frank a few years later. The two of them eventually left the Catholic Church to join a small, ultra-conservative Christian sect.

I don't know when Ma and Dad understood something wasn't quite right with me, but I know they did. They could not *not* have known. My report cards regularly commented, "Doesn't talk or participate." Teachers must have told them that my school friends were the girls in my class. Dad started to spend more time with me, taking me on Saturday walks along the Hudson River. Ma got me into Cub Scouts and offered our house for den meetings. I sang alto in the school chorus. I briefly played the clarinet but was crushed when our dentist made me switch hopelessly to the trumpet.

Looking back these sixty years later, I understand that Ma and Dad were far more progressive than I understood. Ours was one of two Catholic families in an overwhelmingly Jewish neighborhood. When a black family bought the house two doors down from ours, Ma and Dad were the first to welcome them and invite them over for drinks. Later, in 1968, Dad voted for Eugene McCarthy in the Democratic primary, something that left me jaw-dropping astonished when he let that tidbit drop. If the decade had been the 2010s, not the 1960s, might they have been accepting of a child who was exhibiting signs of gender confusion? I now give them that credit. I think they would have. In the 1960s, however, they coped as best they knew how.

Fifth grade brought a change. Already becoming bookish and what we would now call nerdy, I fell in love with the space program and the night sky. I recorded every Gemini launch using Dad's reel-to-reel tape recorder. I lay on the grass in the evening and stared in wonder at the stars. I read *The Search for Planet X* about the discovery of Pluto.[12] I tried to build my own telescope. My grades started to improve, and I once overheard the teacher whisper to Ma on a visitor's day, "See how good he is at math!" By age ten, I had begun to learn that someone who does not fit within social norms gets a pass if seen as smart. Schoolyard isolation, books, and a growing love of the stars had given me that. Nearsightedness and glasses added to the image.

I thrived in sixth grade, already getting good grades and adoring my teacher, Mr. McCandless, the first male teacher in my school career. He exuded gentleness and love in an unstated way that contrasted with what I knew at home. It might have been sixth grade, but story time was a centerpiece of the day. After recess, we would put our heads on our desks as Mr. McCandless read stories and entire books to us over the course of the year. I felt from him the gentle expressive love that Dad, never having experienced it in his own life, did not know how to give.

---

12   Tony Simon, *The Search for Planet X* (New York: Basic Books, 1962).

It didn't last. Gail and Irene had gone on to lives of their own. In 1965, Mary entered the Boston Conservatory of Music to pursue dance, and Chris found a job as an editor in New York City. Our big house was emptying out, and Dad decided he was done with daily commuting. The movers packed us up in the summer of 1966 as we downsized, giving away furniture and our family cat whom I had watched give birth to kittens a year before. I felt sad seeing things go, but I also experienced the excitement of a new adventure. I had no idea what was coming.

3. On Broadway

They say the neon lights are bright
On Broadway (On Broadway)
They say there's always magic in the air[13]

One hundred fifty-five West Sixty-Eighth Street or, rather, Sixty-Eighth Street and Broadway, two blocks north of the new Lincoln Center—that was our address as we moved into an apartment on the thirty-first floor of a brand-new building. The first weeks went by in exhilaration and excitement as I learned how to ride the subway and city buses. I will say this for Ma and Dad. They gave me free rein in the city within a few weeks of our arrival, and I loved to take different subway routes to see where they went. At age twelve, with fifteen cents in my pocket—soon to increase to twenty cents—I could go wherever I wanted.

Now in the city, Dad decided that I should also experience Michigan town life and sent me to spend a week with his sister's family in Monroe, Michigan. My Aunt Irene had spent her teenage years in a convent in Monroe where she stayed, married, and raised three children. My cousin Chuck was a week my senior, and he came back to New York with me to experience city life. Thus began a summer exchange that lasted until we both entered college. I would usually spend a summer month in Monroe, and my cousin would spend a month with us in the city.

The beginning of the school year ripped the glitter off my new life on Broadway. Dad had chosen McBurney School for me, an all-boys preparatory school on Sixty-Third Street that boasted a few greats or near greats

---

13 The Drifters, "On Broadway." Genius. Accessed September 9, 2023. https://genius.com/The-drifters-on-broadway-lyrics.

in its time.[14] I believe Dad, concerned by what he saw in his quiet, introverted son, chose McBurney *to make a man out of me.* Prior to our move, I had been taken to a child psychologist who tested me and recommended McBurney. Here I would be forced into a competitive, rigorous male environment. It would be sink or swim.[15]

I nearly failed all my courses in seventh grade. Most of my classmates had been at McBurney for sixth grade, and I was the outsider who joined them for seventh. Compared with the schoolmates I had known, these boys used rough language and were a rough-and-tumble bunch even if they were from well-off families. Gym class became a torment. I hated having to strip out of my blazer, shirt, and tie to change into a gym outfit as classmates taunted me. Swimming in the nude was even worse. "Your knockers are bigger than my sister's!" I heard that taunt more than once, and it had a double edge for me. I became psychosomatically ill on a regular basis before gym class and would spend the period with the lower school principal until he caught on and started forcing me to go to gym. At the end of the day, I would make only the barest effort to do homework.

Ma was ill. She had come down with hepatitis and took to her bed for several months. Part of my afternoon job at home was to do the laundry. Together Ma and I would watch soap operas. Dad took over cooking dinner with an astounding array of recipes that seemed to include lots of canned tuna. Chris and Mary, who had returned home after dropping out of the Boston Conservatory, sometimes ordered takeout after they were sure Dad had gone to bed.

If Dad didn't understand at first what a hard time I was having, the first report card caused him to jump into action. "Good grades don't prove anything, but bad grades show you're in trouble." That's the phrase I remember.

---

14   J. D. Salinger attended but dropped out of McBurney, later mentioning the school briefly in *Catcher in the Rye*. John Steinbeck's sons were also McBurney dropouts. Several of my classmates including Richard Thomas went on to acting careers.

15   My school trajectory already differed from that of my sisters. All of them had gone to parochial elementary and high schools whereas for me the Catholic part of my education had been consigned to Friday release time from public school and to Sundays after mass. (I was in a release time class on November 22, 1963, when the mother superior entered the room and asked us all to stand and say a prayer for President Kennedy who had just been shot in Dallas.) Years later I asked my sisters why they thought Ma and Dad had chosen parochial schools for them but not for me. They were surprised that I even asked. "So we wouldn't get pregnant, of course!"

Evenings now became seventh grade boot camp with Dad laying out a schedule for each homework assignment and drilling me in particular on math. He sat next to me as I worked the assignments. Between each, we took short breaks for aerobic stair climbing. Living on the thirty-first floor meant there were many flights of stairs to climb. On weekends he took me on long walks across the George Washington Bridge. We rented rowboats and bicycles in Central Park. Looking back, I realize Dad was more than a little concerned for me.

Christmas came and passed without any of the joy I remembered from past years. On New Year's Day I rode the Staten Island Ferry. Alone. I looked out at the New York Harbor that winter day feeling more alone than I had ever felt in my young life. I now understood that Dad was grooming me, his one male offspring, to follow in his footsteps, to be a success as he had been. That thought pushed me to despair. There was nothing in Dad's life that made me want to follow his path.

I hid the fact that I had a paper to write for French class during Christmas break, and I didn't write it. All I did was scribble a few sentences on one sheet of paper. After turning back our assignments, the teacher asked me to stay after class. He tore up the one sheet I had turned in and said it didn't count. He gave me another week and said he was sure I could do this. Not saying a word at home, I spent the next week writing a paper at night by the light of a flashlight after everyone else was asleep. I got a C for my effort, which was far better than the D and D- grades I had been getting.

On one of the first warm days of spring, I saw the math teacher standing at the bus stop. I cringed. I didn't like and was scared of him, but I couldn't get by without him seeing me. He motioned me over. "Mr. McCutcheon, you did much better on today's test. Keep it up." From that point until the end of the year, I got As on every test not only in math but in all subjects other than French in which I was hopelessly behind. With their words, these two teachers changed my trajectory from precipitous decline to rapid ascent. Encouraging words from these two teachers, not Dad's evening boot camp at home, turned me around.

No longer able to lie on our lawn and admire the night sky, I began to hang out at the Hayden Planetarium. I joined the Amateur Astronomers' Association of NYC and in ninth grade was appointed *Meteor Recorder* in its mainly grown-up Observing Group (OG). I built my own telescope in the planetarium basement, and I spent many a night on the roof of our apartment complex doing as much observing as was possible from midtown Manhattan. That telescope went with me for my Michigan summers and to my first solar eclipse in North Carolina in 1970. I came to excel at math and physics and received McBurney's award for best physics student when I graduated in 1972.

In McBurney Blazer (1968)

Mary and her boyfriend Bob introduced me to day hiking in Harriman State Park. Then I learned I could get to the park on my own by bus and convinced several other young OG members to go with me when a possible meteor storm was predicted. Our maps were old, and we got lost going up the wrong trail. We had to camp out in the open with no tents and nothing but cans of tuna for dinner. Paradoxically, from this inauspicious start I developed a love of the outdoors. Short summer backpacking trips in Harriman Park became a part of my life. Like the stars, the hills and forest didn't pass judgment on gender confusion.

My classmates saw me as eccentric but smart. When it became increasingly clear that I had a head on my shoulders, the taunting terror of the locker room ceased.[16] I was never part of the "in" crowd, but in eighth grade I made my first true friend, Michael Korolenko, who has remained a friend for life. Mike was as shy socially as I was when we met, but he had a love for museums and movies and knew the city better than I did. I became a regular weekend visitor at his home in Brooklyn. Eventually we added another two or three classmates to our group, going together to movies, museums, and shows. Walking down Fifth Avenue to see the storefront Christmas displays became an annual tradition.

Still, gender confusion always lurked somewhere in the background. In time it became what I call the *white noise* of my life that could only be drowned out by incessant activity. Male puberty finally came, putting an end to the magical thinking of childhood, but I did not accept it willingly. I even cut my pubic hair when it first appeared and fought the loss of my alto voice. I massaged my breasts incessantly, hoping that somehow, I could make them grow.

I had never heard the word transsexual. Even though we were living in Manhattan at the time of the 1969 Stonewall riots, I had no idea what it was to be gay. *Fag* was a popular insult used by my in-crowd classmates, but I had no idea what it meant. When you come down to it, I didn't know what it meant to be a heterosexual male beyond following Roman Catholic morality to marry and have a family. Male puberty brought no sexual arousal or attraction into my life. Mary set me up on a blind date to take a friend's younger sister to a school dance. I felt nothing. A double date with my cousin in Michigan to see, of all things, *The Bible,* left me equally flat. I felt nothing that could be considered sexual, but gender was something different. I missed the girlfriends of my childhood and the ease of being with them as friends, not dates, without sexual overtones. I wanted that back.

My first realization that there was such a thing as gender transition came, of all places, from Gore Vidal's *Myra Breckinridge*.[17] I discovered it on Ma's bedside table when I was fourteen and began reading it when I was home alone, always taking care to place it back in the same place on the bedside

---

16 By twelfth grade the gym teachers ignored me and allowed me to jog on the track rather than forcing me to be part of the regular program. When I realized that I just had to appear before the gym instructor to be marked present, I began doing just that. After I was sure I had been seen, I would return to the locker room, dress, and cut the rest of the class. My hangout during gym class became the performing arts library at Lincoln Center.

17 Gore Vidal, *Myra Breckinridge* (Little, Brown, & Co., 1968).

table. Then there was the movie biography of Christine Jorgensen in 1970. I never saw the movie. I was too afraid to buy a ticket, but I remember the advertisements.

By 1970, Mary had traded her day job in the city for a developing show business career that had her on the road frequently. When she was away, I got to sleep in her bedroom—where I experimented with everything. One time Ma caught me red-handed in Mary's blouse and skirt. I was on spring break, and it was late in the evening. I was sure both Ma and Dad were asleep, but Ma decided to go to the kitchen for a midnight snack. I was sitting on the couch watching TV and froze in terror. Ma looked and asked, "Why are you wearing Mary's clothes?" Then she went on her way back to the bedroom with a piece of cake and a glass of milk.

I didn't sleep that night. Ma said nothing about it to me in the morning. That day we went together to see *Hawaii* at the movies. I was so nervous that I scarcely remember the movie. As Ma was putting the key into the lock when we got home, I begged her not to tell Dad. Her response was all of two words: "About what?" We didn't talk about what she had seen for another twenty years.

Dad also caught me once in the bathroom with Mary's cosmetics but said nothing. I had taken up amateur photography and was doing everything I could at night in the bathroom-turned-darkroom to see what I would look like with my face superimposed on photos of one or another of my female relatives. Ma and Dad must have seen one or more of those photos even if I did try to hide them in my dresser. It was almost as though they willed themselves not to see what was happening before their eyes. I was successful in school, and that was enough. They averted their gaze.

Even so, I knew *Myra Breckinridge* was a novel and that Christine Jorgensen was one of a kind, or at least so I thought at the time. I found other outlets for what I thought was a hopeless urge. I redoubled my efforts at school. I threw myself ever more passionately into amateur astronomy. I sought escape in literature, losing myself in everything from Dickens and Steinbeck to time travel science fiction and fantasy.

Broadway shows beckoned with their cheap standing room tickets. I went as often as school vacations allowed and saw *Promises, Promises*, *Man of La Mancha*, *The Fantasticks*, and the other great and not-so-great musicals of the day. Mary married Bob and moved out, taking my gender playground with her, but Bob was an Off-Off-Broadway set designer. That meant adding experimental plays to the list even if, honestly, all the shows were so experimental that I don't remember a single one. I recall Mary's own plays better. She appeared in the chorus as a dancer in many summer stock and dinner theater musicals. I remember most of all seeing her in *Gypsy* and *Pajama Game*.

I graduated from McBurney in 1972—not at the top of my class but close enough. The New York City that had terrified and depressed me in 1966 had become home. The glitter and magic of Broadway had returned.

Mike Korolenko and I and the others from our not-the-in-crowd group spent one last evening together, feeling oh-so mature with high school behind us. Our college years called us forward with promise for the future. Despite the excitement, my diary from that autumn contains the following entry:

> I now have the nerve to write something which I have known to be true but have tried to deny for over seven years. I am, mentally, a girl.

The gender confusion, the *white noise* of my life, remained.

4. WahooWa!

The years 1972 through 1976 for me were the years of *WahooWa!* —the rallying cry of the University of Virginia. I traded New York City for sleepy Charlottesville, the home of UVA, the *Princeton of the South*, known also as *The University* or *Mr. Jefferson's University*.[18] Thomas Jefferson's home Monticello is here, and it is said that Mr. Jefferson—he always was and always will be Mr. Jefferson to students—watched through a telescope as the University he designed was built in the valley below his home. In my mind I can see him at the eyepiece, checking to see if his architectural plans were being followed.

For most Americans the college years are a chance to spread one's wings and start living a semi-independent life in a dormitory or apartment and learning what it means to open a bank account, cook one's own dinner,

---

18   UVA had begun admitting women on a quota basis in 1968, but open admissions began only in 1972. UVA alumni sometimes ask me what it was like being a co-ed in that first class. I usually answer, "*It was wonderful*" or "*It was an honor*."

and in general find out what is involved in living on one's own. It is a time of experimentation and wildness along with study and preparation for a future life.

I entered the University to fulfill my dream of becoming an astronomer. I chose a joint major in physics and astronomy. I took my first paying job as a night observer at the Leander McCormick Observatory with its historic nineteenth century, twenty-six-inch Alvan Clark refracting telescope. I worked shifts that went from sunset to 10:00 p.m. or from 2:00 a.m. to sunrise. During those shifts I had the observatory to myself as I loaded photographic plates and maneuvered the telescope to photograph star fields for the Astronomy Department's parallax program to determine star distances. Although Virginia is a southern state, it could get cold in that unheated dome on winter nights. Sometimes I would welcome a bank of clouds that gave me an excuse to retreat to the heated office next door. There I would rummage through drawers and cabinets, a treasure trove of astronomical history. I was always on my own, and I was often dressed entirely in female clothing.

In Charlottesville, I no longer had Mary's wardrobe to experiment with, but I had my own bank account and could buy what I wanted. I was too afraid to go into the women's clothing sections at local stores, but I lived for the mail order catalogs from Sears and Montgomery Wards. I saved my money, placed my orders, and waited for notices to pick up parcels at the post office.

I was young, shy, and scared. I dressed in my modest wardrobe at home and on the three-mile walk to the observatory, always choosing the darkest path where I was sure I wouldn't meet anyone. Terrified of encountering a professor or classmate who knew me, I would turn on my heels and walk the other way if I saw anyone coming in my direction. I did not understand that I could have passed easily with a little work. Back then, contact was to be avoided. If there was a knock on my apartment door, I pretended I was not home. No one was allowed into this secret world, a world that scared me even as I wished it could be my world in reality.

As this was going on in my private life, I took the full math sequence through partial differential equations and physics through quantum mechanics. I studied hard and *took my degree* with high distinction.[19]

---

19 By tradition, no one graduates from UVA. We *take our degrees*.

On Sundays when the weather was nice, I loved to read *The New York Times* in the University's formal gardens. On one such Sunday in April 1975, *The New York Times Book Review* noted that Jan Morris' *Conundrum* had been reprinted as a paperback. The book had been published in hardcover the previous year but had escaped my attention.[20] Now, however, this short notice hit me with out-sized force and left me shaking from excitement. A watershed life event took place: I understood I was not alone. Trans-sexualism was not just Christine Jorgensen, not just a character in a Gore Vidal novel, and not merely rumors. Here was a respected British writer and journalist—a person who had been with Edmund Hillary when he conquered Mount Everest in 1953—who was writing openly and honestly about her transition from James to Jan in midlife.[21]

I found *Conundrum* in the University's Alderman Library and read it cover to cover in a single sitting. I was enthralled and in tears. In the weeks to come, I got the nerve to read everything I could about transsexuality in the University's science and medical libraries. I wrote and wrote about what I learned in my diary. I learned of a Gender Identity Clinic at Johns Hopkins Medical Center in Baltimore and wrote there, receiving back an invitation to come in and talk.

I never followed through. Even when I learned that sexual reassignment surgery (SRS) was being performed at the UVA medical center, I was too afraid to walk through the door. I was the only son of a self-made man who had great expectations for his children. I could not overcome the fear of disappointing him by coming out. In my McBurney years I sometimes wrote notes to Dad, telling him things I was too fearful to tell him face-to-face. I would place the notes in his briefcase, only to nervously retrieve them later for fear that he might actually read them. With that level of fear, how was I going to talk about **THIS** out loud? There were no gay or lesbi-an support groups that I knew of in Charlottesville, let alone transgender,

20 Jan Morris, ibid. Reading Paul Clements' biography of Jan Morris, I am struck by Jan's incessant travel and almost super-human productivity as a journalist and writer. Could this have been the *white noise* of her life in the decades leading to her transition? Paul Clements, *Jan Morris, Life from Both Sides* (Scribe, 2022).

21 Some may cringe at the word *transsexual*. Younger generations have come to see it as a pejorative and are offended by the word. In Russian speaking countries, *transsexual* has been corrupted to mean transgender sex workers and those who appear in *travesty shows* at (usually underground) gay clubs. I, however, grew up with the word and con-tinue to use it, in particular when describing the historical context of my life path.

a word that hadn't even been coined yet. I would feel ashamed to knock on the door of a psychologist. Who would stand behind me? Who would hold my hand? Surely everyone would abandon me, declaring me insane? Maybe they would be right to think of me so?

This, my first non-coming out, turned into my first *purge*.[22] I had been accepted for an internship at the U.S. Naval Observatory in the summer of 1976 and for graduate school at Yale in the fall. In a matter of weeks Ma, Dad, and my sisters would be coming to Charlottesville for my graduation and to pack me up for the move north. I gathered together my small wardrobe, carefully wrapping everything into bundles, and deposited them in a dumpster far from my student apartment, a dumpster from which they could not be retrieved. I tore up my diary.

Looking back today, I wish I could hug that young, scared person who was me in 1976. Little did she know how much she would have to go through, and how many torments lay in store. She didn't know how much she would hurt and how she would hurt those she loved. It's probably good she didn't know what lay ahead. It would have been too much to bear.

I went off to New Haven with a simplistic belief that I could wish my transgender identity away by paying it no mind. Now all I had to do was keep my eyes on the task at hand. Being *cured* seemed so much easier and desirable than dealing with *this*.

But having purged that identity, I fell into my deepest depression since our family's move to New York City in 1966. My interest in astronomy flagged. I studied hard, but the passion was gone. I had been drawn to astronomy by my romance with the night sky, and that passion at UVA had been connected with my abortive coming out. Now I felt out of place in a PhD program populated by hard-driven men, most of them theorists, not romantics in love with the beauty of the night.

My overall interest in living fell to a low that I tried to hide with a smile. I found some relief in baking bread and other kitchen pursuits. I could purge my wardrobe, but I could not purge my mind. It's then that I began to think of transsexuality as the *white noise* of my life. Like the 3-degree background radiation that permeates the Universe in all directions as an

---

22 *Purge* is a term commonly used by transgender persons who attempt to turn away from their transgender identity by removing everything from their lives that could possibly remind them of that identity.

echo of the Big Bang, so too was *this* everywhere. The best I could do was drown out the noise with other noise that comes from over-achievement and overwork.

Like most Americans, I look back with nostalgia at my college years, and I have a special place in my heart for Charlottesville, The University, and Leander McCormick Observatory. For the first time I had tried to be me, and for a brief moment I got close. My *WahooWa* was a shy, scared one. Now I realize that as timid as it was, the voice was really, truly mine.

At the Business End of Leander McCormick Observatory's Historic 26" Refractor in Summer 1976

5. The Russian Revolution. Really.

I conceived ... a love for this great Russian language – rich, pithy, musical, sometimes tender, sometimes earthy and brutal, sometimes classically severe – that was ... an unfailing source of strength and reassurance in the drearier and more trying reaches of later life.[23]

---

23 George F. Kennan, *Memoirs*, as quoted in John Lewis Gaddis, *George F. Kennan* (New York: The Penguin Press, 2011), p. 51.

After two years at Yale, I had had enough. I decided that was it, that I was not PhD material. I took my MS degree in the spring of 1978 with no clear idea what I would do next.

The 1917 Russian Revolution saved me. An incurable romantic, I fell in love with *things Russian* when I saw the movie *Doctor Zhivago* in 1967. The fiftieth anniversary of the *October Revolution* came that fall. It was all over the news and a subject for our eighth-grade history class at Mc-Burney. It pulled me in. I began reading Russian short stories in translation and combed the school library and New York City's used bookstore district for everything I could find about Russian history. How strange, I thought, that a country and a people could evolve to be so different from us in mid-twentieth century America. When I entered UVA in 1972 and had to take a language, I chose Russian. *Things Russian* became the second passion of my life, one that helped me to survive and find meaning when I was not yet ready to come to terms with myself.

I regretted my choice a few times during Russian 101 at UVA. Russian proved harder than any of my physics or math courses, but after two years I was starting to get somewhere. It took me two months to work through Turgenev's *First Love* (Первая любовь) on my own, but I kept going. I wanted to read Pushkin, Tolstoy, Dostoevsky, and Bulgakov in the original. By the time I took my UVA degree in 1976, I had a double major: physics-astronomy and Russian language and literature. A young émigré actress at Yale tried to put together a small amateur theater group, and I was to play Bayan in Mayakovsky's *The Bedbug (Клоп)*. We never did get that production to stage, but I remember some of my lines. Олег Баян от счастья пьян (Oleg Bayan is drunk from happiness). As shy as I was, theater was a forum where I could lose my inhibitions.

At loose ends in the summer of 1978, I heard that Alex Lipson, an eccentric Russian language professor from Boston College, operated a small company called Pioneer Travel that offered summer driving and camping tours across the Soviet Union from the Baltic to the Black Sea. I got the last seat on one of the four VW minivans that summer, and I camped out in Boston's Logan Airport to get a $99 first come, first served ticket on PanAm to Amsterdam.

From the Netherlands we made our way through Germany and Scandinavia, crossing into the Soviet Union from Finland. A few hours later, I found myself walking the streets of Leningrad at the height of the White Nights. I felt I had landed on another planet. Everything, absolutely everything, was different from what I had grown up with. The avalanche of new impressions submerged the *white noise* of my transgender identity.

I remember showing my wallet to the young woman who sat next to me in the theater that first evening in Leningrad. I tried to explain contents that included a driver's license and checkbook, things that to her were exotic. In turn, she and others tried to explain their reality to me. It was the beginning of a cultural love affair that lives to this day.

I have come to think of the transgender journey as one of transitioning cultures, of traveling from one reference frame to another. We grow up in one culture and are expected to abide by its rules and conventions, but if we prepare ourselves for the journey, we can live in a different culture and come to feel as comfortable in it as in our birth culture, at times even more so.

While walking the streets of Leningrad in the summer of 1978, I came to feel on my own skin that the reality surrounding me since birth was not the only reality. I could see that the Soviet system was deeply flawed, but I also saw a positive side that was missing in my own society. Friendships in particular seemed deeper, more passionate than ours. Russians on the street blended to a bland, gray mass, but at more than one kitchen table they showed me that they are vibrant and alive behind closed doors.

By the time we crossed from the Soviet Union to Romania in late August, I knew that *things Russian* were going to play a role in my life. I didn't know yet what role, but a country and a culture had become real to me. I wanted more and would find a way to get it.

6. CSC: The Only Limitations Are the Ones You Bring with You

It was the fall of 1978. Back from my first overseas adventure in the Soviet Union, I was out of graduate school and in need of a job. I would just find something, anything, that would allow me to get by for two or three years and figure things out.

In September, I saw a full-page ad in *The Washington Post* from a company called Computer Sciences Corporation (CSC):[24]

> *Wanted: Physicists, astronomers, and mathematicians with BS or higher degrees who know a little about programming to work on contracts with Goddard Space Flight Center (GSFC).*

The real words of that ad were punchier, but that was the gist of it. I applied and was invited to come to Silver Spring, Maryland, for an interview.

Dr. Malcolm Shuster interviewed me. For the first time in my life, I came face-to-face with a certifiable genius. Trained in nuclear physics, Dr. Shuster had moved to engineering and had made spacecraft *attitude* determination his new career specialty.

No, I'm not talking about the psychology of satellites. *Attitude* is another word for *pointing*. Anyone who has seen Apollo 13 or other space movies has seen someone sitting in front of a console with the word *attitude* on it. Getting a satellite into orbit is only part of the task. It's equally important to be able to point the satellite the right way once it's there. That's what attitude determination and control is all about.

Correction: let's make that attitude *estimation*. That was Dr. Shuster's forte. Nothing can be determined precisely when theory meets reality. The best we can hope for are better estimation methods. Dr. Shuster had developed the *Quaternion Estimator* for attitude determination.[25] His fundamental

---

24　CSC was the second largest software company in the U.S. in the 1980s and 1990s. The CSC brand in the software world was as well-known as IBM in the world of computer hardware. At its height, CSC was the largest provider of mission support systems at GSFC. Founded in 1959, CSC for decades refused mergers and buy-out offers, but by the early 2000s it was in decline. Bought up and split up by other companies, CSC went out of existence as an independent entity in 2017.

25　Attitude can be defined in many ways. One common way is to use three angles; pitch, roll, and yaw; that define a spacecraft's orientation relative to reference axes. Another way is by matrices. Yet another—the one that is most frequently used in spacecraft operations—is via quaternions, a construct first developed by the mathematician William Hamilton in the mid-1800s. A quaternion consists of four elements: a three-element vector and a scalar. With only four elements, quaternions offer an advantage over 9-element 3x3 rotation matrices. A quaternion accomplishes in four numbers what a matrix accomplishes in nine. With little practical application in the nineteenth century, quaternions were rediscovered in the opening days of the space program when, given the limited memory of early computers, a compact form for defining a spacecraft's orientation was needed. Quaternions are also used to transform between reference frames, for example between a sensor frame and a spacecraft's primary reference frame.

work on this algorithm, known popularly as *QUEST*, has been published and re-published in many languages and lives at the center of attitude systems for missions well beyond those managed by NASA.

For a twenty-four-year-old to stand before a recognized genius at a job interview is unnerving. What I remember from that day was being put to the test. Dr. Shuster sat behind his desk, studying my resume. Without looking up, he asked me to summarize everything I knew about numerical methods for integrating differential equations. I responded by regurgitating everything I could remember. A long silence followed. Dr. Shuster looked up and pointedly remarked, "You said nothing about predictor-corrector methods." I answered nervously that we hadn't gotten that far in my numerical methods course. "Why not?" he asked in a tone of reproach. The rest of the interview continued in the same vein for an hour.

There was no way CSC would hire me after this performance, I presumed. Yet I couldn't have been more surprised when the Human Resources (HR) department called with a job offer. I waited until the last possible moment before accepting out of fear that I would be consigned to working with Dr. Shuster.

I started work the Monday after Thanksgiving, moving to Maryland and finding a room in a shared group house with Mary-Pat, Chuck, and an Irish setter who would beg me at night for a taste of my ice cream. On a $14,000/year starting salary, I couldn't afford an apartment of my own.

As I got to see the human behind the genius, Dr. Shuster became simply Malcolm, a man whose severe professional exterior hid a soft inside. A few years later, after we got to know each other better, he asked me if I had ever wondered why I had been hired. I replied that I thought it must have been my academic credentials. Malcolm waved that notion away. "We hired you because I could see that you would do the work of two people."

That's my professional life in a nutshell. I'm not at the genius heights of a Dr. Shuster, but I am a hard worker; a diligent, methodical implementer; and practitioner of methods developed by the Dr. Shusters of the world. Dad had instilled a strong dose of Irish-Scottish-German discipline and work ethic in all of us.

Methodical implementer and practitioner also describes the role of women in science, in particular astronomy, before the 1960s. Before modern digital computing, computers were human. Those humans were almost always the wives or daughters of the astronomers. Many were gifted mathematicians and scientists in their own right, but in the patriarchy of science, they were consigned to supporting roles. Computing was considered women's work. This ethic continued even into the early days of the U.S. space program, as anyone who has seen the movie *Hidden Figures* knows. Women, in particular black women, played a critical role in computing the trajectories and orbits of America's first manned missions.

CSC loved slogans. *CSC: Part of it, proud of it*, was the most common one in corporate advertisements and on posters, but the one I liked most was:

CSC: The only limitations are the ones you bring with you.

How funny I thought that slogan was, how much like the Soviet propaganda I had seen everywhere the previous summer. As the years went by, I came to see it as an ironically truthful description of my own life.

I soon found myself in the Attitude Systems Department working on the attitude system for a scientific spacecraft called *Magsat*. In the first half of 1979, we wrote the entire ground system on punch cards in Fortran 77 to be run on big IBM 360 mainframes. Serving as *punch card librarian* was one of my duties as the new person on the project. We supported the launch on October 29, 1979, which, as we liked to joke with dark humor, was the fiftieth anniversary of the 1929 stock market crash. Unlike the stock market, Magsat did not crash. It went on to become a highly successful science mission mapping the Earth's magnetic field so accurately that the maps could be used to identify anomalies hinting at ore deposits. For a year and a half after launch, our group supported the mission in real time out of the Attitude Operations Office at GSFC. In those days before onboard computers, operations for science missions like Magsat meant around-the-clock support, seven days a week.

I joined the Hubble Space Telescope (HST) project in late 1982. NASA loves its acronyms, and our project was no exception. We were known as PASS, a simple acronym belying the tongue twisting full name: HST Payload Operations Control Center (POCC) Applications Software Support (PASS) project.[26]

---

26 We joked that our project was an acronym within an acronym. "PASS" sounded less suggestive than the alternative of "POCC-ASS."

Over time, I became the leading expert on NASA's *Fixed Head Star Tracker*, a sensor I became so identified with that I was sometimes referred to as *Mr. (sic) FHST*. I also led a team in the 1990s that completely revamped the pointing control for Hubble's High Gain Antennas that had an unfortunate habit of becoming *lost in space* due to incorrect commanding. There are many technical stories I could tell from a project I worked on for over twenty years, but my point here is that working on HST was a challenge, the honor of a lifetime, and downright fun. I still get together with PASS friends for reunion dinners and picnics.

Trying to look cool with a mustache at an Attitude Operations party in 1980

The cool professional in my NASA life, I willed myself to be professional also in my personal life. But then I experienced my first crush on a man. Joe was a soft, gentle southerner from Georgia with a voice that melted my heart. He was also my direct supervisor. Joe was recently divorced, and I sometimes suffered beautiful, sad pangs of *if only*. We spent long evenings together at GSFC preparing for the launch of Magsat, sometimes staying so late that I slept on the couch in his apartment. I would fall asleep with *what if* fantasies. One weekend we went on a long autumn day hike together in Harper's Ferry. It was my first visit to this beautiful confluence of the Potomac and Shenandoah. If I were to choose one adjective today to describe the day, it would be *romantic*.

Come the reality of workday mornings, I ran from those *what if* thoughts. I threw myself into work to drown them out, banishing them as surely as I would edit out FHST data points that failed a data quality test.

Then came *Lifespring*, one of the largest of the self-improvement programs of the "ME Decade." It became the rage at CSC in 1980. One could hardly avoid the hallway conversations about it and pitches from co-workers that sounded like advertisements. Even Malcolm urged me to sign up. I said no. I didn't like the pressure campaign.

Then Malcolm tried a different tactic. He invited me to lunch and described my life to me. He said he knew work was the only thing in my life, and that I had no life outside of work, no friends outside the office. He nailed me with that description. Malcolm urged me again to sign up for *Lifespring* as a way to break out of all work, no play isolation. I still said no.

The next day, without telling Malcolm, I called the *Lifespring* office and signed up.

Lifespring's training known as *The Basic* took place for three evenings and all Saturday and Sunday the next week. By the time it was over, I was on an emotional high such as I had never experienced. The training included a hugging session in which the trainees split into two lines facing each other. With *Pachelbel's Canon* playing in the background, we hugged the person in front of us and then sidestepped to hug the next person. In the course of five or ten minutes, I gave and received more hugs than I had experienced in ten years. Hugs are not common in the lexicon of Scot-Irish emotional exchange. I felt high enough that Sunday night that emotion alone could have put me in orbit. I wanted more.

Lifespring was ready with more. *The Basic* fed into *Intermediate* and then *Advanced* trainings. Today, I look back and think of *Lifespring* as psychology without a license conducted by charismatic facilitators whose real loyalty was to the company's bottom line. "Fan the bonfires of trainee emotions sky high and get them to sign up for more," was the way to keep the dollars rolling in. Yet *Lifespring* influenced me in ways that set my path for better or worse—for both the very best and the very worst—for years to come.

In the *Advanced* training we had small groups in which we were to help each other on our personal issues. I said not a word about *the* issue, but

I complied with my group's suggestion that I date as many women as I could. That was their advice upon learning I was still a virgin, had never dated, had never even masturbated. I became the group's mascot. I loved the attention, and I wanted this to work. Surely by dating women I would find what I had never felt? Or, as Jennifer Finney Boylan wrote two decades later, surely "Love will cure me?"[27]

I went on at least a dozen full-fledged dates over four months. My group cheered and hugged me the day I announced I had lost my virginity.

So what was wrong with this picture? The night when I gave up my virginity, I did not enjoy the experience. It felt wrong, a case of a *Lifespring* friend extending me the favor of a one-night stand. I did everything I had read or been told about, but I found I couldn't care less about the sex act. I closed my eyes and imagined a complete role reversal. Only then was I able to continue, but I felt dishonest.

One evening in late 1980, Malcolm took me to Shepherd Park, a raw strip club on Georgia Avenue near the D.C. line. I had never been to such a club before. The men in this dark club seemed to be having a wonderful time watching, tipping, and yelling encouragement to the dancers. I couldn't understand why anyone would come to such a show. I felt nothing but commiseration with the dancers who wore bored expressions.

One evening I was in the *Lifespring* office, making calls to people who had been to a guest event, trying to convince them to sign up for the full program. It was a sales job that I did not enjoy, but eventually I made one call that was different. The young woman who answered had a slight accent, so I asked where she was from. She was a history graduate student from Brazil doing research for a PhD. I started to talk about my own travels in the Soviet Union.

Helena met me face-to-face several weeks later at another *Lifespring* event. She was seven years older than me and divorced. With brown eyes and red hair, she had grown up within walking distance of Copacabana Beach in Rio de Janeiro, a *carioca* with that soft accent that turns "Rio de Janeiro" into "Hio de Janeiro." She signed up for the trainings, and we began to run into each other again and again. I invited her for dinner at a cafe on Capitol

---

27   Jennifer Finney Boylan, *She's Not There: A Life in Two Genders* (Broadway Books, 2003).

Hill followed by the Soviet film version of *War and Peace* at an art theater. (Given the length of that film, it was a double date of two dinners and two evenings at the art theater.) In early 1981, I joined her at a political rally protesting U.S. involvement in Nicaragua. "Wow," I thought, "Maybe this is what it's about, friendship based on mutual interests and caring?"

Helena had lost both her parents. Her mom was scarcely in her 40s when she passed. Helena, barely in her 20s, was at the bedside when her mom complained of a severe headache. Who could have suspected that such a young woman was suffering a stroke? Helena's dad, a colonel in the Brazilian army, was on duty that night. It was only when he came home in the morning to find his wife unresponsive that the tragedy burst forth on the uncomprehending family. Not long after, Helena married a young doctor and PhD candidate who comforted the family through their loss.

Helena's dad had opposed the 1964 military takeover in Brazil. Already a teenager, Helena remembered how senior officers accompanied by Americans were frequent visitors in the days before the coup. They could not convince her dad to join the plot, and he paid a price in the years following. Never promoted again, he was shunted off to remote bases with his children and wife left behind in Rio. Photos show a sad man who never smiled, a man who had lost both his wife and his career.

Helena's dad had died of a heart attack not long before I met her, and she was still in mourning. Her marriage had also failed. She was alone and at a loss where she was going with her life.

We began to spend more time together as the 1981 calendar moved into spring. Helena did not see me as a romantic prospect, but she enjoyed the release of spending time with me. On occasion we ended long evenings in the same bed, sometimes moving from cuddles to physical sex. I enjoyed the warmth and closeness, but I never said a word about the *reversal of role* fantasy that had entrenched itself in me. Surely, with time, this will go away?

Helena flew back to Brazil in the summer of 1981 to be with her sister and aunts. I took leave that summer to go back to the Soviet Union, this time on a solo journey that saw me rent a car in Western Europe and repeat much of the route from my 1978 group trip. In 1981, I mixed astronomy with *things Russian* to observe a total solar eclipse from a spot on the edge of a collective farm not far from the Caucasus Mountains near Pyatigorsk.

I was there not only to watch the eclipse but to make timings that would help an astronomer friend with his research into solar radius variations. The maps my friend had given me showed minute details down to where power lines crossed the roads. He wouldn't tell me, and I didn't ask where he had gotten the maps; but I made sure to keep them well hidden and destroyed them after the eclipse.

I got back to the U.S. in late August, but Helena delayed her return repeatedly. When she did arrive in November, she felt distant. She made it clear that she saw us as friends only. Then she let it drop that she had met someone in Brazil that summer who was more than a friend. Those words crushed my dreams of a relationship based on mutual interests and caring. My relationship with Helena was over.

Well, not quite over. Fate had another twist in store. Helena left for Boston in December to do archival research for her dissertation. While Helena was away, her sister called me from Brazil. She was frantic. Bruno, the three-year-old son of their brother, had been diagnosed with leukemia. The doctors in Brazil were urging that Bruno be taken to the U.S. for treatment.

I put on my professional NASA hat and jumped into action. After a few days of my own frantic calling, I arranged for Bruno to be treated at the National Institutes of Health (NIH). He arrived in Washington together with his mom Cristina a few days after New Year's Day, 1982. For the next six months, our lives revolved around caring for him. At first, that meant long hours at NIH. Bruno was released in March but had an immune system weakened by chemotherapy. He couldn't play with other children or be in group settings. That meant that Cristina, Helena, and I were Bruno's sole companions, caregivers, and playmates. I still smile at an exhausted but bright memory of a day making a snowman with him on the beach in Ocean City, Maryland. Without noticing, I had slipped into the role of being a parent.

In April, Helena and I took a car trip to visit Ma and Dad at their retirement winter home in Florida. It was to be our last few days together. Helena's brother was coming to the U.S. soon, having procured an assignment to be a security guard at the Brazilian Embassy in Washington. With his arrival imminent, Helena told me we would no longer be needed. More than that, she had decided to return to Brazil for good.

In Florida, Helena gave me the shock of my life. Already in bed, she turned to me and asked me to marry her. Despite the hard work and exhaustion of caring for Bruno, she had enjoyed our co-parenting as much as I had. With Bruno now in remission and with his father coming, perhaps we could create our own family?

Helena had dashed my dreams the previous November, but here she was now, asking me to fulfill her dream. I said yes.

We were married in July 1982 in the backyard of the group house that had expanded the previous winter to include Bruno, Cristina, and Helena. Because Helena was divorced, a *Lifespring* friend who was a Presbyterian minister officiated. Dad almost didn't come because we were marrying outside the Catholic Church, but my sister Irene talked him into it. Malcolm patched together and ran a home brew music system for the event, and my high school friend Mike Korolenko took 8mm movies. The wedding was picture perfect with Helena in a modest white dress and me in a Russian peasant tunic.

But in the middle of celebration, I felt in the back of my mind and in the pit of my stomach that I had made a major mistake, even sinned in the Catholic morality I had grown up with. Lurking inside me, the *white noise* of a transgender identity was still there. It had not gone away. And I had just married a woman without saying a word.

No matter, my inner professional voice reassured me. Work harder. You will find a way. You always have. You will make this work. You must.[28]

7. My Great Purge

Growing up, I remember reading George Orwell's *1984*. That year seemed so impossibly distant and improbable. Yet 1984 did come, and we all survived that year of somber expectations. That distant future now belongs to the past. With the collapse of the Soviet Union, does anyone still read Orwell's *1984*?

Purge is the term used to describe a transgender person's concerted effort

---

28 Helena is, of course, a fictitious name. She has not communicated with me since our divorce in 2010 and my transition in 2011. I strive here to respect her privacy even as I tell the story of my life path. If I appear reticent at times in the telling, it is out of respect for that privacy.

to drive away a transgender identity. Newly married in 1982, I was nearly six years into my personal purge. As the 1980s progressed, I also fell into an all-consuming passion to understand one small corner of the Great Purges, sometimes called the Great Terror, that overwhelmed Stalin's Soviet Union in the late 1930s.[29]

It began with a return to academia. In the fall of 1982, I re-entered graduate school, this time Georgetown University's Russian Area Studies Program (RASP). Over the next three years, I earned an MA degree while continuing my day job at CSC and striving to be a husband at home. This was the beginning of one of the most important phases of my life, one that carried me well into the 1990s.

In 1984, I received a highly valued stack pass at the Library of Congress as I researched the early history of Soviet rocket development for a term paper. At the end of a long Saturday afternoon, I found myself walking past the QB section where I knew the astronomy publications could be found. Having already read a great deal about the Great Purges, I walked over to the publications of Pulkovo Observatory, the main observatory of the Soviet Academy of Sciences, and started to pull down one volume after another. I was curious. How had astronomy fared during the Purges?

Looking at the title pages, I saw that Boris Gerasimovich was Pulkovo director in 1933. The same was true for 1934 through 1936. No director was listed in 1937, and in 1938 an entirely different director had appeared. As the public address system announced closing time, I wondered if there was a story hidden behind this change in director. That was the beginning.

Before I had that chance stroll past the QB shelves in 1984, almost nothing had been written about the fate of astronomers during the Great Purges. As I dug deeper through literature and the archived, personal papers of astronomers, I discovered that astronomy was devastated more than any other science during this period, arguably more so than the well-known case of Soviet genetics. A case of academic fraud and the enmities between young Soviet-educated graduate students and Western-educated senior astronomers made the work of the NKVD easy in a time when mass arrests were being carried out by quota.[30] Over thirty astronomers were ar-

---

29   See, for example, Robert Conquest, *The Great Terror: Stalin's Purge of the Thirties* (Oxford University Press, 1968).

30   The NKVD, the People's Commissariat of Internal Affairs, was the precursor of the KGB, the Committee for State Security.

rested, and the majority died in prisons or camps. Some were executed outright. Only two or three survived to be released.

Research consumed me. I became insufferable to Helena, friends, and co-workers—all of whom were forced to live through the purges with me.

Winter 1987 in Leningrad with the Neva River and the Hermitage in the background

In the end, I wrote a 400-page thesis on the purge of Soviet astronomers. I received my MA in the summer of 1985, but that was not the end. My thesis landed in the hands of Loren Graham at MIT. Loren is America's leading authority on the history of Soviet science, and he urged me to go deeper. With his support, the International Research and Exchanges Board (IREX) gave me a grant that allowed me to spend six months as a researcher in the Soviet Union in the winter of 1987–88. CSC was happy to give me a leave of absence. Space Shuttle *Challenger* had exploded shortly after launch in January 1986, killing all its crew in America's greatest manned spaceflight disaster to that time. Hubble's launch had been planned for October 1986, but now no one knew for sure when, or even if, it would be launched.[31]

I spent most of that winter in Leningrad with shorter stays in Erevan and Moscow. In Leningrad I lived in a small guest house on the grounds of Pulkovo Observatory and spent my days in the archives of the Academy of Sciences. I had already spent countless hours in U.S. archives where I had read many letters sent by Soviet astronomers to their American colleagues in the 1930s. By contrast, the Soviet archives seemed intent on preventing me from seeing anything relevant to the purge years. Gorbachev was in power, and *glasnost* was in the air, but no one yet knew for certain where the liberalizing winds would lead. At the archives, the administrators in charge decided to play it safe and show me as little as they could.

But word got out about the American historian who had come. Before long, the children of astronomers who had perished in the purge years started to seek me out. They invited me into their homes, sharing with me their family archives that sometimes included final letters sent from prison. I used an old-fashioned 35mm camera with close-up lenses to copy what I could in this country that did not yet allow open access to copiers. When I left in March 1987, I had accumulated a treasure trove of new information that I used for a series of publications in the *Slavic Review*[32] and other journals.[33]

In retrospect, I see my research on the purges as my way of learning how others faced repression. Some cooperated with the authorities, giving false evidence against colleagues they knew to be innocent. Others faced down the NKVD and Stalin himself to defend colleagues who had been unjustly arrested. Grigoriy Shain, the director of the observatory in Si-

---

31 In moments of dark humor, we would joke that the Hubble constant, a measure of the expansion of the Universe, was in fact a measure of time remaining until Hubble's launch. As such, it was seemingly well determined: *two years until launch.*

32 "The 1936–37 Purge of Soviet Astronomers," *Slavic Review* 50, No. 1 (Spring 1991), pp. 100-117. For a popular version of the same article, see "Stalin's Purge of Soviet Astronomers," *Sky and Telescope*, October 1989, pp. 352-357.

33 e.g., "Astronomy & the State: U.S. & Russian Perspectives," symposium organized by the Historical Astronomy Division of the American Astronomical Society (R. McCutcheon, D. DeVorkin, S. Dick, L. Doggett, and R. Doel). Held on January 11, 1994. Proceedings published as "Astronomy under the Soviets," *Journal of the History of Astronomy* 26, Part 4, November 1995. For a number of years, I was invited to astronomy conferences as a historian, to history conferences as an astronomer.

meis, Crimea, became my personal hero for his role. He risked his career and life by writing letters and speaking out. More than that, he looked after the children and spouses of arrested astronomers in Crimea, giving them homes and jobs. When one of the few astronomers to survive was released in 1945, Shain brought him to Crimea. Shain stood up to the entire Soviet system of terror and repression but was not harmed. Soviet astrophysicist Iosif Shklovskiy later wrote eloquently about Shain's role in those dark days.[34]

It's easy to look back now to motivations I did not recognize at the time, but I am struck by how deeply I immersed myself in the mechanics of repression and how individuals can resist it if they choose. (Anecdote: In 1986 the welcoming sign for a workshop at the University of Texas said, "Welcome, Repression Workshop.") It became obvious to me that Shain succeeded because he was vocal. He was *out* when others were hiding in corners, afraid for their own skins.

I also learned a lesson about the fragility of life and sudden mortality. In the archives of Harvard University, I held in my hands the last message that Boris Gerasimovich ever sent to a colleague in the United States. Harlow Shapley knew his Russian friend was in trouble and had arranged to get him to the U.S. and out of harm's way. Gerasimovich's March 1937 telegram to Shapley read: *Regretting thanking cannot go.*

Six months later Gerasimovich was dead, executed in an NKVD cellar. For years I kept a copy of that telegram on my office wall. Had Gerasimovich heeded Shapley's advice earlier, had he not dismissed the warning signs, would he have survived and found a new life in the U.S.?

Shain's example haunted me. He stood up and took action in dangerous times. Those who did not were the ones who perished. The lesson was there for me to see, but it would take decades for me to understand that it applied in my own life.

---

34 Iosif Shklovsky, *Five Billion Vodka Bottles to the Moon: Tales of a Soviet Scientist.* Translated and adapted by Mary Fleming Zirin and Harold Zirin, W. W. Norton & Company: 1991. The chapter devoted to Shain is "Kaddish" on pp. 148-156.

8. *Welcome to the Brazilian Matriarchy*

É o pau, é a pedra,	*A stick, a stone,*
É o fim do caminho	*It's the end of the road,*
É um resto de toco,	*It's the rest of the stump*
É um pouco sozinho	*It's a little alone*
É um caco de vidro,	*It's a sliver of glass,*
É a vida, é o sol	*It is life, it's the sun,*
É a noite, é a morte,	*It is night, it is death,*
É um laço, é o anzol.[35]	*It's a trap, it's a gun.*[35]

Helena and I flew to Rio for the holidays in December 1982. Well versed in *things Russian,* I knew next to nothing about Brazilian history or culture, but I had started taking non-credit evening courses in Portuguese at our local community college. I had achieved a level that I call *portugues da cozinha* (kitchen Portuguese).

Time and study might have improved my knowledge of Brazil, but nothing could have prepared me for the family I was now part of. I knew Helena had two aunts and a sister in Rio. To my Scot-Irish ears, that sounded on a par with my having an aunt, uncle, and cousins in Michigan. Although Dad had arranged a summer exchange with my Michigan cousins when we were growing up, I thought of my Michigan relatives as people I loved in the Scot-Irish way through meaningful looks expressed from many states away.

We stayed with Helena's aunts Lia and Lorena in their apartment not far from Copacabana Beach. With no air conditioning, the apartment was oppressively hot. The aunts rarely went out. Lia was divorced, and Lorena had never married. She was living in a mental universe of the past, lost in memories of the one boy she had dated as a teenager. Lia and Lorena were living on the pensions of their father who had been a doctor with the rank of admiral in the Brazilian navy.[36]

---

35   Jobim, Antônio Carlos. "Águas de Março [The Waters of March]." Genius. Accessed September 10, 2023. https://genius.com/Antonio-carlos-jobim-aguas-de-marco-lyrics.

36   At the time, female offspring in Brazil inherited the pensions of their fathers.

The apartment had the feeling of lost grandeur about it. Lorena may have been lost in the past, but her stronger, clear-headed sister Lia also seemed to have lost interest in life. On entering their home and their lives, I was reminded of nothing so much as Miss Havisham in Dickens' *Great Expectations*. What had I walked into? Nothing in my Scot-Irish upbringing had prepared me for this.

Helena's younger sister Alana lived with the aunts and stood out as their opposite. Newly divorced, she was petite, tanned, loquacious, and active. In the sweltering afternoons, she was the one who would tell me to grab my bathing suit to go to the beach with her two blocks away. She was the one who wanted to go out in the evenings, sometimes for a walk or to the movies or once to a samba club. In her, there was life.

We returned to the U.S. in January, and I pushed Brazil away like a bad dream. Six months later, however, the two aunts and Alana came to stay with us in the fixer-upper bungalow we had purchased in Silver Spring, Maryland. They stayed for six months. They did return to Rio, but they were back again within the year for another six months. Eventually the visits lasted a full year.

As time went on, I understood that I had married into a matriarchy. Lia had inherited the role from her strong-willed mother. With time I began to wonder whether Lorena had been kept child-like on purpose. After all, what use is there to being a matriarch if there is no one to rule over? The matriarch's word was law.

I was totally unprepared for the family and culture I had married into. More than this, I had married despite the *white noise* of a transgender identity that I never could drown out no matter how hard I tried through force of will and hard work. By the mid-1980s, I wanted nothing so much as to run away and hide. When I boarded the plane to Moscow in September 1987, I got my wish. At least for a time, I had escaped.

9. Hubble Goes Up; I Go Down

Helena had a teaching job and had stayed behind in Maryland, but she decided to join me at the end of the year. When she did, we had the first full-fledged fight of our marriage. She suspected me of an affair with Ditsui, a young woman who had befriended me in Erevan. The fight erupted on Christmas morning.

An affair? No, not in the usual sense. There had been no physical contact of any kind, and it was beyond my Scot-Irish Catholic sensibilities to consider such a possibility. We had become friends in September when I had time to kill while waiting for MinVuz (Ministry of Higher Education) to get me to Leningrad after I had recorded an oral history interview with astrophysicist Viktor Ambartsumian. That was the whole reason I had gone to Erevan. With that interview behind me, I was itching to get to Leningrad. It took nearly a month for my travel to be arranged.[37] I was at loose ends while I waited.

In Erevan, I lived in a dormitory for graduate students at Erevan State University. Nora Dudwick, also on an IREX research program, was the only other American. Her hallway neighbor, Munzer, was a Syrian physics graduate student who looked at the two of us as naive children lost in a Soviet reality. He took us under his wing, often cooking dinner for us on a hot plate in his dorm room. That's where I met Ditsui. She was Munzer's fiancée who would go with him to Syria after they married.

Engaged to a physics graduate student from Syria who was too busy with his research to give her time, Ditsui became my walking tour guide. In return, I became her source for coffee that I could buy in hard currency stores but that was rationed to Soviet citizens.

I would like to say there was never anything more than that, but I would be lying. I did feel a connection. When I left Erevan in mid-October, I told Ditsui in parting, "If only my life path had been different, who knows? But my life is what it is." We exchanged addresses and wrote to each other by mail several times when I got to Leningrad.

The Christmas morning explosion with Helena erupted when she discovered the letters from Ditsui. Frankly, they were in plain view. Our verbal

---

37 To arrange travel, I had to call MinVuz daily in Moscow for updates. In the end, MinVuz informed me I would have to stay in Armenia. They would not send me to Leningrad. Fortunately, my passport was in my own hands, and I had my own funds. I bought a ticket back to Moscow and stayed for two weeks with the UPI correspondent whom I knew slightly. Salvation came from an informal connection, Viktor Abalakin, director of Pulkovo Observatory outside Leningrad. The U.S. Naval Observatory where I had interned in 1976 had given me a *just in case* letter of introduction to Dr. Abalakin. Director of an Academy of Sciences institution, he was able to *pull rank* on MinVuz and arrange my transfer to Leningrad. All my research success in Leningrad I attribute directly to Viktor Abalakin. Without him, I would have had to pack my bags and return to the U.S.

battle continued non-stop for days. It took the intervention of Zhenya and Vika, my two new Leningrad friends, to pull us apart, talk with us separately, and patch us together for the remainder of our time in the Soviet Union.

Perhaps Ditsui had sized me up as a dupe, an exit strategy from the Soviet Union? Looking back more than thirty years later, I acknowledge that possibility. That she, an Armenian Orthodox Christian, was engaged to a Syrian Muslim already showed desperation. Years later I learned that she had married someone else and had emigrated to Germany.

Our fight on Christmas morning inflicted more emotional hurt than I had ever inflicted on another person. Even in the heat of the fighting, however, I could not bring myself to say that my short relationship with Ditsui was not sexual but, rather, more a friendship between two females. I would not have had the words to explain that.

When we returned to the U.S. in March 1988, Helena immediately fled to Brazil. I expected divorce proceedings. But two months later I learned she was pregnant. Helena returned home and our son Matt was born in November. He had been conceived in the aftermath of our battles in Leningrad. It had taken us six years to conceive a child.

What conflicted feelings I had on the day of my son's birth! I was ecstatic to be a parent. I loved being with Helena in the delivery room. I also felt devastated that I would need to keep something serious hidden away for decades until he grew.

I tried, but I couldn't do it. When the moment came, it came unexpectedly.

By the spring of 1990, I was reaping the fruits of my research on the purge of Soviet astronomers. A major journal article was about to appear, and I was frequently invited to conferences. *Newsday* wrote about my work. When *Sky and Telescope* magazine published my popular article, it promoted my piece with a press release.

Hubble was launched on April 24, 1990. My feeling was one of exhilaration, of chills and goosebumps to be sitting in the control center at GSFC. Out of the corner of my eye I watched on the big screen at the front of the control center as Hubble's solar arrays unfurled. I worked my fingers frantically to fine tune the FHSTs so that they would identify star patterns properly and allow Hubble's attitude to be determined once it was released from the Space Shuttle arm. I was at the pinnacle of my career.

Three months later I was in a psychiatric ward.

I have no clear memory of the events between April and August 1990. I believe it's my own mind's way of protecting me from memories that are still hard to bear.

I do remember I had a one-week research grant at the University of Illinois. I went there to complete my journal article for the *Slavic Review*, but I found I was unable to work. At the time of my greatest career successes and joy at being a parent, the contradictions inside me were yelling, "Enough, this can't go on!" I looked up the unit at Johns Hopkins that dealt with gender issues and called long distance to make an appointment. On the train back to Washington, D.C., I knew I had to talk with Helena.

I don't remember how many days later the conversation came. I don't remember the words that I used—or how she responded—but I know it was a long night. My part of the conversation was fueled by vodka shots for courage. It was the beginning of several long nights.

I soon found myself a *persona non grata* in my own home, not knowing where I would spend the next night. My world collapsed. The secret was out, and Helena's reaction was more devastating than I had feared in my worst nightmares. I stood one late afternoon on a Metro platform thinking that it might be better for everyone if I disappeared from this world.

I didn't jump in front of a moving train, but I had reached my nadir. There was only one person I dared call. My sister Irene had left the Daughters of Charity in 1988 and was now a schoolteacher in Baltimore County. I found a pay phone and dialed her number.

Irene knew I was in crisis from the sound of my voice. She drove straight down from Baltimore and picked me up. I think the sight of me scared her more than my voice. I told her what had happened. Now two people in the world knew. Irene had never heard a story such as mine, but she understood I was in trouble. She drove me to a local hospital.

In the emergency room my story elicited nothing but odd stares. I was immediately remanded to the psychiatric ward under a suicide watch. I didn't know what to expect when I woke up the next morning. In three short months, I had gone from respected engineer and historian to psychiatric patient.

But I felt a comfort at being behind closed doors with the world fading away. I spent several hours each day in a common room, reading a copy of John LeCarre's *A Perfect Spy*. What a story, I thought. Magnus Pym, the main character, spends his entire life being what other people want him to be, always a cipher. I felt a oneness with him.

This was my first encounter with psychiatry, and it was not a pleasant one. I don't remember the name of my psychiatrist. As I recounted my history of gender-confused feelings, he sat stony-faced, never commenting. We met daily for a week. At the last session he pronounced his verdict, telling me, "What you are is overworked and depressed." He was convinced there is no such thing as gender dysphoria, so he prescribed an antidepressant. He released me to the care of Helena, assuring her I would be fine.

Helena did not want to be alone with me that day, and we went to spend the night with family friends. It was an evening of little talking. I went to bed early and just lay there in despair. My first attempt to talk openly about my *white noise* had been a debacle. I wanted to curl up in a ball and disappear. In the distance, the movie *Places in the Heart* was playing on the TV downstairs. To this day, that movie brings back my night of despair but also, strangely, the glimmer of hope that I felt as I heard Sally Field playing the role of a strong woman who perseveres through crisis. Perhaps, just perhaps there will be a brighter day.

But it would not be soon. Helena made it clear that I had to choose. Pursue transition or take the pills. It was also clear that if I went for the former, I would find myself divorced with no access to our son. It was a stark choice—so I chose to stay married, be a parent. I chose to ignore my own desires, to accept the diagnosis of depression, to take the pills, and to go on for the good of all. I went back to work after having disappeared for a week. No one said a word about my sudden absence.

My appointment at Johns Hopkins came several weeks later. I kept it. To her credit, Helena went with me. The diagnosis here was very different from that of the hospital psychiatrist: gender identity disorder of adulthood, non-transsexual. I took that to mean, "Has a serious issue but seems able to cope."

What I did not know in 1990 was that the gender identity clinic I had corresponded with in 1975–76 had long been closed, replaced by the Sexual Behaviors Consultation Unit. That's where I had landed. Its director Paul

McHugh advocated that transgender people do not exist and that those who exhibit transgender tendencies must be cured. Instead of supportive care, what I found at Hopkins in 1990 felt like an adversarial cross examination.[38]

In this, the darkest summer of my life, there were three bright spots. Irene visited me daily and became my main emotional support much as she had when I was a child in New York. Dad was still unapproachable and even proposed taking over my finances since I was *ill*. Ma was different. I asked if she recalled that night she found me wearing Mary's clothes? I'll never forget her words: "Yes. I never understood then how difficult it was for you." It might not sound like much, but in my Scot-Irish emotional universe, this was a watershed moment, a truly significant look from across the room. From that moment I felt closer to Ma than I ever had.

The third bright moment came unexpectedly from Chuck, my housemate from the group house where I had lived when I first came to Maryland. We had not been particularly close. Our politics were too different. I was the progressive liberal while he was an arch, almost reactionary conservative. Still, we had managed to stay in touch.

Chuck happened to come by the Saturday after my release from the hospital. We took a long walk through the neighborhood streets. Near the end, as we walked up the small hill towards my home, I got the nerve to tell him my story. After all, he was bound to find out anyway from Helena. When I was done, Chuck stopped, turned and looked at me. "I believe you," he said. "Maybe you really were supposed to be born a woman." I was stunned. The person I least expected to be understanding was the one person who validated my feelings.

Lost in my thoughts, I almost missed it when Chuck suggested joining him on a group bicycle ride the next weekend. He thought the physical exercise would be a good release for me after the stresses of that long summer.

A bike ride? My college bicycle was gathering dust in the basement, but why not? The next weekend I pumped up the tires, oiled the chain, and

---

38 Johns Hopkins did not reopen a gender identity clinic until 2017. Even in retirement, Paul McHugh continues to advocate that transgender persons do not exist. See, for example, his article *Transgender Surgery Isn't the Solution* in the Wall Street Journal for June 12, 2014 (https://www.wsj.com/articles/paul-mchugh-transgender-surgery-isnt-the-solution-1402615120).

went on that ride with Chuck and his friends. The ride couldn't have been more than ten miles through the Maryland countryside. Thirty-six years old, I was woefully out of shape from a life that revolved around office and archives. I had to push the bike up many of the hills, but I made it.

In the weeks and months to come, I kept riding. I started commuting by bicycle, marveling again at the stars when I commuted home on winter nights. Soon I was riding over five thousand miles a year. To the night sky and *things Russian*, I had added the bicycle as my third passion. I threw myself into bicycle activism, eventually landing on the cover of Maryland's bicycle safety guide.

The year 1990 drew to its close. I had failed at coming out. My marriage was on life support, never to recover fully. I was back in the closet for years to come, but the rhythm of my legs and the quiet of the long road became a solace and a source of peace. Where psychiatry and its pills failed, the bicycle saw me through to a better day.

10. Heaven Can Be Yours Just for Now

NOTE: This blog post appeared in my web journal Trans-gender in State on October 26, 2011. I haven't changed a word. With Gordon Lightfoot's song from his "Cold on the Shoulder" album as backdrop, this is my tone poem to the 1990s.[39] It captures the mood of that decade better than pages of prose ever could, and it still echoes through my head on cool autumn evening bicycle rides, be it in Washington, in Bucharest, in Astana, or in Maine.

All the lovely ladies in their finery tonight,

I wish that I could know them one by one.

All the handsome gentlemen with loving on their minds,

Strolling in to take the ladies home.

Gordon Lightfoot. An old song playing in my head on a frosty autumn morning. Down the hill, up the next on two wheels, spinning the cranks

---

39   Lightfoot, Gordon. "All the Lovely Ladies." Genius. Accessed September 10, 2023. https://genius.com/Gordon-lightfoot-all-the-lovely-ladies-lyrics.

fifteen miles from home to work. All is normal, all is okay in the final decade of the twentieth century.

And it almost was. I had been given a choice in 1990, and I chose the path that would preserve a marriage. Anti-depressants for a year, out of management and back to technical work, attitude determination for Hubble again. The recipe was good, and it almost worked. It was the most normal decade of my marriage. The secret was out, thirty-six years of pressure had been released, the *white noise* of my life had receded. Could it all have been a delusion?

> *Bless you all and keep you on the road to tenderness,*
>
> *Heaven can be yours just for now.*

A Saturday morning in 1991, my son in the carrier seat on the back of my bicycle. We're off, the two of us, to Sligo Creek Park to play by the creek and on the swings. Another weekend it's the Renaissance Festival. Then it's the B&O train museum. It's the age of pumpkin patches, nursery school, and childhood wonder seen again through the eyes of a parent.

> *All the gentle strangers who by nature do not smile,*
>
> *To everyone who cannot hold a pen,*
>
> *To all you heavy rounders with a headache for your pains,*
>
> *Who dread the thought of going 'round the bend.*

1992. "Dad, let's go basement and cut pipe." Our basement becomes my son's weekend playground as I rip out the old plumbing and heating system in our Takoma Park bungalow. He plays with pipe fittings as I cut old steel pipes out of the ceiling and sweat new copper into place. The solder sizzles and burns my fingers. Must finish before the first frost.

> *Bless you all and keep you on the road to better things,*
>
> *Heaven can be yours just for now.*

1994. Monthly IRCHAD[40] meetings at the Naval Observatory for donuts and an international seminar on *Astronomy and the State, U.S. and Russian Perspectives.* Then it's off on a camping and driving trip in an ancient Cadil-

---

40   International Relations Committee of the Historical Astronomy Division of the American Astronomical Society.

lac through upstate New York, Canada, and New England. It's just Helena, my son, and me, a mutual friend joining us mid-way. I see Maine for the first time and fall in love with the state.

> *To all the lovely ladies in their finery tonight,*
> *I wish that I could kiss you while you knit.*
> *To all the ones who learn to live with bein' second-guessed,*
> *Whose job it is to give more than to get.*

Mid '90s. Pointing control lead for Hubble's Mission Scheduling System. Spline algorithms. We throw out everything to do with the High Gain Antennas and start all over again. It's the best technical work I'll ever do. I receive a Space Flight Awareness award, and we go as a family to Kennedy Space Center to see a night launch, stopping at Disney World on the way.

> *Bless you all and keep you with the strength to understand,*
> *Heaven can be yours just for now.*

Cub Scout Pack 432. Pack chairman, newsletter and web-site author and editor, tireless promoter. Webelos Weekend and Pinewood Derby. Then it's Troop 432. Monthly camping trips, weekend hikes, car washes, summer camp, and bicycle merit badge counselor. Take the tandem so the young ones can finish in the back stoker seat if they tire. Swim meets, school events, help with homework, weekend events at the Brazilian-American Cultural Center. Best of all, it's bed-time stories. Nursery rhymes give way to *Huckleberry Finn*, *To Kill a Mockingbird*, and *The Master and Margarita*.

> *To all the little dreamers with a dream that cannot last,*
> *To all the sleeping giants who must wake.*
> *To every man who answers to the letter of the law,*
> *And all the rest imprisoned by mistake.*

College Park Bicyclist Coalition. Become an advocate for bicyclist rights on U.S. Route 29. We win.

Helena's two aunts and sister, marooned with us because of illness. Hopeless, awful, bizarre, and wonderful all together. TV Globo and Brazilian soaps. Little English to be heard.

Bless you all and keep you with the faith to let it pass,

Heaven can be yours just for now.

Summer vacations in Ocean City. Long walks on the beach, jumping through waves. Throwing away money on the boardwalk just for fun. Sand sculptures, Thrasher's french fries, chocolate malts at Dumser's. Summer novels. The sound of the surf that lulls us to sleep.

To all the lonely sailors who have trouble being seen,

To all of you with heartache that remains.

Maybe sometime later you might swim back into shore,

If someone could relieve you of your chains.

1998. An unexpected phone call at work. "Dad has had a stroke, meet us at the hospital." The father with whom I could never speak has softened since my collapse in 1990. I can still see him scooping up ice cream for my son, his grandson, a funny bowler hat on his head. I miss you, Dad. There is so much I still want to tell you. He leaves us three days later.

Gordon Lightfoot. An old song playing in my head on a dark, cold winter evening. Down the hill, up the next on two wheels, spinning the cranks fifteen miles from work to home. All is normal, all is okay in the final decade of the twentieth century.

Bless you all and keep you all on the land or on the sea,

Heaven can be yours, just for now.

11. Calm Century's End

When the red, red robin comes bob, bob, bobbin' along

There'll be no more sobbin' when he starts throbbin'

There'll be no more sobbin' when he starts a throbbin' his old sweet song

Wake up, wake up you sleepy head.[41]

---

41 Woods, Harry. "When the Red, Red Robin (Comes Bob, Bob, Bobbin' Along)." Genius. Accessed September 10, 2023. https://genius.com/Harry-woods-when-the-red-red-robin-comes-bob-bob-bobbin-along-lyrics. This is the wake-up song I sang to my son each morning through the 1990s.

The 1990s were the best decade of my marriage to Helena with all the wonder and hard work of being parents. If there was one thing we agreed on, it was Matt. Helena spoke Portuguese with him at home and later brought him with her to the Saturday children's program at the Brazilian-American Cultural Institute (BACI) where she volunteered. When the time for school came, we chose the French immersion program offered by the Montgomery County school system. In addition to a background in Latin American history, Helena had an MA in French and spoke with Matt as much in French as in Portuguese. I would throw in my Russian sometimes, but since I was the one with a career and work, Portuguese and French ruled at home.

Physically, Matt combined the two of us. His Brazilian pedigree showed in his dark hair and darker skin tone. His Scot-Irish side showed in his prominent nose and rear end, traits that Dad joked about by saying, "We weren't hiding behind any trees when those were handed out."

From both Helena and me, Matt acquired endless curiosity and a thirst to learn about the world around him. When he was a year old, I would give him *crawling lessons* by plopping myself on the floor and pushing myself forward with my arms and legs. I called him *our little guy*, and that became the loving nickname that I use to this day. He's our Guy.

Until he was old enough to join Helena at BACI, I had Matt to myself on Saturday mornings. Those were my favorite times. I'd put him on the back of my bike, and together we would head to a nearby park. Other times we would get in the car and go to a more distant park or museum.

CSC decided to reward me for my technical work on Hubble by promoting me to management. I hated every minute and endured it for only four years. I missed the technical involvement, and I begged to go back to a technical role. I got my wish in 1994 when I became the pointing control lead in a project to re-engineer major portions of Hubble's ground system. I worked a delayed schedule so that I could be at home with Matt in the mornings, and this meant that I was usually on my fifteen-mile bike ride home at night. Many of the new algorithms I devised for Hubble came to me as I pedaled those fifteen miles.

I continued to be involved with Soviet history. In 1994 our IRCHAD group in the American Astronomical Society got funds to hold a seminar on "Astronomy and the State: U.S. and Russian Perspectives." Afterward I served as guest editor when we published the proceedings in a dedicated issue of the *Journal of the History of Astronomy*. I also published book reviews and short historical notes here and there, but I had exhausted my treasure trove of material on the purge of Soviet astronomers. My years of research on the dark period of the Great Purges had exhausted me as well. My time as a historian was passing.

Helena and I agreed on Matt, but we didn't agree on much else. Her aunts and sister were spending more time in the U.S. now than they were in Brazil. Helena's aunts wanted to be with her, but Alana's heart was in Brazil. She wanted a life there, not in the U.S. The aunts came down hard on her. One day in early 1994 Alana came to me for help. A few days later I loaded her bags in the car and drove her to the airport.

At home, no one spoke with me for days. I was seen as a traitor. Several weeks later the aunts announced they were returning to Brazil also. I could scarcely conceal how happy I was. Helena, Matt, and I would have a nuclear American family at last! I even talked Helena into a summer driving/camping trip that took us to upstate New York and then Quebec. It was the best, happiest summer of my marriage. We spent several days at a lakeside cabin in the Adirondacks where I had once spent summer weeks with Ma and Dad and my cousin from Michigan. How wonderful it was to watch Matt splashing in the same water where I had once splashed!

Alas, it didn't last. Shortly after we returned to Maryland, Helena's aunts announced they were on their way back with Alana. No one planned it this way, but this time the return would be for good. Lia became ill and landed in the hospital for weeks with doctors unable to make sense of her symptoms. Helena, Alana, and I took turns spending nights with her in the hospital. It took several specialists consulting together to come up with the diagnosis: tuberculosis of the joints. Lia was released home to us, and a public health nurse came daily to witness her take her medication. Sometime during Lia's illness, their visas expired. Helena's aunts and sister were now illegal immigrants who had overstayed their visas. They would not be going back to Brazil. We embarked on a new home improvement project to convert our basement into a separate apartment for them.

Lia recovered, but Lorena sank even more deeply into her parallel universe of times past. I'm not sure she knew she was in the U.S.

It was Alana, however, who exasperated and angered me even as she brought me to tearful despair. She had given up, given up entirely on a future, on a life of her own. Once the image of a Brazilian beauty on Copacabana Beach, she put on weight rapidly, spending her days eating and watching Doris Day movies. Eventually she became so obese and weak that she could not climb the stairs to the kitchen. She was eating herself to death. Food had become her weapon of choice for departing this planet. The active young woman I had known in Rio in 1982 was gone. Only Matt could still bring a sparkle to her eye. I believe it was her love for Matt that kept her alive.

My exasperation extended to the Brazilian matriarchy. To my Scot-Irish eye, Alana had been groomed to follow in Lorena's childlike, dependent path. The generations were turning over. Lia had stepped down as matriarch. Helena had the role now, and her sister Alana had become to her what Lorena had been to Lia. I could see this as clearly as I could see the algorithms I was developing for Hubble, but I could do nothing. My voice did not count. The matriarchy was a closed system, and I had no place in it.

As the 1990s ended, Helena and I still had Matt as the one island of agreement, but even there we began to disagree on the details. Helena became the helicopter parent and the academic boot camp drill master that Dad had once been for me. Matt had to get the top grades. Nothing less would do. When elementary school ended, he went on to elite private schools for middle and high school. He was up so late each night on homework assignments that I don't know how he stayed awake during the day. I pleaded for Helena to let go, to let him have more free time, fun time, but I was overruled.

It was a rear-guard action on my part, but I did get Matt into Cub Scouts, serving myself as pack chairman. At least there I had a role. Boy Scouts followed. I couldn't have cared less whether Matt went on through the scouting ranks. It was enough to know that he would go on a camping weekend almost every month. I was always the willing parent who would join the Scoutmaster to make the trips happen. I became the bicycle merit badge counselor who took the scouts on their merit badge rides, usually riding solo on a tandem so that younger boys who didn't have the strength to finish on their own could take the rear stoker spot.

Heaven Can Be Yours Just for Now. That's still how I view the 1990s. They were the best years of my married life, of being a parent even as disagreements at home grew. As the calendar turned from 1999 to 2000, the new century beckoned with optimism.

12. No Transition

It is often the inconsequential that brings about the greatest upheavals. The minor thing to which we pay no attention turns out to be a tipping point. Just as the men of genius in Arthur Koestler's *The Sleepwalkers* stumble upon their greatest discoveries not knowing it, so we too, the everyday people, change our life paths not knowing we have done so.

Through the 1990s I devoted myself to family and work. In 1990, a psychiatrist had told me that transgender people do not exist. I took it literally, hoping it was true. If a transgender story appeared in the newspaper, I did not read it. If there was a report on the TV news, I changed the channel. "I need to accept myself as I am," I thought, "and to find the joys that are to be had in that self-acceptance." I tried the different addiction groups such as Sex Addicts Anonymous, wondering if I would find others in the same predicament who were looking for their higher power. I didn't find them. I would leave those rooms scratching my head. I found my peace on two wheels and, increasingly, in long hikes and backpacking trips with Matt's scout groups and with friends. In the mountains of West Virginia, I felt accepted for what I was, whatever that was.

When the transgender *white noise* of my life returned, it did so at startling volume and without warning. It was the summer of 2000. Helena, her aunts and sister, Matt, and I were vacationing on Chincoteague Island in Virginia. I had a fantasy novel with me that I had picked up at the library simply because it was on the new books shelf. I was fifty pages into it before the plot unexpectedly took a transgender turn. This time I continued reading. "It's only a novel," I thought, "and this is no longer an issue for me." I returned the book after our vacation, and I no longer remember the title or the author.

I was wrong. The old thoughts began to return, particularly in dreams, and I felt unable and ultimately unwilling to stop them. Helena realized from my increasing silences that something was wrong. I had to tell her. When I did, it was 1990 all over again.

But not quite. Some things had changed. I was loving my job and work. As the volume of conversations and arguments increased at home, I was delving ever more deeply into developing and applying a new Poisson series method to the creation of ephemerides (predictions of positions) for the major planets and principal minor planets for use on Hubble. It led to a journal article and a paper that I delivered at an international conference. "I'm not crazy and I'm not depressed." This is what I told myself as I rode my bicycle home each evening to continue the previous night's discussion with Helena.

I found a personal counselor, an RN experienced with gender issues. I saw her during lunch hours, but we rarely got around to talking about gender. Our conversations centered around my marriage and the lack of communication in it. It was not a path I wanted to go down, but I soon found myself on it.

"You married the wrong woman," my Russian émigré friend Lenya told me more than once. He already knew of my transgender secret, having been told directly by Helena. "This is nothing," he said, "and if I had known you when you were twenty, I would have cured you within weeks."

Once again, I had hope. Could my émigré friend be right? It's not depression but the wrong choice in partner? Indeed, as good as the 1990s had been, we were living ever more distant lives. Helena's aunts and sister had been marooned with us by illness, and all of Helena's attention was focused on them. I was devoting myself to work. We rarely talked, and all outings had to be with the full extended family.

Another change since 1990 was the Internet. I found a discussion group called *NoTransition* on Yahoo and became a member. This was a group of mainly married transgender people who were trying to find a path without transition that would allow them to preserve marriages without absolutely denying their transgender side. It felt like the right place to be.

I optimistically told Helena about this group and my participation in it. The result was the opposite of what I had hoped for. The volume of our arguments increased. I spent many a night on long insomniac walks through our neighborhood. On one particularly emotional evening, Matt walked into the middle of our argument and, from my own lips, found out what it was we were fighting about. He was devastated.

I moved out in early 2002, confused but convinced that we could not continue with endless fighting under one roof. I moved in with my sister

Irene, made a down payment on a trailer, and thought seriously about divorce for the first time. I talked with a divorce attorney.

My dash to freedom lasted three months. It might have continued, but I could not bear Matt's anger and my own sense of guilt for taking steps that would destroy us as a family. Matt did not want to see me and would call me at night to tell me how angry he was. When I told him I intended to come to a swim meet he would be participating in soon, he told me not to come.

I went anyway. I could not not go. Irene went with me for the first part but could not stay. After that I was on my own, watching Matt swim and seeing Helena at a distance. I couldn't take it. I wrote a short note. "I'm wrong; you're right. Let's talk." I moved back home. As a family, we returned to quieter older patterns and a brief period of honeymoon.

I resigned from *NoTransition*. I looked back at my life and how it played out. I could not come out in college. I nearly crashed for good in 1990. I crumbled again in 2002. "Three strikes and you're out," as they say in American baseball. There is no middle path. Of necessity I will soldier on. I will take this with me to the grave, and I am doing this of my own heartsick free will. My tombstone will read, "Kept the secret to the end. Thank you. Good show and goodbye."

PART 2

The Day My Universe Changed (2002–10)

It is often the inconsequential that brings about the greatest upheavals. I didn't know it then, but in 2002 another inconsequential event was about to change my life's trajectory in ways I never could have imagined. My world did not end. "Three strikes and you're out" did not apply. A new phase was about to begin.

1. A Dinner Conversation

It was a stray comment after a dinner with our friends Bob and Mary on a warm spring evening in 2002. When the time came to leave, Bob made small talk as he waited for Mary to say a long goodbye to Helena.

"I signed up for the Foreign Service exam today," Bob said.

"What's that?" I asked.

"Oh," said Bob, "it's the exam you take to join the State Department as a Foreign Service Officer. It's free to take, and I try it every year to see if I can pass. Why don't you take it also? We'll go together. You've got nothing to lose."

Laughing, I allowed Bob to walk me over to the computer. The next thing I knew, I had registered.

The exam was not until many months later, and I forgot about it. Summer came and with it came those things I like best about family life, a week at the beach and a week with Matt's Boy Scout troop at a scout camp north of Baltimore. The Scoutmaster now knew about my being transgender, but he told me he knew me as a gentle person who loved the troop. It was to be my last summer with Matt at scout camp, and I treasure the memories of the sounds and smells, the heat of the summer, the practical jokes, the lazy conversations, and the gentle friendship of being far from urban life.

Autumn came as relations with Helena spiraled downward. The brief honeymoon following my capitulation in March had ended. I had, in effect, surrendered unconditionally. Already a second fiddle in domestic matters, I now had almost no say in the decision making. This was particularly true in financial matters, where our not-too-abundant retirement savings were now to be diverted for another home renovation and addition for Helena's aunts and sister. I signed the refinancing documents, put down the pen, looked around, and said quietly to no one in particular, "I've just lost my home."

A notice soon came in the mail, reminding me of the Foreign Service exam. I wasn't at all sure I would go, but the night before the exam Helena and I had another fruitless argument. As Saturday morning dawned, I thought to myself, "I can stay home and continue the argument, or I can go take this exam." I took Metro to Catholic University and joined several hundred hopeful exam takers, mostly young people. When it was over, I felt uplifted by the diversion of a task that had been unexpectedly fun.

Six weeks later, I received an envelope from the Department of State. A form letter notified me that I had passed the written exam and invited me to a full-day oral assessment in January 2003.

Again, I was uncertain. The oral assessment would be given on a Monday. That would require a day off from work. It was only the night before the assessment that I decided to go.

I had no expectation that I would pass the oral exam, but I was intrigued. How far will this go? Two dozen of us came for the assessment, a full day of group and individual exercises conducted by expressionless examiners who took copious notes. In the late afternoon the examiners called us in for private talks, one by one. But then an examiner called my name and that of one other person. We followed him into a room and were faced by examiners who suddenly broke into smiles. Of the two dozen assessed that day, it seemed that only the two of us had passed. I was amazed.

The examiners handed me a conditional offer of employment. As I read the fine print, I realized I had taken the day off for nothing. The odds of real employment with the State Department were slim and were contingent on medical and security clearances. *This could drag on for years,* I thought, but then decided to continue the process. After all, they were offering a free physical exam.

Six months later, in the summer of 2003, I received a letter informing me that my clearances had come through. My name was placed on the register of candidates cleared for hiring. In fact, my scores had put me somewhere in the top ten on the *political* register. "Gee," I thought, "Is that significant?"

The Call came within days while I was in my office at CSC. It was an HR representative from the State Department.

"Mr. McCutcheon, could you join the next group of incoming Foreign Service Officers in the orientation class that will start next month?" I was speechless. After a long pause, I answered quietly, "No."

I must credit the Human Resource officer with an ability to read feelings behind the words. "Mr. McCutcheon, is that a real no, or is that an *I need to go home and think about this* no?" I said it was the latter, and she promised to call again the next day.

I did not sleep that night. Almost age fifty, I had been offered a chance to turn my life upside down. Would I take it? I loved my work for NASA, and the people I worked with on Hubble were almost more family to me than my actual family. Still, Hubble had been launched thirteen years earlier, and many of my friends had already left for other projects. More troubling, CSC no longer seemed interested in NASA contracts, so some friends now found themselves on contracts that had nothing to do with NASA, science, or engineering.

I consulted a trusted CSC friend. "Take the State Department offer," she said, "because this company will lay you off one day. CSC is a business, not a family, no matter how many friends you have here."

The HR representative called back the next day. This time I said yes, with a caveat: "I need time to put my affairs in order." I told her I could start with the State Department in the first half of 2004. She assured me she would call again in six months if there were still openings.

The months passed by, and I got ready both financially and emotionally. I bought the suits, ties, and white shirts I had never had to wear at CSC. Joining the State Department would mean a significant salary cut, and I had to save extra hard to have enough to tide over my family.

After twenty-six years with one company and more than half of that on Hubble Space Telescope, the time had come to say goodbye. In March 2004, we took a group photo and went for an emotional farewell lunch. Someone remembered how, in 1979, some had called me *Bobby the Bolshevik* because of my interest in *things Russian*. "Does the State Department know whom they're getting?" someone else quipped.

At the end of April, I rented a small cabin in Little Orleans, Maryland, for a week. I walked for miles along the C&O Canal, went on bike rides through the hills, and lay on the grass at night, marveling at the Milky Way the way I had as a child. *What will my future be like?* I wondered. I was fearful, sensing I had cast my career and family into the unknown.

The stars shone brilliantly. A light breeze from the gentle Maryland night rustled through the branches and caressed my face. Somehow, I decided, this will work. I got up, went inside, and fell into a sleep as peaceful as the night.

Last day at CSC with author seated next to project director Mary Galloway

2. Looking for George Kennan

Great was the year and terrible the year .... It abounded with sunshine in the summer months, with snow in the winter; and two stars stood out prominently in the heavens: the shepherd's star – the evening Venus – and the red, vibrant Mars.[42]

---

42 The opening words of Белая гвардия (White Guard) by Mikhail Bulgakov as quoted by George F. Kennan in the prologue of *The Decision to Intervene* (London: Faber and Faber, 1958).

It would take a transgender Foreign Service Officer to put the names George Kennan and Jennifer Finney Boylan in the same sentence, but there you have it, another first for the transgender world of diplomacy. Just as I admire Jenny Boylan, I have idolized George Kennan since college when I read his books *Russia Leaves the War* and *The Decision to Intervene*. It was through Kennan's writings that I first learned of the Russian writer Mikhail Bulgakov, and it was through Kennan's memoirs[43] that I came to know something of what my new life in the Foreign Service would be like. Although Kennan was writing of his years as an FSO in the 1920s, 30s, and 40s, I was to find that much of what he wrote still applies in the twenty-first century.

I had Kennan on my mind on a Monday morning in June 2004 as I made my way to Foggy Bottom and the heavy, gray State Department headquarters building—known simply as Main State. Kennan had been the State Department's leading expert on Russia and the Soviet Union, the original author of what would become the U.S. policy of containment during the Cold War. On that Monday morning I followed distantly in his footsteps as I walked through the door of EUR/RUS, colloquially known to those who work there as *The Russia Desk*.[44] In the 1930s Kennan had been the *Desk*'s first director.

I had already been working for the State Department for six weeks, but this was taken up fully by orientation training. The orientation class has an official name, but everyone calls it A-100, a name that goes back to the 1920s when orientation was held in room 100 of the State, War, and Navy Building.[45] Most of those six weeks are a blur, taken up as they were by administrative tasks, language testing, and theoretical instruction that would not find practical application for months or years. Most importantly, we "new" FSOs would find out the location of our first postings as entry-level officers.

What would be my first post? When I entered the State Department, I was still officially on leave from CSC. In the back of my mind was the thought that if I were assigned to some dark corner of the globe, I could quit. To my

---

43   George F. Kennan, *Memoirs 1925–1950* (Pantheon, 1983).

44   *The Russia Desk* is the shorthand name commonly used for this office. The official name is Office of Russian Affairs in the Bureau of European and Eurasian Affairs (EUR/RUS).

45   Now the Old Executive Office Building.

delight, however, the State Department assigned me to a year as a political officer on *The Russia Desk* in Washington followed by two years in Moscow. This was exactly what I was hoping for—a chance to use my Russian language and my Russian and Soviet studies background. It was a dream come true.

It didn't feel like much of a dream, however, in the first weeks on the *Desk*. I was one of three political officers in a high-powered office of a dozen people with years of State Department experience. I had gone from being a respected, senior analyst at CSC to being "Hey, you!" I was the most junior person on the *Desk*. I could hardly find my way around the building, let alone navigate politics and policy. One evening my first week I went home and spent the hours staring at the ceiling, wondering, *What have I done with my life? Was it like this for Kennan when he started out?*

The next day I got up and told myself, "OK, you chose this life. You can do it no matter how hard and new it is. You can start over." I resolved I would not let the bucking bronco throw me. If it did, I would get up and start again.

It was the most grueling work year of my life. Handling Russia's external relations with third countries was the portfolio the *Desk* placed into my rookie FSO hands, and those relations ran the gamut from dull and peaceful to a state bordering on hostile. The pace was frenetic. Nothing was predictable. My life revolved around Russia's relations with Georgia and the worsening situation in South Ossetia and Abkhazia. I threw myself into drafting informational memorandums, reports, and instruction cables to FSOs in the political office at Embassy Moscow. I arrived early and stayed late, doing all I could to prove to myself and to others that I could do this job. When NASA friends asked what the new job was like, I answered that it was like launch support for a mission in which everything that could go wrong regularly did go wrong. Moreover, at the State Department there was a new launch every day.

On Saturdays, I headed to my old CSC office to complete a number of projects. Knowing that my salary at the State Department would be significantly lower than it had been at CSC, my CSC managers had arranged for me to work hourly. For a full year, I had only Sundays to rest, but even then, there was no escape as home life simmered ominously at a low boil.

Hubble had been an escape from the home situation, and the work was almost always fun. Now work was hard and exhausting, and the career change had not made me popular at home. "How can you look at yourself in the mirror?" was a phrase I heard more than once from Helena whose progressive political views I shared. She made it clear that she was adamantly opposed to my career change. I had accepted the State Department offer in the certainty that John Kerry would be the next president. Instead, that November a *Desk* colleague sat with me in my office as we both cried during Kerry's concession speech. Had I compromised my own beliefs by working for this administration? What allowed me to continue was the knowledge that when it came to Russia, both Republican and Democratic policies would be similar.[46]

But as the weeks went by, I found I was no longer a danger to myself and colleagues in my immediate proximity. I was listening to *Ekho Moskvy* news radio when Paul Khlebnikov, editor of the Russian-language edition of *Forbes* magazine, was gunned down in Moscow in July. I marched into the office of the *Desk's* deputy director. It was the middle of the night in Moscow, and we phoned to break the story to Embassy Moscow. I had been the first to hear the news.

When I started on the *Desk,* colleagues had raised eyebrows when they saw me with headphones plugged into my workstation. Apparently, the idea of using the Internet to stream live news from Moscow had never occurred to anyone. After the Khlebnikov assassination, no one raised eyebrows. Rather, the *Desk* came to rely on me for the latest news. When several State Department offices became alarmed that debris from an exploded Chinese satellite might damage the International Space Station, I donned my engineering hat and jumped into the group addressing the issue, translating into non-technical language the fact that since the orbital planes did not intersect, there was no threat in the foreseeable future.

I came to be grateful for the people I worked with. Allen Greenberg, the senior political officer, knew how to balance serious business with humor. When I would get tense, a rolling of the eyes from him would tell me to relax. He could even get me laughing.

Gradually, I became known as the junior officer with a depth of ability no one had expected. After six months, I received a Meritorious Honor

---

46   In the early and mid-2000s, most of us concerned with Russia policy nursed the belief that although relations had taken a negative turn under Vladimir Putin, this was a temporary dip. Alas, we were sadly deluded.

Award for my handling of the Russia-external portfolio. I realized that I could do this job. I began to relax and find my own humor, writing an item for our "Daily Activity Report" with the title *Pith Helmet Diplomacy* based on a statement made by Putin. A neighboring office gave me a mock award with a certificate saying, "Best DAR We Wish We Had Written." I extended the joke by distributing Styrofoam pith helmets. Amid the seriousness, we found ways to have fun.

Russia Desk pith helmet diplomacy. Senior political officer Allen Greenberg is third from the left.

Did I think of being transgender that year? If I did, it was only in my dreams. The new career had allowed me to avoid my issues and self-medicate with work. I was too busy to think of anything beyond the basics of get up, get to work, do the job, get home, eat, and go to bed. That's the way it was for twelve months.

Then one day I walked out of Main State at lunch time and stopped short. The cherry blossoms were in bloom. The sun was bright. I walked to the Mall, bought a hot dog, and walked around the Tidal Basin. Spring had come!

Desk colleagues told me to turn my focus to my next task—my transfer to Moscow. Before I knew it, I was at another farewell party with champagne and words of parting.

As I left Main State that day, I reflected on the year. I had switched careers at age 50 and had gone from a senior to a junior position, requiring me to prove myself all over again. It had been difficult, but I had risen to the challenge and succeeded. I had reinvented myself.

Given that I had changed my life at work, might I one day be able to achieve the same rebirth in other parts of my life? In the summer of 2005, I was not ready to think about this possibility, but I was getting increasingly excited about the next adventure. Moscow! I was about to return to Russia, not as a short-term tourist or researcher but to live and work there for two years. In Moscow, I would continue to follow distantly but proudly in the diplomatic footsteps of George Kennan.

3. *Povorot*

Мы себе давали слово	*We all gave our word*
Не сходить с пути прямого,	*Not to stray from the path that's true,*
Но так уж суждено.	*But that's not what fate has in store.*
И уж если откровенно	*Frankly,*
Всех пугают перемены,	*Change frightens everyone,*
Но — тут уж все равно.[47]	*But here it is all the same.*

A mist as thick as a humid July day hangs over my memories of summer 2005, the final summer of my life in Washington. I remember the basic facts, but a veil that cloaks my mind separates me from the details and the feelings.

I finished work on the *Russia Desk* on a Friday and began classes at the Foreign Service Institute (FSI) in suburban Virginia on Monday. My first overseas tour was to be in the consular section at Embassy Moscow, and for two months I went through a training program best described as *Consular Boot Camp* or *Visas 101*. We covered laws and regulations, learned how to use the software systems and take fingerprints, and practiced doing visa interviews.

My life and that of my extended Brazilian family diverged down differ-

---

47 Mashina vremeni. "Povorot [Turn]." Genius. Accessed September 10, 2023. https:// genius.com/Mashina-vremeni-turn-lyrics.

ent tracks. My year on the *Desk* had not increased my popularity at home. Never accepting of my career change, Helena was firm that she would not join me in Moscow and would not even visit. Matt, about to enter his last year of high school, would of necessity stay behind, but there was hope he would come to Moscow the next year.

That summer, I rented a storage locker and began moving into it the possessions I would need to begin a new single life: clothes, papers, kitchenware, books, bicycle, a computer. I would be on my own for the first time in twenty years. I spent hours in thrift stores, buying those things I could not remove from the house.

When I think of summer 2005, it's not training, thrift stores, or storage lockers that come to mind. It's Ma and the time I spent with her. This is what cuts through the misty veil.

Ma had turned ninety that spring, and the family—my four sisters and the grandchildren, nephews, and nieces—had come to mark the day. Ma had become the focus of our lives after Dad died in 1999. She was so strong and so clear of mind. Surely, she was not ninety but still fifty years younger, the way I remembered her when I was a child? I found it hard to recognize or accept her age.

Saturdays and Sundays usually saw me with Ma at her home in Annapolis. I would show off my treasure from the latest thrift store visit. Ma took a coffee percolator I had found for a dollar and polished it up like new, leaving the Farberware label pristine as though the pot was to go back on sale at a retail store. That percolator is still part of my morning coffee ritual.

We would work together in the kitchen to prepare our dinner. She would recount stories of our shared past, like how Ma and Dad met and their years before I was born. The stories continued over dinner and then afterward on her deck in the summer breeze.

Now and again, we would come to my childhood cross-dressing. We both skirted the deep conversation, but each time, as she had in 1990, Ma would say quietly, "I had no idea how hard it was for you...." Then we would move on. With the sun setting behind the trees, I would kiss her goodnight and start for home.

I am blessed by not remembering our final goodbye that summer. Life was becoming more hectic as my departure date came ever closer. Surely, we would have more summer weekend afternoons together when I returned?

My departure day came. A moving truck arrived at my storage locker, and two men needed only two hours to pack everything that would be my material life for the next two years. It is still the core of what I have today.

I said my goodbyes at home, hugged Matt and Helena, and headed for the door. For the first time since I had joined the State Department, Helena showed a softer emotion, something other than anger. She seemed to understand the finality of this moment. She grabbed the car keys and drove me to the Greyhound depot. I would not need a taxi after all. The bus would take me to New York City for two days of consultations before I flew to Moscow. Helena and Matt waved goodbye as the bus pulled back. Soon I was looking at downtown Silver Spring, Maryland, as it slipped away. *When will I come home?* I wondered. *Will I ever call this home again*? To my own surprise, I suddenly felt relieved, and a wave of guilt washed over me.

Then I looked forward and slowly began to smile. I started quietly humming a popular Russian song, Поворот (*Povorot* – The Turn), by the group Машина времени (Time Machine), about the changes in our lives. The only way to know what lies around the next bend in life is to go around that bend. Whatever our fate, we all have within us the strength to go on.

I landed in Moscow three days later. The driver who met me took my two suitcases and held the door. "Добро пожаловать в Москву! Welcome to Moscow!" he said. Then he turned on the radio. *Povorot* was playing.

4. Mission to Moscow

> But when the last visa applicant has left, and the accounts are done, and the door of the Consulate closes behind me, I am George Kennan, and if the government doesn't like it, it can whistle long and loud.[48]

I lived on *Kutuzovskiy prospekt*, one of the most desirable streets in Moscow, the equivalent of Park or Fifth Avenue in New York City. I immediately fell in love with my new apartment, my home for the next two years. I could walk to the embassy in twenty minutes, to Red Square in forty. The theater district beckoned, within walking distance or a quick metro or bus

---

48   George F. Kennan 1928 letter to his sister as quoted in John Lewis Gaddis, ibid., p. 47.

ride away. I walked through old districts and wondered if George Kennan had also walked there seventy years earlier.

Moscow had changed dramatically since the 1980s. Although I had returned to Russia for conferences in 1993 and again in 2003, only now did I take in the radical changes that had occurred. I could see it in every store, the new or renovated buildings, in the theaters, and in the stylish clothing. Most of all, I saw it in the faces of the people. Instead of a gray mass of expressionless faces, in September 2005 I saw people smiling, enjoying their new lives in a country that was freer, government notwithstanding, than it had been at any time in its history. This was far from an American-style democracy, but the fears, the terrors of the Stalinist period that I had spent so many years studying and documenting were gone. Even the silent repression of the Brezhnev years had evaporated. People felt liberated and were living as they never had before.

I, too, felt liberated—from an oppressive personal situation at home. I smiled as I walked the streets of Moscow.

To my surprise, I enjoyed my work in the consular section. The thought of having to conduct visa interviews had nearly convinced me not to work for the State Department. It seemed so foreign to me, so different from anything I had ever done. But after the first tense weeks, I began to relax and enjoy my daily routine. I enjoyed talking with people, hearing their stories as I reviewed their visa applications.

Was I a *good* consular officer? No, I probably wasn't in the State Department's sense of *good*. I tended to believe the stories I heard and to give the benefit of the doubt. A person's story had to be in a universe of its own before I gave the occasional refusal. After all, my own life story would be difficult for anyone to believe. Albeit deeply buried, the transgender *white noise* was always somewhere in the back of my mind as applicant after applicant came to my window.

I remember one case in particular. According to the application, the young woman at my window planned to spend several months at a university in the Midwest. I opened her file and discovered she had been refused twice, one interviewer writing that he suspected the woman was involved in the sex trade. Two refusals like that are usually fatal. But the young woman implored me to take a look at the folder she handed me across the counter. I started turning pages. She was a PhD candidate in linguistics. There was a long CV and a list of publications. I looked to see if any of her publications were included in the file. They were, so I began to scan one of them. It had been published in a peer-reviewed journal. I saw that one of the co-authors was a U.S. professor who had arranged a one-semester collaboration with her. This was the reason she was applying, and I could see no reason why she should have been refused.

I asked about the two previous interviews. "The first consul just looked at me and refused," she said, "and the second one refused me without asking a single question." Incensed, I entered notes into the system deploring how such an error could have been made. The young woman glowed with the biggest of smiles when I told her, "Of course I'm approving your visa. I wish you all possible success in your research." Thanks to my transgender *white noise*, I had righted a wrong and sent this young PhD candidate on her way.

Best of all, in Moscow I had friends. Since my 1990 debacle, friends had been few in number. Those friends I had were required to pass inspection at home, and thus my circle had slowly shrunk to CSC co-workers. Now I could choose my own friends, and I rediscovered the joy of sharing a meal, going to the movies, or going on a trip with friends.

I was a fish out of water as far as the other FSOs were concerned. I was not one of the young twenty- or thirty-somethings looking for a spouse. Neither was I a forty- or fifty-something married FSO with children. Thus, I fell into a circle of locally employed staff (LES) who worked as assistants in the consular section. Almost all of them were women, many of them divorced, and several were around my age. We formed an informal theater club and headed out in the evenings to art exhibits, musicals, comedies, serious drama—even to the puppet theater.

My status as a married man and father made me non-threatening to these Russian women, but it struck them as strange that my spouse had not accompanied me. "She will be coming later, won't she?" they asked. I reassured them that she would, but I knew that was not true. Helena had said she would never set foot in Moscow.

One close friend was Inna, a divorcee from North Ossetia with a son not much older than Matt. We became regular movie, film, and touring companions. I recalled the words of my émigré friend Lenya, who insisted my one problem was that I had not met the right woman. Having turned my back on transition in 2002, I wondered if Lenya might be right. My relationship with Inna remained platonic, never more than a friendship, but it left me confused.

With historian Alina Eremeeva in 2006

I also had friends from earlier visits. Alina Eremeeva, a historian who had worked with me in the 1980s, was well into her seventies but still active. Some evenings I went to her apartment to help with her historical writing. Like so much of the old intelligentsia, she had not benefited from the capitalist windfall of the new Russia and was living in the same simple apartment from twenty years earlier. She had lost her job in the 1970s for daring to write about astronomers who had been purged in the 1930s, and in 1991 she had joined the human chain that protected Boris Yeltsin's Russian White House in the face of troops sent by the coup plotters who sought to overthrow Gorbachev.

One evening Alina served me dinner. As I enjoyed her home cooking, I said, "Next time I'll take you to Yolki Palki," a chain of inexpensive family restaurants. One was across from Alina's apartment, but she had never heard of it. Fourteen years after the fall of the Soviet Union, Alina had never once set foot in a Yolki Palki.

The winter of 2005–06 brought wonderful frosts with temperatures regularly down to -35°C. I had never experienced such cold in my life, but I loved walking through Moscow all bundled up, looking at the brilliant blue winter sky. I went cross-country skiing for the first time. The snow did not melt until mid-April.

I went home for Christmas, 2005, and again for my Matt's high school graduation in May 2006. Then, in fall 2006, I moved out of the consular section and into the environment, science, and technology (EST) section. My original assignment had me doing consular work for two years, but stories had spread that a former *rocket scientist* was doing visa interviews. Science Counselor Dan O'Grady asked if I would consider a transfer. The person who was supposed to take over the civilian nuclear portfolio had developed health issues, and no one else could be found to take the portfolio on short notice. I readily agreed, and the consular section acquiesced.

In my second year, Rosatom, the Russian nuclear agency, became a second home. I spent nearly as much time there as I did at the embassy. I accompanied high-level Washington delegations that came to carry out negotiations on more treaties than I can now remember, and I traveled to such places as the nuclear center at Dubna. Aleksey, an expansive Russian engineer who had been part of the 1986 Chernobyl disaster cleanup, was my local staff assistant who patiently brought me up to speed on issues ranging from plutonium disposition to sunset reviews of Russian uranium dumping. Even more than on the *Russia Desk*, I learned that FSOs are generalists, not specialists, whose job is to understand core issues quickly and report their essence back to Washington.[49] Theater evenings passed into memory as I found myself on the go late into the evening and on weekends. I was tired to the bone, but it was also fun to work in an area that drew from distant memories of college and graduate school physics.

When Secretary Rice visited, I served as the embassy's liaison to her staff, even interpreting between her security detail and representatives of Russia's Federal Security Bureau. When President Boris Yeltsin died, I took up a position as the embassy's site officer at the Cathedral of Christ the Savior. This was to be the first religious state funeral for a Russian head of state since the death of Alexander III in 1894. No one knew what to expect, what the protocol would be. After countless phone calls, I found someone

---

49 Our in-house FSO adage is that we are *a kilometer wide but only a millimeter deep.*

in the Moscow Patriarchate who promised to give me minute-by-minute updates. Standing on the sidewalk before the cathedral, I relayed messages from my inside source to the teams in the arriving American motorcade.

I was somewhat in awe of Ambassador Bill Burns, to me the living incarnation of George Kennan. Embassy Moscow is a large embassy with an American staff that numbered more than 200 in 2005. I can't fathom how Ambassador Burns got to know us all by name, but he did. Even during my first year as a vice consul, he would greet me by name if we passed in a hallway. Later, I sat in to take notes at a number of his meetings, in particular with Rosatom chief and Putin ally Sergey Kiriyenko. I marveled at Ambassador Burns's command of Russian and how he navigated treacherous waters as our relationship with Russia under Putin entered a time of change.[50] Deputy Chief of Mission (DCM) John Beyrle, also with deep Russia experience, did not lag behind Ambassador Burns by a single step.

My sisters Irene and Gail and Gail's husband Pat came to visit in September 2006. First, I showed them Moscow, and then we were off to St. Petersburg. We stayed there with Zhenya and Vika, the friends who had kept me fed in the winter of 1987–88 and who had played a key role in preserving my marriage.

Every other month, I went to Petersburg by express train to spend a weekend with Vika and Zhenya, or sometimes Vika would come to Moscow to spend a weekend with me. I met her brother and sister-in-law who had left Tashkent and moved to the outskirts of Moscow several years earlier. Vika, also born in what was now Uzbekistan, had moved to Leningrad, now Petersburg, with Zhenya decades earlier. Our weekends together were always filled with good food, laughter, and warmth.

I returned home again to the states in December 2006, but this time it did not feel like Christmas. Helena's aunt Lorena had died, and everyone was in mourning. The funeral took place on a cold, overcast day at a crematorium on a commercial strip in suburban Maryland. My mood as dark as the day, I struggled to show empathy even as I was relieved for Lorena. Her struggle was over. Inside I nursed a silent rage at the Brazilian matriarchy that had never allowed her to live a life of her own.

---

50   Bill Burns later headed the U.S. team when the U.S. opened secret negotiations leading the Iranian nuclear deal. In 2021, after the first draft of this memoir was written, President Biden nominated him to head the CIA.

Ma's health also had taken a sharp turn for the worse. In September, she had been rushed to the emergency room in severe pain from gallstones, a condition Ma had ignored for years. Now in pain, she finally allowed the surgeon to remove her gallbladder. The operation was a success, and Ma was home within a week.

Ma's surgery may have been a success, but she was not the same person. Could it have been the anesthesia? By Christmas 2006, she was a scared, pale shell of the strong woman who had polished my thrift store coffee percolator one year earlier. She had lost weight but refused to eat. She remembered the past in detail but could no longer remember what happened five minutes ago. The cold hand of dementia had taken my mother's mind, and she had awareness enough to know it. I could feel her fear in every word. "Please don't leave me," she said again and again.

Irene and Gail had borne the brunt of caring for Ma, but they could not continue even with the help of a live-in nurse. Ma no longer slept, and round-the-clock shifts had exhausted them. Assisted living seemed the only option. We celebrated Christmas with Ma in her own home, and the next day began moving her to a facility a few miles away. I spent the first night with her, unable to comfort her in the strangeness.

Meanwhile, domestic conflict simmered over that Christmas holiday. Matt had his first girlfriend. Helena didn't like her, but I did. I argued that Matt, now a college student, had a right to date whomever he wished. With Lorena's death and Ma's illness in the foreground, we now had conflict over Matt's dating choice in the background.

I flew back to Moscow after the New Year, hoping against hope that I would see Ma in full health when I returned in the summer. In February 2007, I traveled to a provincial town near Petersburg to sit in on hearings for a new nuclear power plant. I wrote my report on the train ride home and polished it the following day, a Friday. As I was preparing to call it quits for the week, the phone rang. It was Irene. "Come home," she said, "Ma was taken to the hospital. She's non-responsive." I was on the plane the next morning.

Ma lingered unconscious for days, but then she rallied. I was the one with her that evening as she ordered me around her room asking for this and that, her mind clearer than it had been in months. I kissed and hugged her goodnight, convinced I would have to reimburse the State Department for the emergency travel ticket that had brought me home in such haste.

Ma did not wake up the following morning. Gail, Irene, Helena, Matt, and I gathered around her as she breathed her last shallow breath. She was gone.

Two more weeks of work went into the funeral and the closing of Ma and Dad's home. Adding to the pain of loss was an argument with Helena. She did not want Matt to bring his girlfriend to the funeral. "Wait a second," I said. "This is my family, my own mom's funeral." For once I stood my ground. Matt's girlfriend stood beside him that day.

There is nothing quite as final in its finality as closing the door of your mother and father's home for the last time, knowing you will never open it again. I arrived back in Moscow on a Wednesday but was not able to compose myself to return to work until the following Monday.

A happier time followed in May 2007. Matt came to visit for three weeks, and he quickly fell in love with Moscow. He delayed his return home for another three weeks, and I took him everywhere. When I was at work, he would go out on his own. Once he spent a night helping sanitation workers clean Red Square, and he invited one of them, a young man from Tajikistan, home for breakfast. For the first time since he was a young boy, my son and I had time alone and began to know each other all over again. When I took him to the airport in early July, it hit me that I, too, would soon be leaving—for good.

The movers came two weeks later and made a quick morning's work of packing me out. When they were done, only the two suitcases I had come with remained. I looked at my bare walls and then took a walk through the neighborhood that had become home to me. There were tears in my eyes. I didn't want to leave. How could two years be gone so quickly?

I already knew my next assignment would be in Uzbekistan, and that made me happy. I would see a part of the former Soviet Union I had never seen before. With rising nationalism in Central Asia, the State Department decided I should be trained in the Uzbek language for six months before going to Tashkent. That meant returning to the U.S. and to FSI, and it also meant returning to Helena and to the house that no longer felt like a home.

As I walked around Moscow in those last hours, I wondered if I would ever see my Russian friends again. I grieved, as I realized I had no wish to return to my old life. I had experienced freedom, a new life. For my own salvation, I could not return to the past.

I boarded my flight back to the U.S. on a bright August day. The Russian fields receded as the plane gained altitude and turned to the northwest. "How am I going to do this?" I wondered. My abortive coming out in 1990 had been a disaster. The period 2000–2002 had been a replay no less disastrous. I had nothing but a history of failure behind me in my personal life. There had to be a way out, a way forward. There simply had to be.

Summer 2007, final days in Moscow

5. *Decision on Gros Morne*

Когда наступит время оправданий,	*When the time for atonement comes,*
Что я скажу тебе?	*What will I say to you?*
Что я не видел смысла делать плохо,	*That I saw no sense in acting badly,*
И что я не видел шансов сделать лучше?[51]	*But I saw no chances to make it better?*

I arrived back in the U.S. in mid-August 2007, but I returned to the old Silver Spring home for a few days only. The days were tense. Helena and I had little to say to each other. The nights were sleepless, and I again started walking the neighborhood streets, not yet wanting to accept the reality that I was right back where I had been in 2004 in the same house, in the same troubled marriage. It was almost as though Moscow had never happened.

Officially, I was on home leave, the time FSOs receive between assignments so that they can re-acculturate into U.S. society. I had three weeks before I needed to report to FSI, and I told Helena I needed to get away to absorb the events of the past whirlwind months. I boarded a plane, flew to Bangor, Maine, and began a two-week driving and camping trip through Maine and the Maritime Provinces of Canada.

Why Maine? A CSC friend had told me as long ago as the 1980s that I would love Maine. This was an active friend who spent a month every summer backpacking in Maine's North Woods. In 1995, Helena, Matt, and I had taken a driving camping trip through upstate New York and Canada with a return route that took us briefly through Maine past Rangeley Lake. That short passage showed me even then that my friend was right. I knew in 1995 that I wanted to return to Maine someday. In August 2007, I seized my chance.

It was time to make decisions. I had not been in the U.S. since February, and I still needed to come to terms with Ma's death. I was 53 and could

---

51 Grebenshchikov, Boris. "Sny o chem-to bol'shem [Dreams of Something Greater]." Genius. Accessed September 10, 2023. https://genius.com/Aquarium-dreams-of-something-bigger-lyrics.

not pretend that most of my life was still ahead of me. Mortality no longer seemed a distant unknown. I suddenly felt old.

As I made my way through Maine, New Brunswick, and Nova Scotia, my mind was a tumult from grief over the loss of Ma, the end of my independent life in Moscow, and growing certainty that I must end my marriage. From the hills of Cape Breton, I looked out upon a steely Atlantic Ocean on a cold, windy day, the gray clouds pressing down. "Will I have the strength to do this?" I was filled with guilt and remorse. Helena had shown an unexpectedly tender side, visiting Ma often in her final weeks. "I should be grateful," I thought as I looked off into the drab distance.

The next day I took the ferry to Newfoundland. Rain, rain, and more rain, my tent and clothes never drying out. Why did I decide to come to such a dismal place? Each morning I threw my wet tent and clothes into the trunk of the car. Mildew became the scent of the day.

The sun was shining as I pulled into the visitors' center of Gros Morne National Park around noon. I asked about hiking to the top. The young volunteer in the visitors' center told me I could make it to the top and back before sunset if I started right away. I replied that I thought I would do the hike the next day. "The sun is shining now, you know," came the reply. I took the hint and put on my hiking boots. After a two-hour rock scramble, I was above the tree line, looking out on the Saint Lawrence Valley. I put my camera on a rock, set the self-timer, and forced a smile.

Standing on that sunny, windy top, looking into the distance, I moved toward a decision. Years of compromise had led to a fruitless dead end. It was time to break from the past, even knowing that the resulting pain would be more intense than anything I had already experienced.

A few days later I camped by a beautiful Maine lake and passed through the town of Lincoln. "This is a place I could call home," I thought, but my days of home leave were coming to an end. It was time to report to FSI.

I pulled into Bangor, returned my rental car, and checked into the airport motel. I placed the call I had been delaying. "I want to live my own life," I told Helena. "That's the way it's been for two years. I want to make it official." I heard silence and disbelief on the other end. Upsetting and combative follow-up calls followed as a sleepless night turned to morning.

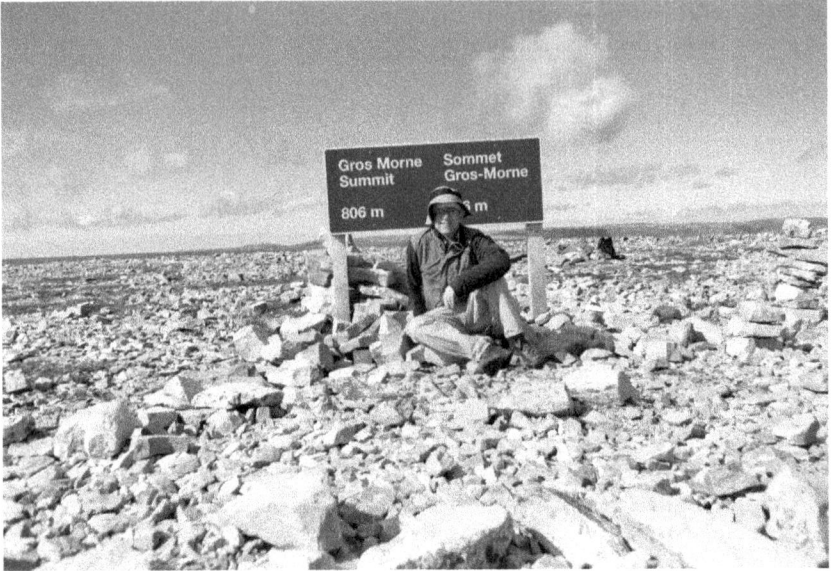

On Gros Morne, August 2007

The conversations continued painfully face-to-face in Maryland. I retreated into a protective emotional shell. It was the only way I knew of not to capitulate yet again, the only way to take action that would allow me to pull away. A week later I moved into an apartment in Greenbelt, a long walk from Goddard Space Flight Center where I had spent so many happy years.

On the first Monday in September 2007, I returned to FSI to begin six months of Uzbek language training. Several FSOs I had worked with on the *Russia Desk* and in Moscow were there, and they all asked how I was doing. Word spread that I was planning a divorce. No one seemed surprised. The only person surprised at my announcement was me. I felt a quiet amazement that after so many years, I had taken a fateful step in my personal life.

Would I have the strength to see it through? I had changed careers at age fifty, had done well in three radically different jobs in three years, and had rediscovered an independent life. If I could do all that, surely I could see this through to the end? I had no idea how difficult the months ahead, the years ahead, would be.

6. I Wish I Was in the Land of Cotton

Passion's always half impossibility,

But lovers that we lose we never dare forget.

Maybe someday there I'll see you in December or in May

In the graveyard of St. Mary's of Regret.[52]

Cotton fields. I bizarrely dreamed of them day and night all through the autumn and winter of 2007, white fields stretching as far as the eye could see. If I could get to those cotton fields, peace and normalcy would follow. That winter, all I could think of was getting to Uzbekistan, today an independent nation but once the Soviet Union's cotton plantation.

I find it odd, but strangely true, that I have found the greatest personal normalcy in places where life was anything but easy, anything but normal: Leningrad in 1978, the Caucasus in 1981, a wintry Soviet Union in 1987–88. The smells and the images from those brief excursions imprinted themselves in my memory in greater relief than years of life in the Silver Spring suburbs of Washington, D.C. If I could hold it together until I got to Uzbekistan, all would be well.

By December 2007, I was taking Prozac for depression, Xanax for anxiety, and Ambien to get a few hours of sleep each night. I had never expected divorce to be easy, but after repeated discussions through the years, I had thought it would be, if not amicable, a field on which negotiation would lead the way. On this count I was very, very deluded.

It had been one thing to live overseas in Moscow, away from Helena in Maryland. It was quite another to know she was a fifteen-minute drive around the Washington Beltway. Our Silver Spring home contrasted starkly with my cheap Greenbelt apartment. Nor did Greenbelt compare well with Moscow.

My task from September 2007 through March 2008 was to learn the Uzbek language. I was the only student, and it did not take long for the instructor Mukhamed-Babur Malikov, once the Uzbek ambassador to the U.S. but now a political refugee, to see I was distracted. My mind was on the divorce.

---

52   Werner, Susan. "St. Mary's of Regret." Genius. Accessed September 10, 2023. https://genius.com/Susan-werner-st-marys-of-regret-lyrics.

Babur was distracted also. Being ambassador to the U.S. was not the highest position he had ever occupied. He had been minister of justice until Uzbek President Karimov sent him to Washington, a blatant demotion that was Karimov's way of telling Babur not to return. From the highest ruling circles in Uzbekistan, Babur had fallen to FSI language instructor. Half of every hour of instruction seemed to go to the story of Babur's life that he told to me in Russian. Distracted as I was, I was happy to be his captive audience. It's a miracle I learned any Uzbek during those months.

Outside the classroom, attorneys and counselors filled my life. Communication with Helena was problematic, but when the holidays came, we decided to try one last time. We spent Christmas together and started marriage counseling. Within a month, however, I could feel that nothing had changed, and nothing would. Helena started a major home renovation that I did not want. The builders and workers took instruction from Helena and did not acknowledge my presence. My role in my own home had become that of a nonentity whose one task was to provide funds.

Helena's life revolved around her sister Alana, whose health had been in steady decline since the Brazilian aunts dragged her back to the U.S. in 1995. In 2004, she caught a bad case of the flu that landed her first in the emergency room and then in the intensive care unit (ICU) at our local hospital. Her blood oxygen level had fallen so low that she was placed on a ventilator.

Alana didn't get off the ventilator for nearly six months. When she came to, she had forgotten all her English, and even her Portuguese had become childlike. Groomed for this role for years, Alana now lived in an alternate universe of her own mind. With legs weakened from six months in the ICU, she showed no interest in physical therapy. She never walked again. When I looked at her, I seethed at the Brazilian matriarchy that had done this to her, had taken away the life of this once young, vibrant woman who twenty years earlier had taken me to the beach in Rio.

In February, I moved back to Greenbelt even as marriage counseling ground on fitfully. Every session began with me insisting, "I want a divorce," but ended with me reluctantly agreeing to meet again.

I left for Tashkent in April 2008 with no resolution at home, but then a strange thing happened. Within weeks I was off the Xanax, Ambien, and Prozac. Life was bearable again. An ocean, a continent, nine time zones, and President Islam Karimov stood between me and Maryland. Only the difficult telephone calls and arguments continued.

Alana's health continued to get worse. She spent her final weeks in a Maryland nursing home, where she passed away in August. I tried to get a flight home for the funeral, but getting anywhere from Uzbekistan is not easy. There was no way I could make it in time. Confronted by Helena in a tense call, I acknowledged that attending would be a matter of duty, a trip I dreaded. In September, I told her that I had made a final decision and would tell my attorney to file for divorce. After that, the lines of communication went dead.

Embassy Tashkent, built during the flowering of the U.S.-Uzbek relationship in the 1990s and early 2000s, loomed large as a white elephant, a veritable ghost ship on the edge of the city. The relationship collapsed in 2005 when troops fired on protesters in the Ferghana Valley city of Andijon. The U.S. and EU demanded an independent investigation, and the Uzbek government retaliated by closing a U.S. airbase that had been supporting our efforts in Afghanistan. It also demanded closure of all regional offices based at the embassy and began rejecting visa applications for senior U.S. diplomats. Entire office suites emptied, shuttered until a better day. In-country for less than a month, I found myself as acting head of the political/economic (pol/econ) office after family medical issues forced the permanent chief to curtail his assignment. With less than four years in the Foreign Service, I was the most senior person in the pol/econ office.

I have a soft spot for Ambassador Dick Norland. I think we all did. He had the unenviable task of saving something from the ruins of the relationship with Uzbekistan. When the government newspaper *Pravda vostoka* printed a photo of him with President Karimov, we took it as a good omen. We knew for a fact he was succeeding when a crew showed up to re-pave the potholed street in front of the embassy on the eve of the July 4 holiday in 2009. After he learned that I knew how to touch-type on a Cyrillic keyboard, Ambassador Norland sometimes stood by my desk and dictated diplomatic correspondence as I typed.

I immersed myself in managing the economic, business, and science technology portfolios. I had no background in economics. Zero. Not even an introductory course. I had both to do the job and fill in gaps in my education. Two local economic assistants worked to bring me up to speed, but the local Scientific Affairs Specialist Bakhtiyor Mukhamadiev could manage quite well without me.[53] Young and energetic, he had an MS degree in water management from Texas A&M. After a month or two, I told him that although my heart belongs to science, I needed to concentrate on economic and business matters. I put in an appearance at meetings when an American face was needed, but otherwise Bakhtiyor ran his own show that eventually led to a U.S.-Uzbekistan Science and Technology Cooperation Agreement.[54]

DCM Duane Butcher arrived in the summer of 2008, and Ambassador Norland used Duane's arrival to take some needed leave time. Duane was thus Chargé d'affaires and I was acting pol/econ chief when Deputy Assistant Secretary George Krol announced he was coming to Tashkent. We frantically put together a meeting schedule and briefing papers. For a day and a half, the three of us used the Ambassador's Cadillac to go from one meeting to another with me serving as notetaker. The gatekeeper at my housing community stared wide-eyed when I returned that night in a Cadillac instead of on my bicycle.

Ironically, I had little use for the Uzbek language I had labored over fitfully for six months. Russian was still the language of diplomacy. I spoke English and Russian 99 percent of the time. Why had I spent six months with Babur at FSI?

A business conference far from the capital taught me why. The conference was in Uzbek. My Russian was of no use here, and so I sat in the back with my LES assistant interpreting quietly into my ear. During a break, the or-

---

53   Technically, Bakhtiyor worked for the Central Asia Environment, Science, Technology, and Health (ESTH) Regional Office. This office, sometimes referred to simply as *The ESTH Hub*, had its own small office suite and library in Tashkent, but there was no American FSO. Bakhtiyor was the only person there. The Hub had suffered the same fate as other regional offices, the victim of the collapse in U.S.-Uzbek relations. The FSO managing the *Hub* was now in Astana, Kazakhstan, supposedly as a temporary measure. He and Bakhtiyor worked together at a distance, joining forces to travel through the five Central Asian countries covered by the Hub. Technically speaking, I was Bakhtiyor's local supervisor, as I managed the economic portfolio. The Department in its wisdom long ago decreed that science falls in the realm of economics.

54   Secretary Clinton signed the agreement on a visit to Tashkent after my departure. It was one of the first tangible signs that the *cold war* between the United States and Uzbekistan was beginning to thaw. Michael Schena at the Bureau of Oceans and International Environmental and Scientific Affairs (OES) in Washington deserves credit for pushing the agreement and for giving Bakhtiyor and me what we needed to get the Uzbek government on board.

ganizers asked if I would say a few words. I agreed, not knowing they had also approached a Russian Embassy representative. He spoke first and in Russian only. Following him, I used broken Uzbek to introduce myself, explain my work at the U.S. Embassy, and say that the U.S. looked forward to increasing business ties with Uzbekistan. Then, I apologized for my poor Uzbek and said I would continue in Russian.

Before I could say another word, the audience applauded and stood to give me a standing ovation. Then the contrast hit me. A U.S. diplomat had just spoken, albeit poorly, in Uzbek, while the Russian representative had spoken only in Russian. For a country trying to break away from a century and a half of Russian domination, my speaking Uzbek signified respect for those aspirations. My months of struggle to learn Uzbek had validated themselves. My address received coverage on Uzbek television news. FSOs are typically told not to make headlines, but this was the type of headline the State Department wants us to make. Never again did I anguish over my months of Uzbek study at FSI.

Meeting with farmers in the Ferghana Valley

Tashkent was not Moscow, and Uzbekistan felt much like being in the Soviet Union. The Lenin statues were gone, but the government newspaper
was still called *Pravda vostoka* (*Pravda of the East*) as it had been in Soviet
times. Independence in 1991 had brought not reform but nationalism and
authoritarian rule under Karimov who systematically pushed aside all opposition. After the Islamic Movement of Uzbekistan carried out terrorist
bombings in Tashkent in 1999, Karimov moved to eliminate opposition
in the literal sense. Uzbekistan became a police state with torture methods
reportedly extending to *boiling in oil.*[55]

High trade barriers blocked almost all Western consumer goods. When
I told local friends of the new economic crisis unfolding in the U.S., they
stopped me by saying, "We've been in an economic crisis since 1991."
Life was difficult. Money was scarce with many employers going months
without paying salaries. Banks frequently did not have cash for weeks at a
time. The largest banknote was 1,000 soum, about $0.50 USD, and shop-
ping trips meant putting money in bags, not a wallet. People hoarded what
money they had, and the shadow barter and black-market economy may
have been as large as the official economy.

Despite this gloom, Tashkent was not a gloomy city, and neither were
its citizens. Impressive historical and modern areas abounded, and the
food—none of it fast food—was wonderful. Outdoor vendors grilled
shashlyk (shish kebab) on almost every corner. Recalling the smell of fresh
fruits and vegetables in open-air markets still causes my mouth to water.

I had friends again. My Petersburg and Moscow friends had friends of
their own in Tashkent. Before I left Moscow, they told me, "We'll put you
in good hands." They did. I found myself invited for dinners, walking tours,
and theater and concert events. Vika, my long-time friend from Petersburg, came to visit in September 2008. She had been born in Uzbekistan,
and she showed me all the places from her childhood.

I look back on the autumn and winter of 2008–09 as a *phony war* in my divorce. My no-frills, bargain-basement attorney did not rush to file papers.
I wrote to Helena with settlement proposals. I took it as a given that she
would keep the family home and cars plus half of our retirement and other

---

55 Although himself a controversial figure, former British Ambassador Craig Murray
gives a good sense of human rights violations under Karimov in his book *Murder in
Samarkand* (Mainstream Publishing, 2007).

assets. I suggested legal separation, not divorce, so that she would still be covered by my health insurance. With Matt now in college and tuition fully paid for, child support was not an issue. There were no replies.

The *hot war* began in the summer of 2009, when my attorney filed divorce papers. Within days, Helena's attorneys sent requests for documents and interrogatories. They were detailed and voluminous. While my attorney had slept through the winter, Helena's attorneys had been hard at work. Their firm was reputed to be one of the ten best family law firms in Washington, D.C. I was badly outgunned and had to find a new attorney who would be a match for this opposition. My life revolved around interrogatories and replies to document requests. My focus on the Uzbek economy weakened.

Transgender issues? They weren't anywhere in view. I had accepted defeat in 2002 and was going to take this to the grave. I was at peace with that.

Helena's attorneys, however, had different ideas. Upon receiving a large package of discovery materials, I experienced a body blow. Throughout, page after page, in black and white, was my transgender history. Even medical records from Johns Hopkins in 1990. These were papers that had gone missing from my files years before. Painfully, I began to relive 1990 and 2000–02. I thought I had done everything possible to conform, but this was not how it had been seen through other eyes. Pages and pages of interrogatories and statements telegraphed a consistent message. As far as Helena's attorneys were concerned, my transgender history amounted to deception.

Rumors began to circulate when Helena wrote a letter, describing her *deluded* husband who thought he was a woman. Inna was one of the first to receive it. She forwarded it to me, asking if it was true. Stunned, I wrote back that it once had been a part of my life. The letter circulated within the State Department, perhaps all the way to the Director General of the Foreign Service. I began to fear for my future in the Department of State.

This brings me to the story of Sophia, my best friend in Tashkent. Her daughter Tamara was my son's age, and together I saw them as the picture of survival through difficult times. Their apartment was spare, and money was little and far between. Sophia and Tamara became my surrogate family and my release from the ever-increasing pressure of divorce.

Nearly my age, Sophia looked ten years younger and had a sense of humor and optimism that had seen her through Soviet rule and the ensuing economic chaos that came with independence. Here was a woman whose interest in me went beyond friendship. I thought again of Lenya's words: "Your one problem is that you married the wrong woman."

It had taken me over fifty years to learn an important lesson. I sat Sophia down at the kitchen table and told her, "There's something you need to know about me." When I was done, she asked, "Is this your past or is this your present?" I answered that I thought it was the past but in truth didn't know; my escalating divorce had consumed me. Sophia calmly replied, "That means you will understand me better, just like my girlfriends."

The response stunned me. Finally, here was someone who accepted me. "I'm a doctor and have seen everything," she reassured me. "We'll work this out together."

Our friendship grew. I went with Sophia and Tamara on regular shopping trips, helping choose their clothes. A shopkeeper once told me she had never seen a man so patiently accompany a wife on a shopping trip. "There's a reason," I thought silently.

Sophia would tell me about her personal life, and I could ask her things I never dared ask anyone. At times, on my own, I began to wonder if life with Sophia was a middle path, a possible life with someone who knew and was not appalled. Could it be? But I resisted commitment.

The divorce continued to escalate, and a date was set for mediation in May 2010 at the end of my tour in Uzbekistan. My work suffered. I could feel it, and I sensed that it was noticed. The divorce dominated my life, sapping both my savings and my energy. When it came time to bid on my next position after Uzbekistan, I did something that the Foreign Service considered unorthodox at best, tantamount to career suicide at worst—I asked to return to the world of information technology, feeling the switch would leave me free to concentrate on the divorce and building a new life.

I got my wish. In October 2009, I learned that I would go to an IT position in Moscow. Sophia was overjoyed, and I told her that once the divorce was final and I had gotten settled, I would invite her to come for a long visit. We could find out if there was a future for us.

Father and son at the border with Karakalpakstan

Matt came to visit twice, and I was relieved to know I had not lost him. We traveled together to the Ferghana Valley, to Samarkand, and even to desert fortresses in Karakalpakstan. We had agreed between us to never talk about the divorce.

I went on long bicycle trips to relieve stress, sometimes forty-five miles completely around Tashkent. In 2009, I rode the back roads for three days from Tashkent to Samarkand. Another time I rode to Khujand, Tajikistan, where I boarded a domestic flight to Dushanbe to support a regional economic conference.[56]

In 2009, I flew twice to Maine. I had received nearly $100,000 from Ma and Dad's estate, the only money not under the cloud of divorce. With my sis-

---

56 Relations between Uzbekistan and Tajikistan were so poor that there were no flights between the capitals. The only way to get from Tashkent to Dushanbe was to go overland from Tashkent to Khujand and continue from there to Dushanbe by domestic flight.

ters as real estate advisers, I bought thirty-five acres with a run-down camp not far from Lincoln, the town I had passed through in 2007 on the eve of asking for a divorce. At long last I had an address of my own in the U.S.

The movers came in late April 2010. I invited friends for a farewell dinner, and then we walked around nighttime Tashkent. I was too distressed over the divorce to connect with my sadness at leaving, but I was grateful for these friends who had supported me as I sank into the morass of litigation. I hugged Sophia, Tamara, and all my friends one last time. Then it hit me—I might never see them again.

That next day my plane rose into the sky, the cotton fields quickly replaced by steppe and desert. Soon I would see Helena across a mediation table, our first meeting in over two years. I would no longer have an ocean, a continent, nine time zones, and President Islam Karimov to protect me. My stomach tied itself into knots all through the long flights. When we landed in Washington, I knew only one thing for sure: I was scared.

7. Pacing the Cage

I've proven who I am so many times,
The magnetic strip's worn thin.
And each time I was someone else,
And everyone was taken in.[57]

Have you ever woken from a nightmare, relieved to realize it was a nightmare—only to find that you are still asleep, waking into a different nightmare? That was my summer of 2010.

Within a week of arriving in the U.S., I had a mediated divorce settlement with Helena. It was finally, unbelievably over even if the settlement was a tough one. I would need to pay over $35,000/year in support for ten years, and our assets would be split 40/60 in Helena's favor. But it didn't matter. With hardship and language pay, my salary in Uzbekistan had been close to $130,000, and it would be similar in Moscow. I could afford this agreement, and I was relieved that we had achieved it through mediation, not in a courtroom.

---

57   Cockburn, Bruce. "Pacing the Cage." Genius. Accessed September 10, 2023. https://genius.com/Bruce-cockburn-pacing-the-cage-lyrics.

I told myself I just had to get through the summer of home leave and training. As any FSO will confirm, our salaries drop to base level when we are on home leave. It can be a hard time, not a vacation at all. My annual salary while on home leave in summer 2010 was less than $90,000. Support payments coupled with payments to my attorney—to whom I owed $25,000—outstripped my after-tax salary. No matter, I thought. I still had $15,000 from my inheritance, and this would see me through until I reported to Moscow in August.

Relieved, I bought a used 1991 station wagon. I drove from Maryland to Maine, taking back roads, camping at night, and visiting places from my past. I hadn't seen my childhood homes in New York in over twenty years.

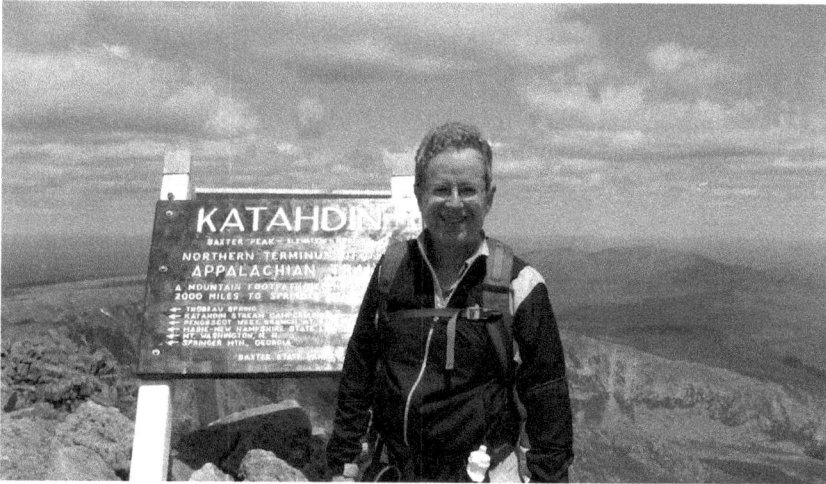

On Katahdin in summer 2010

There had been many changes since the 1960s, but I could still remember street names and directions. I visited our houses in Orangeburg and Monsey and the two-room schoolhouse where I had gone to second grade.

It took me nearly two weeks to reach Bangor. I had five weeks to spend in Maine before reporting back to FSI for five weeks of training. Much of the time went into fixing up my camp, but as often as I could, I was in the mountains. I climbed Katahdin, backpacked in Baxter State Park, and went on day hikes. I bought another bicycle and went on long rides. I had never been in a kayak but had to have one. I enjoyed afternoons on placid lakes under the warm Maine summer sun.

It took several weeks before I realized something wasn't right. I had been offered a *handshake* for my Moscow post a half-year earlier. *Handshake* is an official term in FSO-speak, an agreement by which a post stops looking for candidates and by which the candidate stops looking for posts. The posting becomes official when a candidate is *paneled*. This is usually automatic once a *handshake* is accepted, but I had not been *paneled*. The career development officer (CDO) overseeing my posting told me not to worry but to report to FSI as scheduled. At the end of June, I boarded a plane back to Washington.

Although I had worked over 25 years at CSC in applied mathematics and programming, I had no experience as a systems administrator. I was now at FSI to take courses such as Microsoft Server 2003 and Exchange Server. It was a hot, humid D.C. summer, and my time went into studying and preparing for exams. In mid-July, my CDO told me again not to worry, reassuring me that everything was on track. My new supervisor wrote that he wanted me in Moscow as quickly as possible, and I already had a housing assignment. My community sponsor asked what food I wanted in my refrigerator.

My future began to unravel in July when Diplomatic Security asked to speak with me about the Moscow assignment. I expected a quick conversation, but that expectation evaporated when I was ushered to a table in an interview room where two agents sat opposite me, and a third agent sat in the corner. The interview lasted two hours. The agents grilled me on my post-divorce financial situation. They asked probing questions about my friends in Russia even though I had long ago provided, as required, a list with details on the nature of those relationships. Most incongruous to me that day, however, were the agents' repeated remarks about blackmail. They stressed that a number of U.S. diplomats had been sent home from Moscow after Russian security had attempted to blackmail them because of matters of a *sexual nature*. I said nothing. The interrogation ended with the senior agent telling me I would be informed of a decision regarding Moscow within a few weeks.

With training over, I still had several weeks of vacation. Sophia came to the U.S. for two weeks and went with me to Maine. It was there, in late August, that I got the email telling me I would not be cleared to return to Moscow. I was in shock. Out of training and almost out of vacation, I didn't know what options were left.

The dream had become a nightmare. With a little netbook in my run-down camp, I began looking for a new post. I needed an assignment and needed it fast. I interviewed by phone for IT positions at two posts, Jamaica and Romania, and both offered *handshakes*. The salary at either post would be nothing like Moscow—in fact only slightly more than I was earning while on home leave—but it would be a salary. I knew nothing about either country, but I remembered the beauty of northern Romania from trips in 1978 and 1981. I accepted the *handshake* from our Embassy in Bucharest … and waited.

Again. the process in Washington slowed to a crawl. I was on leave without pay and could get no answers as to why I was not being *paneled*. It was now early September, and I was quickly running through what remained of my inheritance money. One thing was clear: I would default on my support payment to Helena come October. My attorney asked for a modification of support due to reduced salary, but from the other side there came only silence.

I continued to hike, bike, and go kayaking, but my joy at being in Maine was now edged with fear. I felt I was pacing a cage, wondering what would happen. I remembered the lines from a song by Bruce Cockburn—

> *I've proven who I am so many times,*
> *The magnetic strip's worn thin.*
> *And each time I was someone else,*
> *And everyone was taken in.*

I listened to that song over and over. It became my anthem as the leaves turned colors. Still there was no word from Washington.

"OK," I decided, "If I'm to be unemployed, let it end right here in Maine."

On a long hike in Baxter Park, I realized I had lost everything—my home, my savings, and perhaps my career. Everything that one spends a lifetime building was gone or almost gone, and I grimaced as I remembered the famous line from Kris Kristofferson's "Me and Bobby McGee:"

> *Freedom's just another word for nothin' left to lose.*[58]

---

[58] Kristofferson, Kris. "Me and Bobby McGee." Genius. Accessed September 10, 2023. https://genius.com/Kris-kristofferson-me-and-bobby-mcgee-lyrics.

Word came in the final week of September that I had been *paneled* for the Bucharest assignment. After the weeks of waiting, this was a happy surprise, but I already knew I would be cited for contempt when I made only a partial support payment on October 1. My legal bill would continue to grow as my salary dropped to the lowest it had been since I joined the State Department.

I landed in Bucharest on October 5, 2010. My sister Irene had told me many times to stop looking for geographic solutions to life's problems. "Remember," she would say, "Wherever you go, you take yourself with you." But maybe not this time? Could it be that Kris Kristofferson had it backward? I turned the words around:

> *Nothin' left to lose is another word for freedom.*

The day in Bucharest was cold, rainy, and gloomy, but I smiled as I stepped off the plane and kept repeating those words to myself: *Nothin' left to lose is another word for freedom.*

PART 3

Nothing Left to Lose (Oct 2010 – Nov 2011)

In October 2010, I set foot in Bucharest, a city I had never been to, in a country whose language I did not speak. I knew Romania to be the one country in Eastern Europe that overthrew its dictator Nicolae Ceaușescu in a bloody revolution, executing him on Christmas Day in 1989. I recalled that Alex Lipson, the Russian language professor who organized our Soviet Union trip in the summer of 1978, told us Bucharest has "no culturally redeeming value." With those not very comforting thoughts in the background, I headed forth into unknown territory that stretched from the streets of Bucharest to the inner recesses of my own hopes and desires.

1. Kyna

Winter, spring, summer or fall

All you have to do is call

And I'll be there

You've got a friend.[59]

Everything in Bucharest was strange, and I had no ready-made friends as in Moscow and Tashkent. I barely had money for food after being on leave without pay for most of September. It was going to be a long, hard winter. To make matters worse, letters from Helena's attorneys followed within days of my arrival in Romania and signaled the start of a new court battle over support.

Fortunately, my new work in the IT section at Embassy Bucharest was refreshingly laid back, a fact for which I was grateful as evenings and weekends demanded responding to requests for documents and writing answers to interrogatories. My legal bill, already well over $25,000, went higher and higher. My new co-workers knew of my plight; they often paid for me when we went out at lunchtime.

---

59   King, Carole. "You've Got a Friend." Genius. Accessed September 10, 2023. https:// genius.com/Carole-king-youve-got-a-friend-lyrics.

Most of all, there was Kyna, my social sponsor and upstairs neighbor in our modest apartment building at 15A Barbu Delavrancea Street. At the embassy, Kyna headed the medical unit. In the first days after my arrival, she showed me around the neighborhood, and we took more long walks as the days went by. Kyna once had her housekeeper cook and clean for me, and this one-off surprise evolved into a regular event as Kyna came to realize how badly off I was financially. There was a softness and a sense of humor about her that, I came to understand, comes from having lived a hard personal life. Everything about Kyna said, "You can trust me."

By 2010, Amazon had replaced the Sears catalog for anyone wanting to ex-periment with clothes of another gender. Clothing had never been the key issue for me, but it had given me comfort both as a child and in my college years at UVA. I had come to think of clothing as the *attitude quaternion* that takes me from one gender reference frame to another much as I used to transform one spacecraft reference frame to another.

I placed an order with Amazon. Nothing much, only a nightgown and also a skirt, blouse, and shoes. When I opened the package, my fears returned. What would happen if they found out about this at the embassy? I put everything in a bag and started for the dumpster. Ready to throw the bag in, I stopped myself. "Not this time," I whispered. "Not this time." I turned and walked home.

"Kyna, I need to talk with you about something." It was a late November day, and I had come to see her in the med unit. I was nervous, and Kyna sensed it. She closed the door, sat me down, and listened as no one had ever listened to me before. It all came pouring out—my childhood dream, the story of growing up, everything I had kept inside in 1975, my marriage, trying to come out in 1990 and landing in a psychiatric ward instead, and the tumultuous emotional ride of 2000–02.

When I was done, Kyna's first words were, "You need the biggest hug I can give you."

She wasn't appalled. There was no talk of sending me back to the U.S. Rather, Kyna began looking for resources to help me, people to talk to. The only promise Kyna exacted was that I not cross-dress in public, for fear that I might be attacked. I was new to Romania, but I already understood it to be a socially conservative country. The Romanian Orthodox Church played an outsize role in molding social values, and it was no friend to gays and lesbians, let alone to anyone who is transgender.

Kyna

Kyna became my confidante, my protector and promoter. We started walking to work together in the mornings, continuing our conversations about gender and gender non-conformity. Kyna patiently tolerated my early attempts at changing my voice with a grating falsetto. She encouraged me to follow my own way, and she promised to be there for me.

That first hug and those first words of support from Kyna stand out as a key event of my life. What might have happened if someone had hugged me and said those simple words in 1975? In 1990? In 2002? For any transgender person, so much depends on the reaction of the first person one opens up to. It just took fifty-six years for Kyna to become that first person in my transgender life.[60]

I never asked Kyna the meaning of her name during our first winter together. Only later did I discover that it's an Irish name. In Gaelic, Kyna means wise.

2. The Education of a Transgender Rip Van Winkle

> Rise again, rise again!
> Though your heart it be broken and life about to end
> No matter what you've lost, be it a home, a love, a friend
> Then like the Mary Ellen Carter, rise again![61]

In December 2010, I rubbed my eyes and began to wake from a 35-year slumber, like a transgender Rip Van Winkle.

Think of it. In 1975, I had read Jan Morris' *Conundrum* and then devoured everything about transsexualism I could find in the libraries at UVA. I had also reached out to the gender clinic at Hopkins.

Then I lost my nerve. I stopped my search for a new life and purged the trappings of this journey completely. I put my transgender self into a deep slumber. If a transgender story appeared in the newspaper, I did not read it. If there was a report on the TV news, I changed the channel.

I remained in that purposeful hibernation, avoiding anything and everything that had a transgender theme. Even as I told Sophia about my transgender self, I did so with reference to what I knew in 1975. I had never heard the words *transgender* or *gender identity*. The words hadn't yet been invented in the 1970s.

So here I was, yawning, stretching, and rubbing my eyes in December

---

60 As a woman who transitioned later in life, of course I wonder how different my life would have been if I had been born thirty or forty years later. I sometimes envy—what Russian speakers would call good or white envy (белая зависть)—younger transgender persons who have been able to transition at a much younger age with their full lives ahead of them. Then I catch myself. What kind of life would I have had if I had been born earlier, say in 1914?

61 Rogers, Stan. "The Mary Ellen Carter." Genius. Accessed September 10, 2023. https://genius.com/Stan-rogers-the-mary-ellen-carter-lyrics.

2010. As I reawakened, Kyna confessed to knowing little about transgender issues, but she directed me to web sites and literature she thought could help.

My life that December was a triad. I was still learning my new job at Embassy Bucharest. This was the easy part. The hard part was the new legal battle over support to Helena. Even the Christmas-New Year's week disappeared into the legal dark hole of interrogatories.

The third leg of my triad was the self-reeducation of this transgender Rip Van Winkle. So much had happened during my years of slumber. I had never heard of Jennifer Finney Boylan, Mara Kiesling and the National Center for Transgender Equality, or the Human Rights Campaign. I learned that progress had been made; while it was still a difficult path, not all transgender persons automatically lost their careers and families.

"So, are you going to go see her?" asked Kyna. We were walking to work on a December morning when Kyna asked about Iulia Molnar. She was the psychologist at Romania's LGBT+ rights organization, Accept, and I had found her through Kyna. I told Kyna that I would see Iulia the next Friday.

Accept was located on a quiet side street, a long walk from the embassy's downtown location. It was a snowy, slushy day in Bucharest, but there is something welcoming about crossing the threshold into Accept with its many cats, its smiling volunteers, and the always ready teapot. Iulia met me and walked me to her office.

For an hour, I told Iulia the story of my life, from the childhood dream through my divorce and uncertain future. Iulia listened quietly. When I was finished, she offered gently, "I think it's time you finally gave Robyn permission to live her life." She urged me to attend an upcoming transgender congress, promising to put me in touch with the organizers.

Of all the organizations that I learned of, the most important was Gays and Lesbians in Foreign Affairs Agencies (GLIFAA). I had been dimly aware of GLIFAA from the moment I joined the Foreign Service, but I had steered clear of it. In December 2010, I was still uncertain whether GLIFAA knew anything about transgender issues, but that changed quickly when I found an article on the GLIFAA website by Dr. Chloe Schwenke, a senior adviser on African development issues at the U.S. Agency for International Development.

It was a pivotal moment for me. Chloe had transitioned gender two years earlier in 2008. She had been one of the lucky ones; while she lost her job, she had preserved her marriage and family. Chloe had been working for a USAID contractor. After being let go, Chloe went to GLIFAA. Together they began a lobbying effort to have gender identity added to the employee non-discrimination policies at State and at USAID. That effort was ultimately successful. Secretary Clinton signed the policy reform in the summer of 2010, and President Obama then appointed Chloe directly to USAID. Together with Amanda Simpson and Dylan Orr, Chloe was one of the first high-level transgender appointees in the U.S. government.[62]

Chloe's existence was to me like the proverbial apple falling on Isaac Newton's head. Maybe my career was not over? We began a correspondence that lifted me as I continued unhappily through my deepening legal battle.

Not all was brightness, however, on this resumed transgender journey. Over Skype I watched myself die in Sophia's eyes. First, there was the realization that we would not be together again soon. I didn't have enough money to buy her an airplane ticket to Romania. Even if I could have bought a ticket, there would be nothing for her in Bucharest. She spoke no Romanian or English. Long-distance, I did my best to comfort her through her mother's final illness and death.

In December, I broke the news that I had started down a transgender path on my own. This was not something we would figure out together. "I now know this is not only my past," I told her. "I don't know yet where this road will take me, but I need to follow it." I felt brutal in my honesty, and I knew the words hurt. I had dashed Sophia's dreams and hopes. It was faint comfort, but I knew this was the conversation I should have had with Helena decades earlier. Although late, I was coming to understand that the pain one inflicts on others by keeping one's true identity hidden is cumulative, mounting ever higher until the moment of disclosure. Better to be open from the start and limit that pain. Honesty is an act of caring.

On New Year's Eve, I took a long walk to the center of Bucharest. I watched happy couples rushing to parties. It was the first time I had spent New Year's Eve alone in many years. I took stock. My financial situation was bleak, and my legal bill was growing with no end in sight. My relationship

---

62   Chloe eloquently chronicles her own life journey in *SELF-ish: A Transgender Awakening* (Red Hen Press, 2018).

with Sophia had been redefined as a friendship. All of these were reasons to be depressed, but as I watched the fireworks at midnight, my spirit lifted. Thanks to Kyna and Iulia, I had support and guidance. In Chloe's example I had found inspiration. As I watched the sky blaze in colors, it was Iulia's words that echoed in my mind:

I think it's time you finally gave Robyn permission to live her life.

"Maybe, just maybe," I thought to myself, "maybe in 2011 I will." The self-imposed, decades-long hibernation of this transgender Rip Van Winkle had officially ended.

3. Fortochka

Чуда хочется настоящего ни на что, ни на что несмотря ...	I want a miracle no matter, no matter what ...
Что принесёт мне белый ветер этого января?[63]	What will you bring me, white January wind?

Kyna was reaching down a hand and helping me up from the ice. One moment we had been walking and talking, and then my legs went out from under me. I lay there, sprawled out with a surprised expression and feeling what would soon become bruises.

Kyna's hand lifting me up is another image that stays in my mind years after. It may only have been an icy path on the way to work that morning, but she was also helping me find balance on the unsure, risky path to a new life.

"So, are you going to tell anyone?" Kyna resumed the January morning conversation. "I guess I'll have to," I replied, "but I don't know when."

We were talking about the upcoming transgender congress that would take place in Brasov, several hours to the north of Bucharest. As promised, Iulia Molnar had put me in touch with the organizers. I was getting ready to go for two weeks of training in the U.S., and the congress would happen shortly after I got back. Only Kyna at the embassy knew I was going. Should I tell anyone else?

---

63 Yashchenko, Zoya. "Belyi veter yanvarya [The White Wind of January]." Bgvmusic. Accessed September 10, 2023. https://bgvmusic.ru/creations/albom-varenie/belyj-veter-yanvarya.html.

"I think you may want to tell someone," Kyna said. "What if a group of skinheads breaks up your congress and you land in a hospital and then a newspaper headline?"

Kyna was right, but I was nervous and delayed telling anyone.

During those January walks with Kyna, I opened my *fortochka* (форточка). In Russian, the *fortochka* is a small window inside a much larger one that is opened with the first thaws that presage the coming of spring. I was now opening the *fortochka* that I had kept closed most of my life.

Opening the *fortochka* meant I would have to start talking with people beyond my inner circle of Kyna, Iulia, and Chloe. I would have to be honest with people who might not be accepting. With memories of past rejections vividly replaying in my head, I was scared.

We all called him the G-Man. He was my new co-worker, freshly arrived in Bucharest in December. Until then I had worked on my own, but the G-Man and I would now share the work and our small, cramped office. We would get to know each other intimately whether we wanted to or not.

The G-Man was a naturalized U.S. citizen, Chilean by birth. He was ten years younger than me, neither tall nor short, of solid build with a wide face and a swarthy Latin complexion. Balding, he often wore a beret and had a deep, resonant, almost professional singing voice. I found him elegantly handsome, but I also knew my life could be heaven or hell, depending on the relationship we developed. We began a slow dance of coming to know each other.

The G-Man once owned his own company and had become modestly wealthy in the 1990s. He sold his company, planning never to work again, and set off on a bicycle journey across the U.S. When the dot-com bubble burst in the late '90s, the G-Man lost most of his life investments and found himself in need of a job. He made his way to the State Department a year after I did.

Talk of bicycling initially helped us form a bond. My CSC/NASA career fascinated him, and he never tired of hearing my stories. I began to open up slowly. We talked about my divorce and ongoing post-divorce litigation, about his family in Chile, and about his wife and two children who would be joining him in a few weeks. He was also a patient educator who helped me learn my job day by day.

One morning, as I walked into the office, G-Man's mouth dropped.

"What in the world happened to you?" he asked as he stared at my face. I had gone the night before for my first-ever electrolysis session with an electrologist who, it turned out, knew nothing about electrolysis. My face looked as though I had fallen off my bicycle and suffered road rash. I couldn't hide it. I told the G-Man that I had had a *shaving accident.* I could not come up with a better cover story, and I had to repeat it many times to others throughout the day.

The G-Man liked to tell stories and jokes, and he warned me to stop him if he ever went too far. For the first several weeks I laughed often at his un-ending storehouse of tales. I needed the laughter, and the G-Man provided a good release. But then, one day, he started to tell a new story from his past. It went something like this:

> I had a job once where the boss came around introducing a new employee. I was busy with something and looking the other way. I heard him say "I'd like you to meet Di-ane." I said hello and turned around to shake her hand. Would you believe it, it was a man! She was in a dress, but I knew that underneath it was a man. No one else did, but I knew. I can sense these things ....

My face must have gone pale. The G-Man trailed off in mid-sentence and looked puzzled. My mind raced. What was I going to do? Was I going to run from myself yet again?

We both fell into a silence, a heavy silence that seemed to last a lifetime. I broke the silence in a whisper, looking the G-Man in the eyes and saying slowly, carefully, "I could be Diane, the woman you are talking about."

I don't recall what the G-Man said in response. I was too nervous to re-member, but I felt we had turned a corner. Over the next several weeks, our slow dance together continued to evolve. Bit by bit, I told the G-Man my story. I knew I had before me not Kyna but my co-worker—a suave, somewhat macho guy rooted in Chilean culture. This conversation was going to be different.

"Haven't you ever gone out of your mind with sexual desire?" the G-Man asked one day.

"Never," I said.

"Not even once?"

"No, not even once."

I told him about my sexual life, such as it was, in which the roles always seemed perversely backwards. I simply did not enjoy male sex. I wanted to be the woman in the relationship.

"Haven't you seen how guys flock to a beautiful woman like moths to a flame?" the G-Man asked. "What do you feel when you look at a beautiful woman?"

"I feel she is lucky."

"What do you think of when you look at her face?" the G-Man continued to probe.

"I think of the great job she has done with her makeup and hair and wish I could ask her how she did it. I'm envious."

The G-Man paused, puzzled understanding registering on his face. I had broken through. This was not a passing fancy, some momentary short circuit in the brain that a female sex partner could fix. This was different.

The G-Man became my educator, explaining to me what sex is like for a man.

"Did you ever notice how the local staff guys become jittery if we sit too long in a meeting?"

"Sure, I've noticed that."

"It's because they're all smokers. They have to have their regular fix. Without it, they can't work, they can't do anything. It's the same with sex. Without sex, a man can't live."

We continued our discussion over the weeks and months to come as we deepened our conversations on sex and gender. I don't know if the G-Man ever understood me fully, but I know that I eventually won his heart. The G-Man had unexpectedly become a protector.

Kyna and the G-Man. Now there were two at the Embassy who knew.

Kyna continued to worry about my going to the transgender congress in Brasov. She pushed me to tell someone in our Regional Security Office (RSO), the people whose job it is to keep us safe while in-country. I had already upset the RSO in Tashkent when I set out by bicycle to Tajikistan without telling anyone. What would be the reaction if anything unusual happened while I was in Brasov?

It took me days to get the courage. When I did, I approached our regional security officer (RSO) in the hallway and said I needed to have a conversation with him. He seemed to be expecting me, but he stopped me from speaking in the hallway. Instead, he told me to come to our secure conference room in the afternoon.

When I came, the RSO was waiting with two assistant RSOs. I sat down opposite them at the conference table. Notepad ready, the RSO asked what I wanted to talk about. My confidence was rapidly deserting me. I stammered:

"With my divorce now final, I'm moving ahead to explore an area of my life I never could before. I'll be going to a transgender congress in Brasov in early March. I'm slowly coming out as the T in LGBT."

His response floored me.

"Gee, Bob, that's another one of your fancy NASA acronyms, isn't it? Could you spell it out?"

As I left the meeting, I wondered if I had put the stake through the heart of my limping career. Could emails already be on their way to Washington about this FSO who suddenly blurted out the word transgender? The RSO remained expressionless throughout, but from his even tone I again got the feeling that he had been waiting for a confession of some kind.

Later, when doing a check of communication equipment in one of the secure conference rooms, I accidentally discovered that Diplomatic Security in Washington still had me under investigation. Someone had left behind meeting notes. I couldn't help but read them when I saw I had been the subject. The agenda? Whether I should be recalled on security grounds.

As best I can tell, Diplomatic Security did not end its investigation until late 2011. I have no way to know for certain, but I believe my openness with the RSO played a key role in ending it. By coming out as transgender,

I had removed a secret that had blackmail potential. Foreign security services do use personal secrets as leverage when targeting Americans who have access to classified information. As long as I had my *deep dark secret*, I could have been a target.

On February 5, I boarded a pre-sunrise flight at Bucharest's Otopeni Airport, bound for Washington and two weeks' training at FSI. Outside of training hours, Chloe Schwenke had agreed to meet me in person. I had also made an appointment with Martha Harris, a well-known counselor on gender issues, and I had scheduled a session with an electrologist a few blocks from my hotel. Romania's January white wind and snows had not yet produced a miracle in my life, but they had given me the opening, the *fortochka* that I wished I could have had decades sooner.

4. Liftoff!

Поехали! [64]   *Here we go!*

It is February 17, 2011, sometime after 4:00 p.m. The clock is counting down the final seconds.

Hair. Blow dryer, brushes, and an hour of combing and fussing. Thank goodness it's been months since a haircut, so I have something to work with. Barely OK but yes, hair is GO. Check.

Face. Triple-blade razor, concealer, and foundation. Good thing I'm more gray than dark. No beard shadow. Change to a new pair of glasses. Not as bad as I expected. Face and hair are GO. Check.

Purple blouse, sweater, and brown slacks from Macy's. Shoes. Why did I wear thick socks when I bought these shoes? Wad tissue and shove it in so they won't fall off. Hair, face, and outfit are GO. Check.

Brown handbag over shoulder. Cosmetics in bag. Did I move everything to my new wallet? Hair, face, outfit, and handbag GO. Check.

Vital signs: Heart pounding. Pulse racing. Nervous stomach. Sit for a moment and get centered. HOLD!

· · · · · · · · · · · · · · · ·

---

64   Yuri Gagarin's words as he lifted off in Vostok 1 on April 12, 1961, to become the first human in space.

I landed at Washington's Dulles Airport on Saturday evening, February 5. On Monday I was to begin two weeks of training at FSI. That was during the day, but in the evenings I had a series of meetings and events set up to find out, at long last, about myself. "It's research," I thought, "no different from any other research project I've worked on." It's just that this time I was both the researcher and the research subject.

From Dulles, I caught the express bus to Rosslyn. I sat next to another U.S. government traveler, and we made small talk about flights, long connection times, customs, and jet lag. What would he have thought about my real journey?

From Rosslyn it was a quick one stop by Metro to Courthouse station and a five-minute walk to my hotel—home for the next two weeks. I checked in, dropped my bags, and walked back into the evening to Azure Dream Day Spa. I had learned that cosmetician Leila Espari was opening a new spa, and I called her from Bucharest. She invited me to her grand opening party that would take place the evening of my arrival.

I walked in to find Leila's celebration in full swing with much of her extended Iranian family in attendance. A table was set with appetizers, drinks, and sweets. I seemed to be the only non-relative there, but the joy and hope of the evening was infectious with animated conversation, kisses, and hugs all-round. Within minutes I felt I had been adopted into the family.

When the party began to wind down, Leila took me into a treatment room. She took a close look at my unshaven face and assured me, "This isn't going to be bad." She recommended laser treatment for the dark hair and electrolysis for the white. I had my first laser session then and there.

Sunday morning, I was back for electrolysis. For an hour and a half, I lay there as Leila used her needle to remove hairs one by one. The pain was not as bad as I expected—nothing like the pain inflicted by the inexperienced Bucharest electrologist who had left me bloody and red with road rash. Being with Leila felt right.

Visiting Leila became part of my daily routine. In the days to come, nobody asked me about shaving accidents.

. . . .

Vital signs. Heart still pounding. Pulse still racing. "Am I really going to do this?" HOLD?

· · · · · · · · · · · · · · · ·

Wednesday evening, February 9. Shannon Doyle, from the Washington Metro Area Gender Identity Connection (MAGIC-DC), met me in my hotel lobby. Her spouse Mary was with her. The wind dug into our faces that frigid evening as we walked a few blocks to a Thai restaurant. Shannon was tall with long hair, just a few years older than me. Mary, shorter, glowed with her own quiet beauty. They were both retired from the Department of Justice, where Shannon had worked in IT and Mary had been an attorney. Mary supported Shannon through transition, and now Shannon was supporting Mary as early Alzheimer's placed its cold hand on her. I could feel the love between them, and I felt deeply sad that Helena and I had never experienced this.

"Shannon," I said, emotionally overcome, "before tonight I never knowingly sat across from a person who has felt what I have felt my entire life."

It was true. Childhood cross dressing. Trying to come out in college and not being able to cope. Purge. Marriage. Career. Family. Coming out to Helena in 1990. Psychiatry and disaster. Purge and hide again. I was 56 years old, had known I was different in 1960, but only now was I at last sitting with a kindred spirit.

I learned much about Shannon's story that night, and the conversation continued on the weekend when Shannon and Mary invited me to their home for dinner. I realized I was in the presence of two of the most balanced, loving, normal people I had ever known. This was no longer an academic research project. I understood from Shannon and Mary that being transgender is normal. I felt it with my whole being. I wanted the peace that Shannon had found.

· · · · · · · · · · · · · · · ·

Vital signs. Heart and pulse calmer. Stomach not so nervous. GO. "Ten, nine, eight, seven, six, five, ..."

I stood in front of my hotel room door, literally doing a countdown.

Did Alan Shepard feel like this? Did Valentina Tereshkova?

"Four, three, two, one ...."

I turned the knob, walked into the hallway and then to the elevator. No one around. The elevator door opened. Still no one. I stepped in. Another count. "Four, three, two, lobby."

The elevator door is going to open, and I'm going to die.

The door opened. I stepped out into the lobby. No one stopped and stared. No one pointed.

Then I was on the street in broad daylight. In college in 1975, I had always tried to avoid people, but here I was on a sidewalk in Courthouse, Virginia, in plain view, dressed as I wanted to be, as I needed to be. I started up the street.

I panicked when I saw a familiar face in the distance. Could this be a colleague I worked with in Tashkent? He was coming my way. I quickly turned down a side street and stopped to calm myself.

A moment later I was back on the main street in the late-afternoon rush, people all around. I suddenly had trouble with my shoes and stopped to put in more tissue.

Up and walking again, I made my way to Leila's spa. Leila tended to my hair, giving it a bit more style, and gave me a thumbs up.

"It's just like riding a bicycle!" I gasped to myself in self-realization as I walked towards the Courthouse Metro station.

In 1975, I had gone forth as myself in the shadows, scared to death what would happen if anyone recognized me. That's also how I drove a bicycle in the early 1990s when I first became a daily commuter. I hugged the curb, trying to stay out of everyone's way—which resulted in repeated mishaps and injuries. As I gained experience, I learned that bicycle safety means taking one's rightful place in the traffic flow and being visible. Now I was applying that same, hard-learned rule to life: Be visible, be assertive, and join the traffic. I had as much right to walk down that street as anyone.

Minutes later I was in the Metro station. The platform was crowded and so were the rush-hour trains. If anyone noticed me at all, I didn't notice that they had. I went to the end of the line and up to the street again.

By now I was flying, giddy, excited. All inhibition had fallen away in less than thirty minutes. I was in orbit, weightless and in ecstasy, part of a miracle that was beginning to unfold.

I made my way to the Banyan Counseling Center to see Martha Harris, a counselor versed in gender issues whom I had learned of through Chloe Schwenke. This was my third visit. On the first two visits I had still been in guy mode, but I quickly sensed this would be different from my psychiatric experience in 1990. Martha encouraged me to talk about myself, and I did not feel that I was being sized up for the proper antidepressant dosage. With Cheryl Wheeler playing on her stereo and two cats in attendance, I felt I had been welcomed into a home, not a therapy center.

On this third visit, Martha greeted me with a smile. "Good evening, Madame." I kicked off my shoes and got comfortable on her couch. In less than an hour, after decades of hiding, I no longer asked if. Rather, I asked how and when.

I did not want the night to end. For a few hours I had gone into orbit, did not die, and had become me.

. . . .

I planned to spend a few days with my sister Irene in Maryland before flying back to Bucharest. I called her before checking out of my hotel.

"Irene, do you think you could take a surprise today?" Shannon had warned me that the words *transgender* and *surprise* do not go well together, but I took the risk.

"Will I recognize you?" Irene asked. It was my faithful sister, back in 1990, who had taken me to the hospital and visited me there daily. Back then, I think she had been as much in shock as Helena, but that had changed in the years since. We had become closer, and I had come to lean on my big sister for support as my marriage began its prolonged, tortuous decline.

On that windy Saturday I lugged a suitcase and a carry-on bag through the city. The Metro was closed in the city center, and I had to shuttle between stations by bus. The wind, bags, and unexpected Metro transfers undid my hour and a half of prepping at the hotel. Some people did look quizzically in my direction. But I couldn't care less. I felt wonderful, and that was all that counted.

Irene gave me a hug when I arrived at my final stop. She still recognized me. In the car, I told her the story of my past two weeks. I told her about Leila, about Shannon and Mary, about Martha, and about taking flight on Thursday.

That night we went out to dinner as sisters, greeted by the waiter who called us *ladies*. Two teenage girls in the next booth kept sneaking peeks and giggling, but I refused to let it bother me. Before going to bed, Irene acknowledged my rebirth by giving me some of Ma's jewelry and scarves. I was overcome by emotion. The same sister who had delivered me to my first psychiatrist in 1990 had accepted me.

The following week I met Chloe Schwenke at USAID. I arrived in guy clothes, as I didn't have the nerve to go as my new self into a government building where I would have to present my ID badge. I recognized Chloe as she got off the elevator, and she had no trouble recognizing me.

"You must be Robyn." Chloe's voice was at once feminine and professional. She stepped back, got a good look at me, and told me how lucky I was to be short and of small build.

I behaved like a star-struck teenager in the presence of her favorite Hollywood actress. "I can't believe I'm really sitting with you, Chloe," was the thought going through my head. "You are real. You really exist. Here you are at USAID, and here I am sitting across from you." Chloe was no longer articles on the Internet and responses to emails but a real, physical person. She had taken the transgender road and had fought for her right to exist. She had prepared the path for me. Thanks to Chloe, I would find a way forward. Our half hour coffee passed in what seemed like a minute.

· · · · · · · · · · · · · · ·

On February 27 I sat in Dulles Airport, waiting for my flight back to Europe. I knew nothing in my life would ever be the same. My time in the U.S. had been a suborbital hop, not much more than Alan Shepard's fifteen-minute flight, but I had been in space and knew I would return. I was free. I had found my future, and nothing would stop me from getting there.

5. *Stepping Out in Bucharest*

What's that I feel now beating in my heart?
I've felt that beat before.
What's that I feel now beating in my heart?
I feel it more and more.
It's the rumble of freedom calling,
Climbing up to the sky.
It's the rumble of the old ways a falling,
You can feel it if you try.[65]

I arrived back in Bucharest on March 4, 2011, elated over my two and a half weeks in the U.S. and sad that it was over. I had promised Kyna I would not be public in Bucharest. Our little FSO worlds overseas are like fishbowls. It is nearly impossible to hide. Rumors travel quickly.

I didn't unpack until the next day. As I did, I wistfully looked at the clothing I had purchased at Macy's. "Well, why not? It's Saturday, and I'm at home." A few minutes later I looked at myself in the mirror and did what I could with my hair. Then a thought occurred to me. I called Kyna and asked if I could come upstairs. Without saying about what precisely, I told her I needed her professional opinion.

When Kyna opened her door, she gasped and took a step backward. "I need a vodka," she said. She sank into a chair and pointed to the refrigerator. "You need one too."

I poured two shots. Kyna told me to take a few steps back and turn around. "You look lovely," she said, a compliment I never expected to hear in my life.

Kyna continued, "I'm going to the theater on Sunday evening. You're coming too."

"But you told me I should never appear in public as Robyn," I demurred.

"I know, but you're fine. Let's go together."

65 Ochs, Phil. "What's that I Hear?" Genius. Accessed on September 10, 2023. https://genius.com/Phil-ochs-whats-that-i-hear-lyrics.

I asked if anyone else would be joining us. The answer was yes, Laurie, Ray, and Natalie from the embassy. I objected, but Kyna said she was sure it would be okay. Still, remembering Shannon's dictum that *transgender* and *surprise* do not fit well together, I called each of our theater companions. I explained that my life was moving in ways that might surprise them. To the point, I was coming out openly as transgender and planned to go to the theater as myself. To my relief, no one objected.

The next day I bought a blow dryer and spent two hours on hair and make-up to be ready for a night at the theater. But when I went upstairs and rang her bell, Kyna was in a nightgown. "I'm sick," she said. "I can't go."

My heart dropped. All of that work for nothing. Then Kyna surprised me. "But you're going," she said. "I've already called a taxi." Now my heart was beating loudly in terror. I couldn't see myself going without Kyna at my side to support me.

Kyna loaned me a suede jacket for the evening. Then she threw a coat over her nightgown, led me outside to the waiting taxi, pushed me in, and told the driver where to take me. I was sure the driver would look in his rear-view mirror at this unusual-looking woman, but he never did. To him, I was just another fare.

Fifteen minutes later I stood in the lobby of a downtown Bucharest theater. Natalie, Ray, and Laurie had yet to appear. I waited alone, in shock to think I had stepped out in Bucharest as Robyn. A few people gave me quizzical sideways glances, but most paid me no attention.

Natalie appeared ten minutes later, waving from a distance. When she got closer, she exclaimed that I looked fine, and so did Laurie and Ray when they joined us. We moved to our seats, and an evening of African dance began.

A friend of Laurie's from the Canadian Embassy came over during the intermission. Laurie introduced me as Robyn. We shook hands, and she asked how long I had been in Bucharest. As far as she was concerned, I was a diplomatic colleague, a woman newly arrived at the U.S. Embassy.

Three hours later I was home again, my Cinderella evening over all too quickly. The next day I returned to work in professional male dress that was beginning to feel strange on my skin.

The following Saturday, Tudor Kovacs from the Romanian office of Population Services International (PSI) came in his car to take me to the transgender congress in Brasov. One of the most visible gay activists in Romania, Tudor had funded the congress through his PSI budget. A young Romanian trans woman was already in the car when he came for me. Getting to Brasov meant a long drive through spectacular Carpathian Mountain scenery, and my two companions spent most of the drive playing the role of tour guide for me, the American who had not yet gone any significant distance outside the capital.

Despite the scenery, my mind was on what was to come. I was both excited and nervous. What would I find at this weekend get-together that Tudor had dubbed the First Romanian Transgender Congress? The sun was already setting as we arrived in Brasov and checked into the hotel Tudor had chosen for the weekend. With no events planned that night, I went to my room and spent the evening with a book.

In the morning, I went to the small conference room reserved for us. The chairs were arranged in a circle, and most everyone else was already seated. In all, there were nine transgender women and two transgender men, and I was by far the oldest in the room. We took turns at introducing ourselves. Looking around, I said I must be old enough to be the mother of everyone in the room. I looked at the two youngest and added that I could be their grandmother. One was still in high school. Tudor translated my comments into Romanian, and no matter how accurate the translation, the group response seemed to be one of puzzlement and disbelief that a U.S. diplomat could be transgender.

The transgender minority in Romania differed greatly from the community I was coming to know in the U.S. Most of the transgender women I met that day were self-medicating with birth control pills, but the two transgender men said they had little difficulty buying testosterone and steroids. With the rapid physical changes brought on by testosterone, they had an easier time blending in as long as they did not need to show identity documents. There was no easy way to change gender in Romanian identity papers—doing so required court battles that sometimes lasted years. Few had succeeded.

As the morning wore on, I realized I wasn't the only foreigner in the room. Monica was from Moldova, that portion of Romania that was swallowed by the Soviet Union after the Molotov–Ribbentrop Pact of 1939. Monica was in her thirties, a decade older than the Romanian transgender women in the room.

Despite the language barrier, I felt a quiet but authoritative presence when Monica began to speak. While others were still questioning and searching, she was leading a committed group of activists that had met several times with the Ministries of Health and of Justice. Romanians tended to look down on Moldova as backward, but thanks to Monica, a discussion of transgender rights was taking place in Moldova that had yet to happen in Romania.

During the break I walked up to Monica and started to introduce myself in English. I had already gotten used to Romanians speaking at least some English, but I understood quickly that Monica speaks hardly a word. She started to walk away, but then I remembered that fifty years of Soviet occupation had made Russian obligatory in Moldova. I called after her in Russian. She turned around, surprised that an American could speak Russian. We started to chat. When it was time to reconvene in our circle, we sat next to each other. Monica served as my personal Romanian-Russian interpreter for the rest of the day, relieving Tudor of the need to interpret every word into English.

An evening dinner marked the end of this small event that Tudor had grandly dubbed a congress. As conversation continued well into the night, I thought about what my new companions were facing. Each of the transgender men and women I had met that day had more courage than I had shown in the U.S. when I was their age. The Romania of 2011 was as socially conservative as U.S. society had been in my youth. I was in the presence of pioneers, the Jan Morrises of Romania, struggling to find acceptance in a society that has no understanding of them.

The congress over, I was back at the embassy on Monday. Without realizing it, I had begun to live the classic double life. I was *good old Bob* in the workplace, but on weekends and evenings, I was Robyn. Fear and nervousness melted away as winter turned to spring. I became ever more comfortable going through the normal activities of life. Even clothes shopping at Bucharest department stores was not a problem. Rarely did I get a sideways glance. If anything, I seemed to attract less attention now.

With Kyna and Natalie, spring 2011

On a warm spring Saturday, Natalie, Kyna, and I went for lunch at a Lebanese restaurant in our neighborhood. As we walked down the street, I saw Curtis Presson, our information management officer and my direct supervisor, on the sidewalk ahead of us. By now I had told him I was coming out as transgender. I had no fears in that regard, but I was surprised when he paid no attention to me. Natalie was the first to realize that Curtis had not recognized me. "Curtis," Natalie said, "I don't think you've met Robyn yet, have you?" Curtis's eyes grew wide with amazement.

The circle of those in the know grew. Some had only a theoretical knowledge as I told them one by one. Others had the experiential knowledge as well. I was getting my wings, socializing comfortably with friends on the weekend. By summer, a dozen or more knew with certainty the path that I was taking.

Was it all easy and straightforward? Well, not always.

One day, I got a call from Kyna, asking to meet her in the med unit. When I came, she closed the door and asked what I had been wearing on Sunday. I described the outfit. Apparently Jeri, our DCM, had recognized me when

I unknowingly walked past her house. My Sunday outfit matched what she had seen, and she had asked Kyna if I was mentally stable. Could I be persuaded to relinquish my position, accept *compassionate curtailment*, and return to the U.S. and take care of *my problem*?

"Look, people know I'm your friend," Kyna explained, "so no one will take my word for it when I tell them you're fine." Kyna arranged a telephone interview with the State Department's regional psychiatrist in Vienna. We talked about Hubble, space, Russian history, and what it is to be transgender, quite a contrast to my previous experience with psychiatry in 1990. Kyna later told me the psychiatrist had expected to speak with a very troubled person, not someone who was accomplished and successful at work. No one bothered me further with proffers of compassionate curtailment.[66]

After that episode, I had no more reason to hide. I wasn't yet ready to make a global announcement, but neither would I worry about who knew and who didn't.

I also made a work decision. Prior to the Brasov congress, a closeted transgender FSO friend in the Senior Foreign Service (SFS),[67] had told me to remember my roots as a political reporting officer. After the congress, I sat down and wrote a three-page cable on Romania's transgender minority. I wrote it, as Russians in the Stalin period would have said, for the desk. I had no intention of showing it to anyone.

After the curtailment episode, I changed my mind. I took the report, dusted it off and improved it, and submitted it officially for clearance. The process took months, quite a contrast to the usual days or weeks needed for clearance, but in mid-summer the cable was released officially. To the best of my knowledge, that is the first State Department report ever written specifically on transgender issues.

Becoming myself—that was my spring of 2011. What had seemed impossible now felt normal and right. The pain of earlier failures in 1975–76, in

---

66 I learned later that the DCM had more than just compassionate curtailment in mind. Rather, she asked the Department to recall me for conduct incompatible with diplomatic status. In an earlier time, her request likely would have been acted upon. Thanks to Chloe Schwenke and GLIFAA, however, gender identity was now included in State Department non-discrimination policies. Gender identity could no longer be construed as incompatible with diplomatic status.

67 The Senior Foreign Service is to the Foreign Service what the Senior Executive Service is to the Civil Service.

1990, and 2000–02 faded into the past as though they had happened in another lifetime.

6. Stepping Out in Court

Are you going away with no word of farewell,
Will there be not a trace left behind?
I could have loved you better, didn't mean to be unkind.
You know that was the last thing on my mind.[68]

It was June 1, 2011. The venue—Circuit Court in Rockville, Maryland. Robyn's day in court had come.

My divorce had been finalized in the summer of 2010, but waves of new litigation washed over me after I lost my clearance to serve in Moscow. First, I was on leave without pay for a month. Then I scrambled to find the replacement posting that took me to Bucharest with a salary one-third lower than in Moscow. I could not meet my support payment of over $3,000/month, and I asked for an adjustment. Helena's attorneys cited me for contempt.

Interrogatories and replies to document requests dominated my long winter of 2010–11. Requests to open negotiations were rebuffed. Overtures made while I was in the U.S. in February were ignored. I flew to the U.S. again in early May for a settlement hearing mediated by a retired judge. My attorney Lisa was optimistic that everything would be resolved.

Lisa was wrong. The day started badly with the settlement judge deciding we should not all meet together in one room. The passions, at least on Helena's side, were still heated. Instead, the judge shuttled between two rooms. After going back-and-forth several times, he proposed a settlement based on my salary. I agreed quickly, but Helena and her attorneys would not budge. By noon the judge gave up, and the hearing ended without a settlement. Instead, we would go to trial later in the month.

Hours of preparation and written answers to still more interrogatories filled the next two weeks. When not preparing for court, I went on long

---

68   Paxton, Tom. "The Last Thing on My Mind." Genius. Accessed September 10, 2023. https://genius.com/Tom-paxton-the-last-thing-on-my-mind-lyrics.

walks with my sister Irene. I also went into downtown Washington several times. One day as I was going up the escalator at a Metro station, two men pointed and started laughing. *Passing* in Washington seemed more difficult than in Bucharest and more difficult than I remembered from the previous February. The stress of the coming trial was sapping my confidence.

I was back in court a few days later for a hearing on a motion to dismiss that Helena's attorneys had entered. They contended my support agreement was non-modifiable and that the court should cancel the trial and order me to pay back-support.

I did nothing at this hearing but sit and observe. Helena was not in the room. Lisa did the talking, as did Helena's attorney. When the judge almost granted the motion, I was confused. According to the terms of the agreement, he observed, support could be modified in the event of death, debilitating illness, or involuntary unemployment, but there didn't seem to be anything that covered a severe drop in income.

"Yes," Lisa said to the judge, "but it is our contention that my client's ex-spouse and attorneys may have played a material role in this reduction of income. They are not innocent victims."

The judge cut her off. "Alright, I won't comment on the merits of the case, but I will allow it to go forward to trial. Motion dismissed."

Outside the courtroom, Lisa turned to me and said, "Our case sucks. The judge almost granted their motion." Then she added, surprisingly, "Would you be comfortable coming to trial as Robyn?" I responded, "Sure. But why?"

Lisa said it was the last thing Helena's attorneys would expect. Moreover, she told me of a transgender family law attorney in Montgomery County who was well known to and respected by all the judges. The fact of my being transgender would not be an issue in the courtroom.

In the days to come I arrived at Lisa's office in a skirt and blouse, giving her a chance to get comfortable with the new me. Together, we worked and prepared. Lisa put Helena's outing letter at the center of our strategy. If that letter had gone all the way to the State Department's Director General and then to Diplomatic Security, could it have played a role in the denial of my Moscow posting? It seemed likely.

My sisters Gail and Irene went with me for the trial on June 1. We found the trial room and waited outside. Lisa soon joined us. I excused myself to use the restroom. As I started back, I heard a familiar voice, more accurately a gasp.

"Oh, shit. Oh sh-i-i-i-i-t. . . ."

It was Helena. We had been married for twenty-five years. Helena had known I was transgender since 1990, but this was the first time that she had met Robyn face-to-face. In years past I would have melted and surrendered in the glare of her disapproval, but those days were over. On June 1, 2011, I felt calm. I knew who I was and why I was in court.

I returned to Lisa and my sisters, and we entered the trial room. The judge entered and glanced at me, my appearance not fazing him in the least. He addressed us evenly, saying, "There is no reason this case should be in my court. We can go to trial if that's what we must do, but first I want you to try one last round of negotiating." I breathed a sigh of relief. Lisa's strategy seemed to be working.

The judge sent us off to separate rooms, and for two hours the attorneys shuttled back and forth, the judge serving as arbiter. When Helena's attorney entered our room, he looked fixedly at Lisa, averting his gaze. He did not want to look at me.

Things started to move. The opposing position of no negotiation began to soften and flow. Back and forth, yes, no, and how much and for how long? A lump sum? A buyout? Well, maybe. Why not? How much?

In the end, that's what we did. We threw out the old agreement that called for monthly support until I was age 65 and replaced it with a lump sum buyout. It would be a hefty payment, over $200,000 out of my retirement savings, but the legal hell that had lasted for nearly four years would come to a close. I could live with this. Deal.

We went back to the courtroom. The judge summarized the agreement. Helena and I both stood and affirmed our acceptance.

My sisters rushed forward and hugged me. Then I hugged Lisa. Four years of torment that had hounded me across oceans and continents came to a final, negotiated end on June 1, 2011. It was over.

Was it Lisa's strategy that did the trick? I think it did. One look at me had convinced Helena's attorneys that I was out of my mind. Better take what they could get now, as I might soon be in a psychiatric ward.

As relieved as I was, I was also conscious of the material wealth I had lost. The family home had gone to Helena, while I had the dilapidated camp in northern Maine. At age 57, I was left with less than $75,000 in retirement savings. My four-year legal bill to Lisa had climbed to nearly $70,000.

My closeted trans SFS friend had warned me earlier, "Don't walk the transition path unless you are prepared to lose everything." In the material sense she had been right, but that was the furthest thing from my mind in the Rockville courtroom on June 1, 2011. My sisters had accepted me, and more and more friends in Bucharest and in the U.S. had embraced me. As far as I was concerned on that June day, I had gained everything.

7. *My Guy, My Son*

Newborn cry in the morning air
The past and the future are wedded there
In this wellspring of my sons and daughters
The bone and blood of living water
And, though Grandpa's hands have gone to dust
Like Grandma's pump; reduced to rust
Their stories quench my soul and mind
Like water from another time.[69]

On June 2, 2011, I sat nervously in an Irish pub near the Courthouse Metro in Arlington, Virginia. I had again pulled on my guy travel clothes and had slicked back my hair, trying to look normal. I fidgeted with the menu, reading it line by line to calm myself. Court was one thing. This was going to be harder.

The door opened, and in walked Matt, dressed in his bicycling clothes. Twenty-two years old, he was now a young man, slightly taller than me with hair cropped short. On the eve of my day in court, my sister Gail and

---

69 McCutcheon, John. "Water from Another Time." Genius. Accessed on September 10, 2023. https://genius.com/John-mccutcheon-water-from-another-time-lyrics.

I had sat in a large gymnasium at the University of Maryland to watch him graduate.

Young man although he now was, I still called him by the nickname I gave him when he was *our little guy* crawling on the floor of our Silver Spring bungalow. He joined me and gave me a hug. What was I going to say to him? How was I going to give him *this* news?

I marveled at the adult at my side. Better educated than I am, Matt is gifted in everything from languages to literature to music to math to science. To my own surprise, he had taken after me in many things and was about to go to work for Lockheed, the company that built the Hubble Space Telescope, the project I had worked on for two decades before joining the State Department. An accomplished athlete who excelled as a swimmer, he rode bicycles with me as he was growing up. Then he joined the cycling team in college. Like me, my guy is now a bicycle commuter and does not own a car.

He also takes after Helena in many things. She, not I, pushed him to excel academically. Thanks to her, Matt is fluent in French and Portuguese and briefly considered a college major in classics as his interests extended to ancient Greek and Latin. He also plays piano and classical guitar.

I expect Helena would agree that the best thing about our marriage was our son. Fight as we did through the years, we always agreed on that score even as we fought over the details. Out of a troubled, painful marriage, Matt took the best of both of us—and is more than the sum of the two of us.

Matt had a very wise formula for dealing with our divorce. "When I'm with you, I don't talk about Mom; when I'm with Mom, I don't talk about you." He managed to do this even as the heavy litigation artillery boomed. The divorce and everything surrounding it fell outside the bounds of his relationships with us.

It did, however, put me in an awkward position. The divorce documents loudly proclaimed my transgender status, but the divorce was out of bounds in my conversations with Matt. During the winter of 2010–11, I became concerned about this enforced silence. When Matt and I talked by telephone, I could say only that my personal life had taken an important turn that I needed to discuss with him once litigation was behind us.

That day had come. Here we were, father and son, ordering lunch at an

Irish pub in Arlington. When the waiter took the menus, I inhaled deeply and began a prepared speech. "Guy, I need to tell you now what I've wanted to tell you for months ...."

Matt stopped me. "Dad, I know."

"You mean, you know that ...."

"Yes, I know. It's OK."

Matt had overheard our argument and learned of my transgender identity in 2001. How much else had he picked up since then even as I strove to do what is expected of a husband and father? Over lunch I found he already knew far more than I could have guessed.

"Dad, it's alright."

And it has been. I'm still Dad and always will be. It's what I'm proudest of from twenty-five years of marriage.

Lunch over, we hugged each other goodbye, and I watched as Matt rode off on his bicycle. There he went, our Guy, the wisest, most loving and accepting young man I know.

I turned on that bright June afternoon and walked slowly to the Metro with a light and happy step. A few days later I would fly back to Bucharest. With my son's love and acceptance as support, no obstacles remained. I now knew that this, my fourth lifetime transition attempt, would succeed.

8. Mâine

Some luck lies in not getting what you thought you wanted but getting what you have, which once you have got it you may be smart enough to see is what you would have wanted had you known.[70]

On Saturday evenings in the 1980s, during the first years of my marriage, I would listen to Garrison Keillor on Prairie Home Companion. Thinking back to those years, I remember languid Washington, D.C., summers and the growing fear and then painful certainty that I had deluded both myself and Helena through marriage. I had no idea when I gathered the courage

---

70   Quote attributed to Garrison Keillor on his radio show *Prairie Home Companion*.

to speak in 1990 that I was beginning a process, boarding a roller coaster that would ride on for twenty-one years.

The roller coaster came to a halt on June 2, 2011. Matt, with his acceptance, had stopped it. The words spoken, I watched as he rode away. "I'm free," I thought. "Incredibly, improbably, I'm free. My life is my own to take where I will."

Before returning to Bucharest, I spent my remaining days in the U.S. in an airy dream world that had become reality. On June 5, I drove to my special spot, the Big Schloss outcropping on the border of Virginia and West Virginia. Looking out on the valley below as hawks rode the thermals, I swallowed my first tablets of estradiol and spironolactone, the first to begin the feminization of my body and the latter to block the action of the male hormone testosterone. Hormone Replacement Therapy (HRT) had started.

The people closest to me in my life accepted that I would transition gender. My sisters were relieved about my decision, after watching my decades of pain. I began reaching out to old friends and co-workers by letter and phone and email. The email subject line usually read, "Put down that cup of coffee before opening this message." For the next several months, I peeled the onion outward from the center as I moved to more distant friends and colleagues with whom I might cross paths again one day.

How many countries had I lived and worked in? Where were my co-workers from Embassy Tashkent now? From Embassy Moscow? From the *Russia Desk*? I had to find each one. Everyone needed to hear this in my own words. No one was to be surprised by a rumor through the grapevine. A few never wrote back, but most did. The best notes came from female friends and colleagues, many of them from my NASA years. Several responded with the words, "Welcome to our world."

Then it hit me. "Why not start a web journal?" I had written a travelogue for friends and family when I served in Russia, carefully maintaining a list of email addresses and sending updates every few weeks. Now I would write a travelogue of a different sort. Family, friends, and colleagues could follow me on the journey of a lifetime. *Transgender in State*, my personal declaration of independence, was born on July 4, 2011.[71]

71   https://attitude-analyst.blogspot.com

Jeri, the DCM who had wanted me gone from Bucharest, departed in spring 2011 and was to be replaced by Duane Butcher in the summer. I had served under Duane in Uzbekistan and decided it was best to write to him before he arrived. I took pains to word my letter carefully, explaining that this was not a sudden decision but a lifelong process that was coming to fruition. Duane replied to my email quickly, expressing initial surprise that changed to full support as he read through my letter to the end.

How does one manage gender transition inside a U.S. embassy? Ours being a government facility, the answer should be obvious: by committee! At Embassy Bucharest we called it the Gender Transition Committee (GTC). Duane opened our first GTC meeting with the words, "Gender transition should be treated no differently in an embassy community than any other life event." That was Duane's take from the start, and his lead set the tone for everything that was to come.

As human resources officer, my friend Natalie chaired most GTC meetings. Peter represented our med unit following Kyna's departure in May and proved as supportive as she had been. Curtis was there as my department head, as was our management counselor and our equal employment opportunity officer. The front office was represented, as was our security office and the consular section.

We had two big worries. How will the local Romanian staff react to the news that an American supervisor is changing gender? Also, how will the Romanian government react? Some on the GTC worried that I might come to physical harm in the streets of Bucharest.

Everyone on the GTC understood the eyes of Washington would be on us. We studied the experience of NASA, USAID, and other U.S. agencies and departments. In May, the Office of Personnel Management issued guidance on gender transition in the federal workplace. Still, we knew that as instructive as those experiences and guidance might be, things could be different for us. No FSO had ever transitioned gender while posted overseas.

Our embassy was scheduled to move in the fall from downtown Bucharest to a New Embassy Compound (NEC) on the outskirts of town. We decided that we should not announce my transition until the NEC move was behind us, reasoning that one shock to the embassy community at a time was enough. We settled on November 10. We decided that I would speak personally to the local staff in our IM department and that I would follow this with an email letter to all embassy staff. A special *Hail and Farewell* notice would appear in our embassy newsletter, the *Dacian Dispatch.*

At the eleventh hour we thought to include the embassy's press officer in the GTC. It was good that we did. On November 8, Washington instructed Duane as DCM to ask me to delay my transition announcement. Although we had been keeping the State Department apprised of our plans for months, it seemed no one in Washington was paying attention. That changed when a friendly Romanian journalist asked if she could write about my transition. When her article went to Washington for clearance, the State Department woke up in nervous alarm. The concern was that the Romanian government would learn of the transition from the press account and that this could lead to questions at the daily press briefing in Washington.

Duane would have none of it. As I learned later, he asked that the State Department put its request in a front channel instruction cable. Given that gender identity was now included in the Department of State's non-discrimination policy, Duane knew the State Department would not do this. At the same time, Duane swung into action to address their concerns. He kept the GTC at the embassy late into the evening of November 9 as we prepared press guidance and went back and forth with Washington on revisions.

For me the night was a sleepless one. I tossed and turned with nervous anticipation. Would our actions be sufficient for the State Department?

I learned the answer the following morning after I parked my bicycle in the embassy garage. Taking out my cell phone, I saw there was a text message from Duane. It consisted of a single word: "YES." Duane followed this with a text to the full GTC: "We won!" My fears evaporated as my heart soared. We were going forward with our plan for the day. The State Department had agreed!

Curtis called a staff meeting of the IT section for 10:00 a.m. He opened by talking about our move to the NEC but quickly moved on. He asked if everyone had seen the updated non-discrimination statement, translated into Romanian just days before, to which gender identity had been added. Did everyone understand what it means to be transgender? The local staff shrugged their shoulders. Curtis offered a short explanation and described what it meant for management policy. He stressed that because of this change, all eyes were on Embassy Bucharest. I looked around the table and saw puzzled expressions. Curtis paused for dramatic effect and said, "The reason Washington is looking at us is sitting in this room. I would like to introduce you to Robyn."

There were looks of incredulity around the room, and a few jaws dropped. Now it was my turn to speak. How could I summarize a lifetime in only a few words that they would understand? My fears returned as I explained that I had known since childhood that my gender identity and sex assigned at birth did not match. Despite my nervousness, my words must have gotten through. By the time I finished, the shocked expressions had changed to ones of compassion. I could see a tear or two. Our Romanian staff surprised me by telling me how brave I was, and they followed those words with handshakes and hugs.

My email announcement to all embassy staff went out at 10:30 a.m. By the time we walked out of our staff meeting at 11:00, everyone knew. The *Dacian Dispatch* appeared at 2:00 p.m. with a hail and farewell unlike that ever seen at a U.S. embassy. Congratulatory emails poured in, capped by a message from Ambassador Gitenstein's wife Libby with the simple words, "Welcome, Robyn." With those words from Libby, I knew that our embassy community had embraced me warmly and fully. My emotions reached a high they had never known before. Finally, at age 57, I had found complete acceptance.

Two days later I came out formally into society at the annual Marine Ball. The marines who once used to greet me with the words, "Good Morning, Sir!" stood in a receiving line in their dress uniforms and now greeted me with, "Good Evening, Ma'am!" as they each presented me with a rose.

I danced the night away like I had never danced before. I felt like Natasha Rostova in *War in Peace* going to her first ball. The dreams kept secretly for more than fifty years were coming true.

Lessons learned? There have been many, but I will list just two.

Be open, visible, and predictable. I learned this the hard way. In the past, I hid in the shadows rather than come to terms with being transgender. It took me until the sixth decade of my life to apply a lesson I learned from bicycling. *Those who hug the curb for fear of cars are the ones who get hurt. Taking the lane and being visible and predictable is far safer.* I applied that lesson in 2010–11. Everyone knew what I was doing, and I did it openly and visibly with a smile on my face. That smile alone may have convinced many I was doing what was right for me. Happiness is contagious and wins allies.

Farewell Robert, Welcome Robyn!

Robert Allen McCutcheon

Robyn Alice McCutcheon

A Message to Friends and Colleagues from Robyn

The time has come for me to make a personal announcement concerning a major life change that will affect my day-to-day appearance: I am a transgender person who is transitioning from male to female. Beginning Monday, November 14, I will be coming to work as Robyn. Some of you may find this confusing or unusual, so here are answers to a few of the concerns and questions that may be on your mind:

YES, please do call me Robyn, as that is my new legal name.
NO, my sense of humor has not changed. It's still impenetrably based on engineering and science.
YES, please do use feminine pronouns (*she, her*) when referring to me.
NO, you will not see me commuting by bicycle through most of the winter
YES, I will be coming to work in professional dress appropriate to a woman of my age.
NO, I have not given up my membership in the American Astronomical Society.
YES, I will still jump to resolve your computer problems.
NO, I don't know if Herodotus had anything to say on the subject of transgender.

This may be the first time you have ever met a transgender person, so it's only natural to have questions. Feel free to ask them directly. HR and MED will be happy to hear from you. Gays and Lesbians in Foreign Affairs Agencies (GLIFAA) for which I am Bucharest post representative, is another resource. OPM's Guidance Regarding the Employment of Transgender Individuals is well written and is official policy for the Federal workplace.

To those at Embassy Bucharest who have known and helped me on my way down this path for nearly a year, I am eternally grateful. Peace to all.

"Dacian Dispatch" for November 10, 2011

With Natalie (L) and her sister Suzie (R) at the 2011 Marine Ball in Bucharest

Failing once or twice or even three times is not the end. That's the second lesson. When I failed to embrace my transgender self in 2000–02, I thought life was over. I believed the baseball adage about three strikes and you're out, but now I was my own living proof of how wrong I was. Life is not a baseball game.

In the spring of 2010, I thought I would be going to Moscow, only to have that post pulled away. My career as I knew it was over, or so I thought. Coming to Romania was an accident. I needed a job, and Embassy Bucharest had an opening. I arrived with a single suitcase on a cold and rainy October day.

Garrison Keillor was right. Some luck lies in not getting what you thought you wanted but getting what you have. Coming to Romania is what I would have wanted in 2010 had I known. *Romania, te iubesc.*

In a funny way, Garrison Keillor was also wrong. When all seemed lost in 2010, I repeated to myself, "If I'm to be unemployed, let it end right here in Maine." In saying those words, I was thinking of a refuge, a reclusive life in Maine away from the world.

The Romanian language has a word spelled like Maine, but it comes with an accent over the "a": Mâine. It means tomorrow. In Bucharest in November 2011, my dreams for tomorrow came true.

127

The GTC with (L-to-R) Peter Chordas, Rob Dalton, Micah Savidge, Natalie Koza, Ambassador Mark Gittenstein, Author, Duane Butcher, and Curtis Presson

PART 4

A Romanian LGBT+ Folk Hero? (Nov 2011 – June 2013)

On Monday, November 14, 2011, it was time to go back to work at Embassy Bucharest. My career would go on. Life would go on. The difference was that my *deep dark secret* no longer lurked in the closet. The transgender *white noise* in my head that had followed me from childhood was gone. What would life be like now?

As I would find out quickly, I had become something of a *rock star* in Romania and in the Foreign Service. Well, let's make that a minor rock star or, as I prefer to think of it, the person performing on a satellite stage at a folk festival with a few groupies arrayed on the grass. That is the new life I walked into on the Monday after the Marine Ball. It was as though I had arrived in Bucharest and in the Foreign Service all over again.

1. What Do Uranium and a Transgender FSO Have in Common?

NOTE: This article appeared in my web journal Transgender in State on February 12, 2012, which accounts for the 2012 time frame of reference. It was later reprinted in Diplopundit on April 4, 2012 (https://diplopundit.net/2012/04/02/ what-do-uranium-and-a-transgender-foreign-service-officer- have-in-common/).

Quite a lot, come to think of it.

There is the radioactivity to begin with. When I first tried to speak of being transgender in 1990, I might as well have been radioactive judging from the speed with which some people in my life ran in the other direction. Even in this much more welcoming and enlightened second decade of the twenty-first century, some may have preferred to deal with radioactivity rather than with the announcement of my intent to transition in the work- place overseas. Special handling seemed called for, much as it might have been for an international shipment of uranium.

But just as with uranium, being transgender implies energy. We need large stores of potential energy that we turn to kinetic as we walk the transition path. I tell everyone that today I feel far younger than I did two years ago. It's as though I'm fifty-seven going on twenty-seven.

Being a transgender FSO takes the analogy further. Like uranium, I have found that a transgender FSO can find herself in more demand than she ever expected. It has been my greatest post-transition surprise over the past three months.

For the coming weekend I will be judging twenty-six finalist essays on the theme of *tolerance*. Embassy Bucharest is holding an essay contest in honor of Human Rights Day, and the essays were submitted by Romanian high school students. Last weekend I judged twenty-eight essays in the first round. Over 300 essays were submitted in all, and I am one of a dozen volunteer judges.

Then there is a GLIFAA colleague in Washington who thinks I should be able to pull together enough information to write a report about LGBT+ issues among the Roma people. Thanks to my former career, I believe I am better placed to report on LGBT+ issues on the Moon than among the Roma, but to my own surprise, I may be on the verge of having enough information to write a cable. Whether I do or not depends on three gay Roma men. One is in Bucharest, another is in Prague, and the third is in Dubai. Well, maybe I had better stick to the Moon.

Next, there is the transgender chapter for the twentieth anniversary GLI-FAA retrospective. I wrote a draft over the holidays and got edits and clearances from everyone who was anyone who had anything to say on the subject ... except for one. I was simply going to turn it in to the editor, but then the one missing person sent me an archive of emails and other documents going back to 2007.

My first reaction to the sight of this archive was an ardent wish to run for the hills. Then I started to go through the couple of hundred pages of material . . . and was enthralled. There's enough here for a book, and I've only got a couple of pages. The archive covers everything that went on in GLIFAA's successful lobbying that culminated in gender identity being added to the State Department's *Statement on Discriminatory and Sexual Harassment* in the summer of 2010. If it hadn't been for a core group of committed people, Robyn might not be writing to you from Bucharest today. Looking at these documents, I feel I'm a historian working in the archives in Leningrad again. Instead of running for the hills, I feel honored to be reading these papers. Now all I need is about 40 hours a week to devote to this ....

Let's see, what else? Oh, yes, this is LGBT+ history month in Romania, and last Sunday I was a *book* in a *living library* event organized by Accept. When I was first told that anyone who wished to would be able *to check me out* and *read me* for 15-20 minutes at a time, I had to chuckle. The thought of a transgender person willingly offering herself to be *checked out* and *read* was too humorous. In the end it was a fun evening as I was *checked out* and *read* multiple times, mainly by young gay and lesbian Romanians for whom a transgender person is nearly as exotic as an extraterrestrial. This book from the foreign literature section learned as much from the evening as did her readers.

Yes, like uranium, a transgender FSO can be simultaneously radioactive, energetic, and in demand. Please just don't put me in a centrifuge. Although I wouldn't mind being enriched, I believe I'm already as refined as I can be and can't be improved. As long as my half-life is long, I will continue to live as a young fifty-seven going on twenty-seven.

Now, where did I leave that stack of essays on *tolerance*? . . .

2. New Life, New Stories

How do you want to be remembered,
A blazing fire or dying ember? [72]

I had expected to go forward with my life quietly, but in the days after November 10, I started receiving congratulatory emails from FSOs around the world. GLIFAA named me its Post Representative for Bucharest. The Romanian language article about my transition at Embassy Bucharest attracted notice in the Romanian LGBT+ community. Then I wrote *What Do Uranium and a Transgender FSO Have in Common?* in my web journal. It was picked up and re-published in *Diplopundit*, one of the most widely read Internet journals about FSO life. After that, it seemed that every visit-

---

72 Kennedy, Pete and Maura. "Life is Large." Cowboy Lyrics. Accessed September 10, 2023. https://www.cowboylyrics.com/tabs/kennedys/life-is-large-4712.html.

ing group from Washington wanted to meet me. In spring 2012, I learned that GLIFAA would give me its annual Equality Award for being the first FSO to transition within an embassy environment.

I stood in a minor spotlight. Almost as a sleepwalker, I had crossed into activism. All I had to do was look around in Romania to know how difficult life was for the LGBT+ community, in particular for transgender persons. Could my example, my actions, help them in some small way? I felt I also had a moral responsibility to advance the rights of others like me in Romania. I didn't know what I could do as a run-of-the-mill mid-level FSO, but I had to do something.

With little to do in the IT section, I threw myself into political reporting and outreach. I had no one telling me what to report on, and I had no taskers from Washington to satisfy. I was able to design my own program, going places and reporting on issues for which other FSOs might not have access, time, or interest. Titles of my *cables*[73] from that time give a flavor where that reporting took me:

> *Transgender Community Comes out of the Shadows*
>
> *Roma and Gay: A Triple Stigma*
>
> *Anti-LGBT+ Protesters Win a Battle, Lose a War?*
>
> *LGBT+ Film Festival in Cluj*
>
> *LGBT+ Issues not on Radar Screen at Ministry of Health*
>
> *LGBT+ Education in Schools*
>
> *European Transgender Participation Symposium*
>
> *Bucharest Pride 2012: Hope and Optimism*

I mentioned the first of these, *Roma and Gay*, in *What Do Uranium and a Transgender FSO Have in Common?* It broke new ground. The Roma minority has long suffered discrimination in Romania. For this reason, there is an unwritten rule that all Roma must adhere to a code of conduct that is beyond reproach. Some Roma leaders said outright that being gay was not

---

73   State Department reports submitted from posts overseas are still called *cables*, hearkening back to the days when those reports were, in fact, sent as cables. Today these reports are sent electronically over Department intranet networks and are in fact emails, sometimes including attachments, with Department-specific metadata included in the headers. Technology has changed, but the tradition of calling these reports *cables* remains.

possible for Roma, and this meant that finding gay Roma to talk openly about their lives took patient effort. Washington liked the cable and sent what we FSOs refer to as a front-channel *kudos cable*.

I became active with Accept, Romania's leading LGBT+ rights organization, sometimes speaking at their events, and I worked with the British and other friendly embassies to publish joint statements in support of LGBT+ rights in Romania. I organized the embassy's participation in the Bucharest Pride marches in 2012 and 2013. For the first time, our embassy community marched behind our own U.S. banner to show our solidarity with Romania's LGBT+ community.

After Ambassador Gittenstein departed in 2012, Duane Butcher became Chargé d'affaires. Already a strong ally, Duane used his influence to advance LGBT+ issues. When the Ministry of Education threatened to shut down an after-school LGBT+ discussion program at a leading Bucharest high school, Duane brought the issue up in his next meeting with the minister of education. Roxana, a facilitator of the after-school group, told me the following week that the program would continue. The school principal had told her quietly that closing the program might provoke an international incident. Duane's conversation with the minister had made the difference.

Another example of Duane's support came in 2013 when he convinced the Bucharest city authorities to authorize a new, more visible route for the annual Pride march. It would now be in the city center, walking down the Bucharest equivalent of embassy row. Accept had designed the new route, but its application to the city had languished without answer until Duane stepped in.[74]

I traveled widely in Romania during the year and a half from November 2011 until my departure in June 2013. I traveled both to cover LGBT+ issues and to see as much of the country as I could by bicycle. Of all the countries I served in, Romania with its Carpathian Mountains and the rolling hills of Transylvania felt most like home. There was even local maple syrup on sale in the *Mega Image* chain of grocery stores.

---

74   The first Pride march in Bucharest took place in 2005, but there were numerous counter-demonstrations and violent clashes. Those incidents lessened after 2010, but the annual marches still did not reflect a party atmosphere like in Western Europe or the U.S.

Before I knew it, I was traveling outside Romania. First, it was to speak on LGBT+ issues at the U.S. Embassy in Tirana, Albania. Then it was to participate in a panel on transgender issues in The Netherlands organized by Transgender Europe (TGEU). I traveled by train or bus several times to neighboring Moldova to meet with LGBT+ activists, marveling that crossing the River Prut meant exchanging English and my limited Romanian for my much better Russian.

Irina Nita at the Bucharest Diversity March in 2012

Beyond work and an unexpected spotlight, there was something else. My relationships with people had changed. The burden of a torturous secret and the resulting tension were gone. Even Duane Butcher saw it. One day several months after my social transition at the embassy, Duane stopped me in the hallway. He had a twinkle in his eye and said he had been spying on me as I had been talking with several other women in the embassy atrium. He added that although he knew he had done the right thing in supporting my transition, now he *really knew*. From a distance he had watched me conversing and interacting with others. He said I now seemed easygoing and natural in a way that attracted others, something he didn't remember seeing in me before.

That was also true outside embassy walls. My apartment became more than a sanctuary for trans community events. People would knock on the door at any time. It could be my Scottish friend Rupert looking for *a spot of tea*. It could be Manuela with her writing projects. It could be Sasha and Patrick to talk about trans life in Romania. Irina Nita, executive director of Accept, sometimes came with her teenage son for an evening of stargazing with my little telescope. There was Olympia, who would become an emotionally adopted daughter. There were Thanksgiving dinners, Christmas get-togethers, and *just because* dinners. Most of all, there was life, a new life with new stories to be told.

3. Rupert: To Peris(h) by Bicycle

NOTE: This article appeared in my web journal Transgender in State on September 15, 2012, which accounts for the 2012 time frame of reference.

"We are going to perish by bicycle." Rupert Wolfe Murray got my attention with those words.

I would not be a bicyclist today if I were not transgender. My life as an adult cyclist began in 1990. I just had spent a week in a psychiatric ward, a consequence of my attempt to speak openly of being transgender. As I succumbed to pressure and retreated to the closet, I fell into a deep depression. I owe my emotional survival to a friend who both accepted me and offered an outlet for my conflicted feelings. By inviting me to join him on a weekend ride with friends, he put me back on two wheels for the first time in many years.

Since 1990, the bicycle has been my primary mode of transportation. Before joining the Foreign Service, I rode seven thousand miles per year, most of it as a daily commuter. My annual mileage has dropped to half that since going overseas due to shorter daily commutes and good public transit, but in Bucharest the bicycle continues to give me the wings I need to live as a mobile woman of the modern age. Day and night, my Rivendell Atlantis takes me everywhere and is an extension of myself.

Back to Rupert, whom I know to be very sane and not prone to talk of sudden death.

"No, not perish, but Peris(h)," Rupert said as he spread out the map. "It's a small town north of Bucharest." Looking at the map, I realized I had already been there in 2010 on the weekend after I had first reassembled my Atlantis. It had been a chilly November day, and the ride had been a solitary one.

We headed out on Saturday morning into weekend traffic not much different from what I was used to in Washington, D.C. In Romania as in the U.S., weekends are the time for families to run errands. Traffic was as heavy as on any weekday.

But not for long. Within thirty minutes we entered an oak forest on Bucharest's northern edge. On the road I set the pace, but in the woods, I lagged behind. My Atlantis is a touring bicycle built for the road, and I have little off-road riding experience as it is. Rupert waited patiently for me at key turning points, and a number of times he had to wait longer still as I dismounted and walked around ruts, mud, and other obstacles. But in the saddle or on foot, it was a lovely end of summer day to be in nature, outside the city.

Out of the woods and back on the road, we pushed on northward. As we did, I watched Rupert with his shirt blowing in the wind and realized my perceptions of male beauty are changing. He was downright handsome in the saddle, at once the talented writer I knew him to be but also the athletic bicyclist with leg muscles showing as he spun the cranks.

Then we were in another forest. This time we were on a dirt road, not a forest path. We should have suspected something from the smooth surface and the barricade that we walked around. There were no vehicles on the road, and the only sounds were those of the forest and of our wheels on the gravel.

That quiet ended when a pack of barking dogs bounded around the bend to tell us we were not welcome. We dismounted, walked around the bend, and discovered we were at the gate of a run-down military facility. Rupert asked in Romanian whether we could cross to get to the road on the north side of the woods. The guard's gestures alone were enough to tell me the answer was "No!" Instead, we backtracked, exited the woods into a field, and stopped for lunch in the shade. After that we walked our bikes across a harvested field, the remains of sunflowers at our feet.

Rupert Wolfe Murray on our ride to Peris(h)

Country roads took us the rest of the way to Peris(h). The accent is on the first syllable, and the "s" is a Romanian "s" with a cedilla underneath that is pronounced "sh." So why go to Peris(h)? I learned the answer when we pulled up to a Romanian home on a side street. A woman walked out to the gate to greet us. She spoke in American English with a Texas accent.

Rupert introduced her as Nancy. She welcomed us in, and soon we were seated on her porch sipping Coca Cola.

Nancy's husband is a Romanian artist and architect. They designed their house themselves, and artwork hangs everywhere, even in the bathroom. Nancy had worked at a university in Texas in the late 1980s when she met her husband, at that time a political refugee on the run from Ceausescu's regime in its brutal final years. Now they live on the plot of land in this small Romanian town that had belonged to his family before World War II. Their love has transcended nationality, culture, and politics.

They also live in Romania for practical reasons.

"Here my pension is worth something," Nancy told me. "I wouldn't be able to live on it in the U.S."

That part of Nancy's story caught my attention. I lost most of my savings through divorce, and I am now less than seven years away from mandatory retirement for age from the Foreign Service. Might I decide to spend my retirement in Romania or Moldova? That idea is starting to sound reasonable.

Nancy's two grandnieces arrived, and the conversations turned to their jobs, parties, and boyfriends. I could have been on a front porch anywhere in the heartland of America.

The autumnal equinox is soon approaching. I saw from the clock that it was 6:00 p.m., time to leave if I did not want to be caught on the road after dark. Rupert was staying in Peris(h) for the night, but I had things to do on Sunday. Reluctantly, I got back on my bike and went on my way, this time entirely on-road. I paused a short distance outside Bucharest where the highway crosses the railway tracks on a tall, arching bridge in Buftea. I stood and watched as the sun sank to the horizon. I thought back on the distance I had come since I last crossed that bridge in 2010. I looked at the odometer. My entire trip today would be 100km, but in my heart I knew that the odometer lies. In the two years since my ride to Peris(h) in 2010, I have journeyed a lifetime, a distance no odometer can measure.

I looked again at the setting sun. Then I turned on my lights, threw my leg over the top tube, and pushed on for home and the future that awaits me.

4. November Postcards

> NOTE: *This article appeared in my web journal Transgender in State on November 28, 2012, which accounts for the 2012 time frame of reference.*

It's been a very busy several weeks in Bucharest, my hometown, leaving little time to write. These are my weaving together of incomplete jottings, my postcards for November 2012, if you will, before December intervenes and brings the first snows with Christmas and 2013 not far behind.

Riding the CfR Rails on the Bucharest-Brasov-Cluj Line

Clickety-clack, the slow CfR train just passed through Rupea, bound for Bucharest another four hours down the line. Alexandra, Monica, and Olympia doze in our second-class compartment as I write and watch the Romanian countryside pass by our window, a countryside of rolling hills, farms, and woods. The landscape reminds me yet again why I feel so at home in Romania, so strong a resemblance it bears to the countryside of the northeastern United States. We are halfway home to Bucharest, but I feel I could step out of the train and find myself somewhere in New England.

We journeyed the other way three days ago, departing from Bucharest's North Station an hour before sunrise. Our destination was Cluj-Napoca, eight hours and a different historical reality away. A part of the Austro-Hungarian Empire until 1918, the city still proudly bears witness to the days of grand empire. Historic buildings carry carved inscriptions in Hungarian, and the feeling is as much Budapest as it is Bucharest.

It's not my first visit to Cluj. I was here in 1978, *en route* back to Western Europe from the Soviet Union. As I stood on the central square in front of the Roman Catholic Saint Michael's Cathedral on Thursday afternoon, I remembered the scared young student, then deep in self-denial, who had stood on the same spot 34 years earlier.

On the train to Cluj with activist Alexandra Carastoian

How very different this present visit. The four of us had come to Cluj for Romania's largest annual LGBT+ film festival, now in its ninth year. A small group of volunteers working with a shoestring budget has pulled off what some say is in the top ten festivals in Europe. From Monday through Saturday, movies attracted a couple of hundred moviegoers and activists to the heart of Transylvania, coming from as far away as the UK and Spain. The movies ranged from locally produced documentaries to art movies from Thailand, Israel, and Portugal. A few played to standing-room audiences. After screenings, many flocked to Delirio, Cluj's sole LGBT+ club, for an after-party. Our Bucharest foursome was seriously impressed.

Living Libraries

November 20, 2012. The evening was dark and chilly as I made my way from the Embassy to Accept, the Romanian LGBT+ rights organization. This is one day of the calendar known to all transgender persons. It's Transgender Day of Remembrance (TDOR), the day when we remember those who have died in hate murders over the preceding twelve months for daring to live as their true selves.

What a difference a year can make. When I went to the TDOR observance at Accept a year ago, I was the only transgender person who attended. We watched a short film, and then I spoke to the small group about what it means to be transgender.

This year I was not alone. Eight members of Bucharest's transgender community turned out. Moreover, they organized the evening. Posters announcing the evening had been hung in several locations, and thirty or so allies came. The names of those who had died were scrolled on the projection screen, and the transgender symbol hung on the wall, covered with origami flowers. The heart of the evening was a living library, something I had first heard of during LGBT+ History Month last February. When the time came to leave, we did so in groups. We knew that several people had been attacked in the street the previous week after attending an LGBT+ play and discussion evening at a Bucharest university.

Two nights later on Thanksgiving Day, several of us did a reprise of the living library at a Bucharest high school. Joined by several LGBT+ Romanians and expats, we told our stories to small groups of students. This living library was even more gratifying than the one two days earlier on

TDOR. The students with whom we spoke are Romania's future. In another decade or two, they are the ones who will be leading the country.

Thanksgiving

I spent the rest of my Thanksgiving Day cooking. I had announced a Thanksgiving Open House for Saturday the twenty-fourth, and several late evenings had already gone into cooking and baking.

Two years ago, Thanksgiving was a lonely affair. I was newly arrived, knew almost no one, and was immersed in post-divorce litigation. In 2011, I hosted several close friends for a warm evening celebration, but this year I decided to take the leap and hold a Thanksgiving Open House. I had no real idea how many people might come and how much I should cook. "Never mind," I thought, "Turkey, ham, and pumpkin pie freeze well." I prepared an extra-large batch of Harvard beets and a fresh supply of Brazilian black beans, just in case.

My doorbell began ringing shortly before 4:00 p.m. More than twenty friends came through my door that evening, many bringing flowers, a bottle of wine, *tsuica*,[75] or a dish to share. After the feast we turned up the stereo volume and began dancing to everything from classics to LGBT+ music to traditional Roma tunes. The last guest left around 2:00 a.m.

Sunday brought with it the peace that follows a holiday evening as Olympia and I gradually brought the apartment back into order. Another friend who had spent the night worked with us as we drank coffee and ate leftover pumpkin pie. Then we lounged on the couch and watched a movie as the autumn cold kept us in the comfort of indoors.

Tonight will be another evening for friends when we gather to eat leftovers. In Romania, as in the U.S., it all tastes so much better the day after.

· · · · · · · · · · · · · · · ·

Those are my November postcards from Bucharest, where all the women are strong, the men are good-looking, and ... if you are a fan of Garrison Keillor and *Prairie Home Companion*, you know the rest.

---

75   *Tsuica* is a traditional Romanian plum-based spirit that can contain up to 65% alcohol by volume. Vodka is tame by comparison.

5. *Olympia*

There but for fortune,

Go you or go I.[76]

We first met in Brasov in early 2011. There we were, Olympia and I, together in a small hotel meeting room for the event that Tudor had ambitiously dubbed The First Romanian Transgender Congress. I was taking my first uncertain but determined steps on the road of transition. So was Olympia.

Olympia is a week younger than my son Matt. She studied the same math I once used as an attitude analyst on the HST project. In 2011, she worked for a European geospatial imaging company that was taking advantage of lower salaries paid to technical workers in Romania. Olympia plays classical and modern guitar, is a whiz with computer graphics design, and sometimes gigs as a DJ at clubs and parties.

When we met, Olympia was almost finished with undergraduate studies at a Bucharest university. She lived at home with her parents in a provincial city about a hundred kilometers north of Bucharest, and most of her coursework was done online.

In the summer of 2012, Olympia wrote that she would be coming to Bucharest for her exams. Could she stay with me for two weeks? I agreed. It would be better for her than a sweltering dormitory in the hot Bucharest summer. Also, it would be fun for me to have company and to cook for someone other than myself. Outside of my work and her exams, we could watch movies, have friends over, or go on city walks.

Olympia was *in the closet* to her parents, but they suspected. During the two weeks she was with me in Bucharest, her father went through her room and found articles of clothing and transgender literature. When Olympia returned home, he beat her severely, screaming, "Why can't you just be gay?" Olympia called me in tears, and I insisted she get on the bus back to Bucharest. That night I saw the bruises on her back.

That's how it started. Olympia stayed with me nearly a year until I left Bucharest in June 2013. My apartment was large enough for a family. Olympia got the second bedroom and became the surrogate daughter I never

---

76   Ochs, Phil. "There but for Fortune." Genius. Accessed September 10, 2023. https://genius.com/Phil-ochs-there-but-for-fortune-lyrics.

had. She began calling me "Mom," and I began calling her "Daughter." At first it was in jest, but with time it became more than words. We became family.[77]

That year we did most everything together—cooking and entertaining, going grocery shopping, participating in LGBT+ events, and spending afternoons walking around Lake Herestrau. Evenings ended with hugs and wishes of "*Noapte buna. Somn uşor. Visa placute pureci sa te sarute.*"[78]

As in any family, it's not all peace and love. We were different. We came from different cultures. Most importantly, I was an American living in a diplomatic bubble, and I would be leaving. I could protect Olympia for a time, but she would remain behind when I left.

Two months before my departure, Olympia started dating a lesbian woman and began to question her gender identity. She came to me in the morning after a date night and told me she had decided to stop hormones. She would try living again as a man.

In Romania, many transgender women end up as sex workers, a hard choice in a country where life is difficult for all whose gender identity does not conform with societal expectations. Few are able to transition fully and live normal lives. Identity documents reflecting one's true gender identity are nearly impossible to obtain. But without those documents, life for a transgender person can be a living hell.

Perhaps I was wrong to have taken Olympia under my wing, giving her refuge that was only temporary. The hope was that she would find work as herself. Despite many interviews and letters, it did not happen. She lost her job in spatial imaging when she came to Bucharest, and there was no going back now that she was in transition. In the U.S., perhaps, a person in transition is employable. In Romania, a transgender applicant is more likely to be met with strange looks and barely suppressed laughter.

I was supportive and rational when Olympia told me of her decision. That support lasted until the night when I came home to find a young man in

---

77   FSOs are not free, willy-nilly, to invite anyone they wish to live under their roof. They are required to inform of intent to cohabitate and to apply for member of household (MOH) status for the person they are inviting. I will have more to say about MOH later, but in the case of Olympia, the RSO at Embassy Bucharest, an ally ever since my coming-out, waived all formalities.

78   Good night. Sleep tight. Don't let the bedbugs kiss you.

my apartment. I never could have imagined what Olympia would look like as a man. My heart broke into a million pieces. I sobbed for days.

Olympia was now Octavian, a typical young Romanian man who became more masculine by the day as testosterone reasserted itself in his system. *Testosterone revenge* gave Octavian an insatiable appetite. I couldn't keep enough food in the refrigerator.

Both sides now. Looking back seven years later from 2020, I can see that Olympia and Octavian gave me the gift of understanding. Through them I now know what a parent or significant other goes through when a child, spouse, or sibling announces that he/she is transgender and intends to transition. For the unsuspecting, declaration of a transgender identity can come as a shock. Whether we admit it or not, gender has much to do with how we perceive others. Changing gender changes those perceptions. My own sisters, accepting of me today as they are, have told me they had to grieve the death of a brother in order to welcome the birth of a sister. I know this today, but in 2013 I was in a million pieces.

It was Sasha who helped me through. A young trans man and an up-and-coming leader in Romania's LGBT+ community, he attended my farewell party. It happened on an evening when clearly, I was not holding myself together. He took me to my room, closed the door, and sat me down on the edge of my bed. He quietly but firmly asked, "Robyn, if you can't deal with this, what hope is there for the rest of us who are rejected by our families?" He rebuked me and demanded that I be a grown-up and get a grip on myself. It was a needed lesson I will never forget.

For my remaining weeks in Romania, I let Octavian be Octavian. What other choice did I have? It was his life to live, not mine. A week before I left, he found an apartment of his own, and an embassy friend with a car helped move him in. When my departure day arrived, Octavian accompanied me to the airport, holding my hand and hugging me until the last minute.

Olympia and I are still close. I have visited her three times in Romania, twice in Bucharest and once in Constanța. She spent several days with me in Copenhagen in 2016.

Why do I still call her Olympia? You see, by the time I returned for my first visit in 2014, she was Olympia again. To my surprise, she had money and took me out to dinner. After a couple of days, she confessed that her income came from being an online sex performer. She was working at a Bucharest studio owned by a shady outfit back in the U.S. that caters mainly to American men. Olympia was earning good money, had even become something of a star.

The money didn't last, and by 2017 I was helping when she did not have enough to pay her rent. Apparently, the American male appetite for online sex performers is fickle; the days of stardom for transgender sex performers had passed.

Olympia may soon be Octavian again. At age 31 and with little future in the sex performance business, she has few options. Like many Romanians and Moldovans, she may go to Western Europe to find work washing dishes or do other manual labor. Without a passport showing her to be female, it's Octavian who will have to take that step.

Did Olympia's year with me help her sense of self? I may never know the answer. The only certainty for me is that whatever the gender, I still care about this young person. She deserves a better life than Romania has given.

6. A Vagina Monologue with Elbows

In summer 2011 I found LaserMed, a clinic with a good electrologist. In time, I started calling Mirela *the miracle electrologist of Bucharest*. At less than $25/hour, she charged a third or a quarter the going rate for electrolysis in the U.S., and I found her to be every bit as good and gentle as Leila in Virginia. Visiting Mirela became part of my daily after-work routine throughout summer 2011, with my visits decreasing in frequency as we made progress. Mirela was up-front with me that full facial electrolysis would take three years, but that meant I could get the bulk of it done during my remaining two years in Romania.

Hair was a problem. Now grown out, I didn't know what to do with it. My straight-haired sisters who once envied my curly hair now recommended that I straighten it. I did. Sometimes several times a day. As a bicycle commuter, I carried a straightening iron with me and did touch-up straightening after every ride. It took but a hint of wind or humidity to turn my carefully straightened hair into a bees' nest of frizz. Only later did I discover and take the *curly girl pledge*. I cut my hair back to manageable length and threw away the straightening iron. Now hair care is simple. I let the curls air dry into the pattern they choose for the day.

Clothing in Bucharest was easy and fun. Olympia went with me on many shopping trips and was my friendly adviser and critic. To this day, I have many of the shoes that I bought in Bucharest. They were cheap, stylish, and of good quality. According to Bucharest friends, many Italian shoes are actually made by Romanians who work as shoemakers in Italy.

I thought of voice as my final frontier, a barrier that seemed insurmountable. Far from the alto it had been when I was a child, my voice was baritone with the intonation pattern one would expect from an engineer. Droning monotone would be a charitable way to describe it.

Quantum physics teaches us, however, that a particle has a non-zero chance of penetrating a barrier even if, according to classical physics, it lacks the energy to do so. So it turned out to be for me with voice. I found Linda Siegfriedt, director of the transgender voice program at George Washington University in D.C. We worked together over Skype on Saturdays, and I would disappear into the isolated server room at Embassy Bucharest twice a day to practice the pitch glides, oral resonance, and intonation exercises that Linda assigned. Within three months Linda was asking me how it was that I was managing to progress so quickly. To my own surprise, I found the exercises not at all difficult. It was as though I was rediscovering an alto that had never really left me. It had simply been masked over for decades. I told Linda that in me she had a motivated learner. Knowing how to use my tongue and lips to produce sounds of languages other than English may also have played a role.

Now I come to my vagina monologue. Retired today in a rural part of Maine, I chuckle when religious conservatives describe themselves as traditional. When I hear this, I want to jump in and say I'm with them. I'm traditional too! Traditional transgender, that is. To be precise, I'm a transgender woman in the transsexual tradition of the 1960s.

I've written already about how, as a child, I would hide my penis between my legs under the water in the bathtub and will it to disappear. As an adult, I never enjoyed seeing myself naked in a mirror.

In 2012 I could do something about it at last. I began researching surgeons for what once was called *sexual reassignment surgery* but now is usually referred to as *gender confirmation surgery* (GCS). I corresponded with a number of surgeons in the U.S. and visited two of them when I was on vacation there in 2012. I settled on Dr. Sanjuan Kunaporn in Phuket, Thailand. Surgery in Thailand would be at least a third less expensive than in the U.S., and Thai surgeons are as experienced or more so in GCS than their U.S. colleagues.

Cost was a big part of my decision. Divorce and post-divorce litigation had left me nearly broke. Frugal by nature, I was seeing my finances rebound some by late 2012, but I knew it would take years for them to recover to their 2007 level.

Cost was one reason, but there was another: Monica. We had become friends at the transgender congress in Brasov in 2011. She came to Bucharest that spring, and I visited her in Moldova in early 2012. I could not see myself going for GCS without her.

The Soviet/Russian historian in me had returned. Much of the world rejoiced when the red Soviet flag came down for the last time on December 25, 1991; but Monica was not one of them. She had good reason not to be happy. At age twenty, Monica had gone through all the psychiatric boards of the Soviet medical system and had been approved for GCS in early 1992. When she appeared at the Moscow hospital for check-in, however, she was told to go home, that she was now a citizen of independent Moldova, not Russia. It nearly destroyed her as she retreated into depression and isolation.

Monica resurfaced months later, accepting that surgery, so nearly within her grasp, was now an impossible dream. She returned to the university, earned her degree, and became a respected teacher of Romanian language and literature at one of Moldova's best high schools.

Only in 2001 did she decide that the time had come to try again. Surgery was still out of the question, and there were no endocrinologists in Moldova who would help her. She did it by herself, studying the medical literature and beginning hormone therapy on her own. She was fired from her teaching position when physical changes began to manifest themselves. Supportive students and parents rallied to her cause but to no avail. The Ministry of Education barred her from teaching in any school in Moldova. After that she eked out a living as a freelance translator and writer.

Having spent so many years researching the fate of repressed Soviet astronomers, I came to see in Monica not only a friend but also the last chapter in my personal Cold War. I was powerless in the 1980s and 1990s to do anything other than research and publish, but in Monica I had before me a human being who was herself a casualty of the Soviet system and its collapse. I had it in my power to do something tangible, to right a wrong. I knew I could not go to Thailand without her.

Throughout 2012, I conducted a fundraising campaign on Monica's behalf that collected the nearly $12,000 needed for GCS in Thailand. A number of people contributed, and I chipped in what I could. Over half the needed funds came from a successful American transgender businesswoman living in Germany.

Monica and I boarded a plane on January 21, 2013. After three flights we arrived in Phuket and checked into the Aspasia Resort on Kata Beach. We had a rest day to relax and walk on the beach before moving on to the serious business at the Phuket International Hospital (PIH), our home for the next two weeks.

Monica and I shared a room, and I served as Monica's interpreter. English was the language of communication with Dr. Kunaporn and the senior nursing staff, but we soon found out that the nurse assistants have a knowledge of English that is best described as theoretical. This led to amusing moments on things as simple as placing our daily breakfast order. For example, Monica liked hot tea with breakfast, and I wanted cold juice. We developed a morning mantra in which we slowly and carefully repeated _HOT_ TEA and _COLD_ MANGO JUICE. Despite this best effort at communication, one morning the breakfast trays brought us iced tea and a steaming hot glass of mango juice. Frustrated as we were, we burst out laughing.

GCS itself was surprisingly painless. For a traditional transgender woman like me, the joy of sensing there was no longer an unwanted bulge between my legs was beyond words. Embassy Bucharest friends sent flowers, and Peter from our med unit stayed in close contact with Dr. Kunaporn. Our Foreign Service community had joined together to support and celebrate me on this journey.

The difficult part of recovery was the tedium of three days' enforced bed rest. How many DVDs could one watch? How much reading could one do while squirming to find a comfortable position? Since I had some breast augmentation in addition to GCS, I was limited to 180 degrees of rotation. I lay pretty much flat on my back with my freedom of motion limited to rolling onto one side or the other. Even that had to be done carefully, as it tended to tug painfully at stitches under my breasts.

I had also decided to have some facial feminization surgery (FFS) done in Phuket. In 2012, I sent photos to PIH's cranial-facial surgeon Dr. Rushapol Sdawat. We agreed on a number of procedures that included face and neck lifts, forehead lift, and reduction rhinoplasty. I didn't want to overdo this, but I did want to soften some features. The guiding principle was that I needed to come through FFS with it still being evident that my sisters and I come from the same Scot-Irish family.

FFS hurt far more than GCS. When I came to, I was in an ICU in some sort of machine that alternately compressed and released my legs, apparently to keep the blood flowing. My head was tightly bandaged, and I couldn't see. My mouth was as dry as the Sahara. I spent the night in the ICU, and Monica was beside herself with worry, not knowing what had happened to me. In the morning Dr. Rushapol stood by my ICU bed and fed me my first post-surgery meal the way a mother would feed a child, mouthful by mouthful. Bandaged and without sight, I could not feed myself.

It was many days before the bandages came off, but even then, my eyes were swollen and my head was in a state of perpetual headache. It took many days more for the pain and swelling to pass. When I could finally see straight, I almost wished I could not. My face looked as though not one but more likely ten Mack trucks had run over it. I was all shades of black and blue and yellow and orange, and my eyes looked as though they were staring out from two purple abysses. It now dawned on me belatedly that doing GCS and FFS back-to-back had been overload. It was like inviting two independent trucking companies to drive eighteen-wheelers over my body as many times as they wanted. With total time in surgeries just shy of twenty-four hours, it's no surprise that I also suffered a dropped left foot.[79]

---

79 Drop foot after a long surgery is not common but also is not unknown. One theory as to the cause holds that the nerves that control the muscles in the foot are damaged during the surgery. Another holds that the muscles themselves are weakened or stretched out of position. Whatever the cause, after my surgeries I was unable to lift my left foot at the ankle and had to be very careful walking so as not to trip over my own foot.

But the pain did pass. I started walking the hospital hallway, lifting my left foot carefully while holding onto the railing. In time I started to get feeling and motion back.

After two weeks, Monica and I were released to the Aspasia Resort with regular post-op visits back to PIH. We had to follow a rigorous regimen of dilating our newly created vaginas three times a day for the first three months after surgery. This dominated our days, but I wanted to get out and moving as quickly as I could. With motion returning to my left foot, I started walking the length of Kata Beach at sunset, sometimes buying fresh fish from the daily catch that the fishermen grilled on the spot. With the pain of surgery fading into memory, I looked out on the Andaman Sea and felt at peace. The life journey had been worth it.

Still looking like an accident victim but enjoying a sunset walk on Kata Beach

On our final full day in Phuket, we closed out our financial accounts at PIH. The young woman going through my paperwork got to the last page and couldn't help exclaiming, "You spent over a million Thai Baht!" That's about $35,000 with FFS accounting for the largest portion. For months thereafter, I boasted to friends that I now had a *million-baht body*.

Did having this *million-baht body* fill me with flights of exaltation? No. It simply made me feel normal. I could look in a mirror and not avert my eyes. Everything reflected back to me was as it always should have been. I could look at myself with amazement and quiet joy.

Prior to her transition, Jennifer Finney Boylan asked a woman friend what it's like to have breasts.[80] She was surprised to get the response that it's akin to having elbows. They're just there. Finally, in Phuket, I got my elbows.

Monica and I flew back to Bucharest on February 19. From there Monica continued on to Moldova, and I returned to my Bucharest apartment where Olympia was waiting. After a day of rest, I was back at Embassy Bucharest. For the remainder of my time in Romania, I was up at 5:00 a.m. to dilate my new vagina before work, often with Olympia joining me in the bed to watch old movies as I dilated. I dilated again during the lunch hour. Thankfully, our med unit had a second examination room that Peter reserved for me. I dilated a third time in the evening. With nearly three hours of every day going into dilation, there wasn't much time for anything else during my final weeks in Bucharest.[81] One of my greatest joys was the day when I was able to sit again on my bicycle without pain. I even participated in a weekend rally for bicyclist rights in Bucharest. I was in the saddle again.

That's my vagina monologue, the story of the journey Monica and I took together to Phuket to complete life journeys we had set out on as children. If I have disappointed in the telling of those weeks together, in their lack of deep drama and pathos, the explanation is simple. All the drama and pathos happened before Phuket. Our journey there was a completion, an exclamation point at the end of a sentence that spanned decades. We had our elbows at last.

---

80   Jennifer Finney Boylan, ibid.

81   I was able to reduce to dilating twice a day when I left Romania in June. Six months later I was down to once a day. Now, in 2021, I dilate at least weekly. Dilation is a fact of life for anyone who acquires a vagina late in life.

7. The Carpet, Too, Is Moving Under You

You must leave now, take what you need, you think will last.
But whatever you wish to keep, you better grab it fast.[82]

NOTE: *This article appeared in my web journal Transgender in State on May 24, 2013, which accounts for the 2013 time frame of reference on the eve of my departure from Romania.*

It's all over now, Baby Blue. The old Bob Dylan tune plays in my head. For weeks I have put off the thought of leaving Romania. Surely, I thought, there is more time, more time for everything? Alas, the answer is no. In three weeks, I leave Bucharest for good.

Personal life in the Foreign Service is both exhilarating and cruel. When we first join, our eyes are filled with the wonder of impending adventure, the chance to live and work in other countries, to experience other cultures. That joy never fades. I still experience it.

The cruel side comes two or three years later, when we must leave the homes we have made in countries we may never have expected to visit in our lifetimes. I was misty-eyed when I left Moscow in 2007. I was sad to leave Uzbekistan in 2010. Nothing, however, compares with the emotions I am experiencing in my final days in Romania. It's the warmest home I have known.

This is the country that saw my rebirth. It is filled with friends who supported and walked me through every twist and turn. I feel I have a sister in Chisinau. The memory of family life with Olympia in Bucharest will stay with me for the rest of my life. Wherever I go, I meet friends who are more like aunts, uncles, and cousins.

When I roll my bicycle out the door this morning, it will be my last ride to work in Romania. Day in, day out, the bicycle has gotten me around Bucharest for over two and a half years. The route that I could ride nearly in my sleep will not seem humdrum today. Tonight, the bicycle comes to pieces for cleaning, servicing, and packing.

---

82 Dylan, Bob. "It's All Over Now, Baby Blue." Genius. Accessed September 10, 2023. https://genius.com/Bob-dylan-its-all-over-now-baby-blue-lyrics.

The dismantling of this life begins in earnest on Saturday. Friends will help me go through my apartment to divide what is to be kept from what is to be given or thrown away. That which is to be kept must be divided between unaccompanied air baggage (UAB) and household effects (HHE). I will personally pack anything too fragile, important, or emotionally valuable to be entrusted to the movers. I must pack two suitcases containing everything I will need for the next two months.

Pack-out. The movers come a week from today. In the course of a day, my home will be transformed back into furnished but sterile government housing. The pictures will be gone from the walls; anything that made it home for three years will be loaded into trucks and driven away. I will be left with my two suitcases and a *departure kit* consisting of a few basic housekeeping items and kitchenware.

With author and activist Kevin Sessums

Once the movers have carried out their destruction, I will have two weeks left in the country. If there is a bright side to the sadness of leaving, it is that the first week of June will be a celebration. It is GayFest week, Bucharest's celebration of LGBT+ Pride. It will be the second Pride of my life. Accept has a full week planned culminating with the Diversity March on June 8.

The Embassy is involved, having arranged a video conference with former Ambassador Michael Guest. We're also bringing Kevin Sessums, author of *Mississippi Sissy*, to Romania for the week, and we will co-host a Pride reception with other diplomatic missions. I had a hand in many parts of this, but I feel particularly good that more hands are involved this year than last.

Then it will be my last week. At work, I will run around collecting signatures on a departure checklist and writing up notes for the person taking my place. There may be a last party or two. That there will be hugs and tears goes without saying. Bob Dylan will continue to reverberate in my head:

> *You must leave now, take what you need, you think will last.*
>
> *But whatever you wish to keep, you better grab it fast.*

Then, I will close the door of my Bucharest home one last time, rolling my two suitcases to the waiting car that will take me to the airport. But what will last is not to be found in those suitcases. It is to be found in my heart and in my memories of the people I have known and loved and who have known and loved me in return.

PART 5

Freight Trains, Arms Control, and LGBT+ Diplomacy on the Potomac (July 2013–Sept 2014)

I landed in the United States on June 14, 2013, not having spent more than a few weeks in the U.S. since 2008. Now, for the first time since my year on the *Russia Desk* in 2004–05, I was to have a one-year tour at "Main State." Still grieving my Bucharest home, I made my way north to Maine for a month and planned to spend the time coming to terms with this new life in my home country.

Saying I had a house in Maine would be misleading. The thirty-five acres I purchased in a lake region town in 2009 had a run-down, off-grid, three-season camp on it that could never serve as a year-round residence. I had already found a local builder who would tear it down and replace it with a small but modern, on-grid house.

During that month I climbed Katahdin for a second time and spent hours kayaking. Matt came to visit for two days, our first significant alone time together since I came out to him at an Irish pub in 2011. We hiked and fought our way upstream through shallow rapids in a tandem kayak lent by a friend. The ties that bound us were still there.

Then, in the proverbial blink of an eye, the month was over. It was time to report to Washington.

1. The Other Side of the Tracks

I signed for the apartment while still in Bucharest, sight unseen. The apartment had to be within walking distance of a Metro station and biking distance to Main State in Foggy Bottom. I wanted it to be affordable but not a dump. In signing the lease and returning it by email, I got what I was looking for but not quite what I expected.

"How do you live here with all the racket from the trains?" I asked my new neighbor the day I saw the apartment for the first time.

"You'll be surprised," she said. "Within a week, you won't even hear them."

It had never occurred to me that an apartment near a Metro station might also be near the tracks. My new apartment was a 15-minute walk to the Takoma Metro station, across the D.C. line on the Maryland side. The Metro tracks were right outside my bedroom window. Worse still, so were the CTX freight and commuter rail tracks. The tracks were so close that the blinds would rattle each time a train went by, blowing wildly if the window was open. Metro shuts down for a few hours every night, but freight never sleeps. Neither did I the first week.

I had no furniture.[83] My sister Irene loaned me a folding chair and card table, and I had my sleeping bag and air mattress from Maine. It would be a week before my UAB arrived and a month until the HHE came. It would take a month to get Ma and Dad's furniture out of storage where it had been since I left for Uzbekistan in 2008. My living conditions that first month made an undergraduate dormitory look luxurious by comparison.

Time proved my neighbor right. The round-the-clock train racket faded to the background. My UAB and HHE did arrive, and so did the furniture. The apartment was tiny by overseas Foreign Service standards even if it was, on paper, a two-bedroom apartment. I had reasoned that the second bedroom would be my storage room, cheaper than renting a storage unit. It became my warehouse with narrow crawlways zigzagging between boxes. I never unpacked most of them, but I spent many late evenings searching through them in usually vain attempts to find *something* that at the moment seemed indispensable.

I now lived on the other side of the tracks from the house I had owned for over twenty-five years until divorce. It was a scant ten-minute walk away—that is, a ten-minute walk if I had been able to walk directly across the tracks. I had chosen the location not only because it was cheap and near a Metro station. The area was familiar. I knew all the stores. My doctors were nearby. I wouldn't have to spend the year learning a new area only to go overseas again just as I was getting comfortable.

There was another reason. I needed to face this oh-so-familiar territory

---

83   I did not know it at the time, but I could have stayed in furnished temporary housing until my HHE arrived. On this, my first posting back to Washington, I still had much to learn about State Department transfer allowances for FSOs.

156

where I had lived much of my life. I needed to make it mine again. It did feel strange at first to walk streets I had once wandered vainly at night in search of a future, but with time the Twilight Zone feeling passed. Now I walked them as the liberated person I had become.

Time went on. Friends came for dinner. So did Matt and his girlfriend. Sometimes I sat alone on my small balcony on a rickety lounge chair and watched the trains go by.

It was on a rare snowy winter evening that I realized this apartment was truly home. I had just rolled out of Main State on my bicycle, after 11:00 p.m. A light snow was falling. As I pedaled up Virginia Avenue and then onto Rock Creek Parkway, there was not a single car in sight. A thin layer of white covered the roadway. What on most days was a busy car commuter route had become a silent, beautiful, enchanted forest with wet snow hanging heavily in the trees. I pedaled as slowly as I could, wanting to make the moment last.

When I arrived in Takoma Park, the bicycle was dirty and caked with snow. There was no way I could bring it into my living room. I spent an hour bringing rags and buckets of warm water out onto the stairwell. When I rolled the bicycle inside, I looked around and said quietly, "This is home."

A boyfriend entered the picture. John made an impression as soon as he sat down opposite me at the first and only speed dating event of my life. He was the rarest of breeds, a D.C. native who had lived his entire life in the area, had never been overseas, and didn't even have a passport. He worked in IT for an insurance company, but he knew the world! Books had taken him everywhere. When I told him I had lived in Uzbekistan, he knew what I was talking about. That knowledge alone made him stand out from most Americans who have no clue where Central Asia is located.

John was half a head taller than me, fit, and Irish handsome. We came from the same Catholic childhoods and expectations that go with Irish or Scot-Irish families. We both understood that significant looks from opposite corners of the room are every bit as meaningful as demonstrative, voluble Brazilian outbursts of emotion. We also clicked on our love of movies, theater, and long walks. In short, we were a good match.

John and I became constant weekend companions. Often, he would wait for me at Main State as I finished my shift. Since my job for the year actually did involve shift work, that meant he was picking me up sometimes at midnight or at 8:00 a.m. Late suppers, early breakfasts, movies, theater, and quiet evenings interrupted by noisy trains became the norm. We went hiking in the George Washington National Forest. Another time we spent a three-day weekend in New York City, walking all the way from the Cloisters to the Brooklyn Bridge and then across to Brooklyn Heights.

In John, I also had a sexual partner. We had our first night together before I managed to come out to him about my past. I knew he would find out eventually. I intended to tell him, but events on a romantic evening got ahead of my good intentions.

I was terrified the next morning to tell him there was something important he needed to know about me. I sat him down for another cup of coffee. He listened in silence as I told him the condensed version of my life. When I was done, he looked up and asked, "Is that all?" When I said yes, he added, "I was afraid you were going to say it was over between us." My relief knew no bounds. I had been terrified that John would reject me because of my past, but it turned out John had been afraid I was sitting him down to say this was the end!

John, as I learned, was no stranger to LGBT+ issues. He had been married nearly as long as I had, but his wife had come out openly as lesbian after their two daughters were grown. They had, however, managed to stay on good terms. Through his personal experience and through his reading, John understood the meaning of sexual orientation and gender identity. For him, my being transgender was no issue at all.

The year, more precisely fourteen months, went by quickly. My little apartment was but a refuge from the busiest year I was yet to have in my FSO life. It was, however, the year in which I faced returning to the area I had called home for over twenty-six years. By the time the year was done, it had become home again. Life does go on. Dreams do continue even on the other side of the tracks.

2. *How I Learned to Stop Worrying and Love the Bomb*

And you tell me over and over and over again my friend,

Ah, you don't believe we're on the eve of destruction.[84]

It's called the Nuclear Risk Reduction Center, but everyone working there calls it by its acronym, NRRC, pronouncing it N-E-R-K. It's an operations center that functions 24/7, 365 days a year to carry out U.S. monitoring and reporting commitments for a whole bunch of arms control treaties, in particular our nuclear treaties with Russia. Training to work in the NRRC includes a week at the Defense Threat Reduction Agency, where a screening of Stanley Kubrick's classic 1964 black comedy *Dr. Strangelove* serves as the lunchtime entertainment on the first day.

The NRRC dates back to an agreement with the Soviet Union in the waning years of the Cold War, a confidence building measure that was the brainchild of Senators Nunn and Lugar. There is a NRRC in Moscow staffed by the Russian government, and there are NRRCs in the capitals of other post-Soviet countries. Over time, a number of multilateral arms treaties under the auspices of the Organization for Security and Cooperation in Europe and the Organization for the Prohibition of Chemical Weapons were added to the NRRC's monitoring responsibilities.

The NRRC became my workplace home for the year. I served there as a watch officer, part of the team that staffs the NRRC all hours of day and night. The routine on the Watch was to work a shift for six days, then rotate to the next shift after a break. In the course of a month, a watch officer works the full twenty-four-hour schedule, first on day shift, then on evening shift, and then on the overnight shift. Each shift has its own rhythm. The day shift means dressing in a professional wardrobe and briefing both staff officers and front office staff. The evening and overnight shifts are more relaxed, and weekends allow for comfortable shirts, blouses, and slacks. We lovingly referred to the latter as *NRRC weekends*.

A watch officer processes up to three dozen treaty notifications during a shift, some of them involving very technical translating from Russian or other treaty languages. Although we loved the quiet of our *NRRC week-*

---

84   Sloan, P.F., recorded by Barry McGuire. "Eve of Destruction." Genius. Accessed September 10, 2023. https://genius.com/Barry-mcguire-eve-of-destruction-lyrics.

ends, other shifts scarcely allowed time to run to the bathroom, let alone grab a bite to eat. I rarely knew in advance what a shift would bring.

Each shift can have its surprises. An uneventful Sunday morning can be interrupted by an impending Russian missile launch. Such notifications send watch officers scurrying to put the Pentagon and other government agencies in the know. That's the whole point of the NRRC's existence: no surprises. By constantly monitoring and processing treaty notifications, the NRRCs in Washington and Moscow ensure there are no surprises, that *Dr. Strangelove* doomsday scenarios cannot happen. Joined by the Hot Line at the Pentagon, the NRRC is one of the best examples of diplomacy and arms control at work to make the world safer for all of us.

Our work on the Watch increased greatly in February 2014. Soldiers without insignia began filtering into Crimea, but it was clear they had Russian backing. By the end of March, Russia had annexed Crimea. In the aftermath, separatist forces appeared in Donetsk and other parts of eastern Ukraine. During a quiet overnight shift, a notification from Kyiv jarred me to full attention. The one-page notification was, in essence, saying that Ukraine had observed Russian troop movements on its eastern border and feared a full-scale invasion. As quickly as I could, I translated the notification to English, taking care to convey the nuanced emotions behind the words. I had to get it right. U.S. reaction depended on my accurate translation.

That's life on the Watch in the NRRC: long periods of routine, sometimes tedious, interrupted by moments of high anxiety. For someone like me who grew up with the fear of nuclear holocaust, it was the right place to be. No, I did not learn to stop worrying and love the bomb, but during my NRRC year I know I did my part to make the world a little bit safer, a little more distant from the eve of destruction. I finished with a Meritorious Honor Award ... and with my name on a plaque as *NRRC Watch Officer of the Year.*

3. Madam President

I joined the Foreign Service in 2004, but I was barely aware of GLIFAA when I began transition in Romania in 2010. In September 2013, I somewhat nervously became its president. The NRRC may have been my day job, but it was as GLIFAA president that I used every skill I had as a communicator, a researcher, a writer, and a negotiator. I had become leader of one of the best known, oldest LGBT+ organizations in the federal government.

The Department of State had not been kind to its gay and lesbian FSOs. In the 1950s, it tried hard to identify and root out all gay FSOs in the so-called *lavender scare*.[85] Security interviews bordering on interrogations kept widening the circle of incrimination. The *lavender scare* stripped clearances from FSOs found to be gay and drove them out of the State Department. It destroyed their careers. Some committed suicide.

Overt persecution of gay FSOs may have waned after the 1950s, but it had not ended in any official sense. Policy held that being gay and *in the closet* left an FSO open to blackmail. Perversely, being gay and *out of the closet* was seen as little better, an opening for foreign intelligence services to leverage to their advantage. The State Department did not dismiss FSOs from the service for being gay as such. Rather, it took away their security clearances. Without a clearance, an FSO ostensibly had failed to maintain *worldwide availability*. After a year or so, the State Department selected gay FSOs out of the service for failure to maintain that availability.

Against this still hostile backdrop, in 1992 a brave few founded *Gays and Lesbians in Foreign Affairs Agencies*. Within a year GLIFAA's advocacy achieved is first goal of reforming the security clearance policy that had been used to root out gay FSOs. Two years later, Secretary Warren Christopher issued a statement prohibiting discrimination based on sexual orientation.

GLIFAA's next worry was domestic partners. As far as State HR was concerned, the partners of gay and lesbian FSOs did not exist. Partners could not travel to post on an FSO's government orders. If they went at their own expense, it was with a tourist passport and no status granting the privileges and immunities (*Ps & Is*) enjoyed by FSOs and their families. Accompanying partners risked their lives in countries that harbored hostility towards gays and lesbians.

---

85   Few women served as FSOs prior to 1970. In annual performance appraisals, the State Department rated FSO men on the characteristics of their wives as diplomatic hostesses. The State Department required that FSO women who married resign from the service. It wasn't until the Palmer Case of 1968 and its following class-action suit that women finally obtained the right to serve on a par with men in the Foreign Service.

The first step forward for domestic partners came with a member of household (MOH) policy announced by Secretary Madeleine Albright in a cable transmitted during the holiday lull on December 26, 2000, so that it would attract little notice. Under the new policy, the State Department acknowledged the existence of domestic partners. It would not pay their moving expenses and there were still no *Ps & Is*, but partners could reside in government housing at post, obtain permanent embassy or consulate visitor badges, and use post facilities such as the medical office.

GLIFAA wanted more and got it in June 2009 when Secretary Hillary Rodham-Clinton ordered a new policy that extended family benefits to registered same-sex domestic partners (SSDPs) to the maximum extent allowed by law. Thanks to GLIFAA, gay and lesbian FSOs and their families were now accepted and enjoyed many of the same privileges as their straight colleagues.

This was the backdrop when outgoing president Ken Kero-Mentz turned over the chair to me in August 2013. I had become only the second woman and the first transgender woman to serve as GLIFAA president. Gulp. Could I really do this?

There I was, a woman with a full-time job in nuclear security and arms control at the head of an organization with *Gays and Lesbians* in its name. I had no personal experience of what it is to be gay. My post-transition sexual orientation was leading me on a more-or-less heterosexual path. When I attended the first GLIFAA happy hour in my new role, I set foot in a gay bar for the first time. As much as I enjoyed the party atmosphere, I felt myself a fish out of water.

I needed some education, and I knew my GLIFAA board needed it also. It wasn't lost on me that I was taking up my position at the moment Allyson Robinson was losing hers. In October 2012, Allyson had become executive director of OutServe-SLDN, the military's equivalent of GLIFAA.[86] As such, Allyson was the first transgender person to lead an organization advocating for LGBT+ issues broadly rather than specifically for transgender issues.

It had not gone well. In part this was because OutServe-SLDN had succumbed to its own success. Following the 2011 repeal of the *Don't ask,*

---

86   Servicemembers Legal Defense Network (SLDN).

don't tell (DADT), OutServe-SLDN lost much of its reason to exist. It lost most of its funding, declared bankruptcy, and closed its headquarters in July 2013. Allyson announced her resignation the same day.

GLIFAA is tiny compared with OutServe-SLDN just as the Department of State is tiny compared with the Department of Defense. The issues of gay and lesbian FSOs had never captured the public imagination the way DADT had. Unlike OutServe-SLDN with its abundant funding and professional staff, GLIFAA is a volunteer association funded by membership dues. The scales are entirely different. Still, I was worried.

I had lunch with Allyson in August 2013. Although everyone had tried to present a united front, Allyson confirmed there had been tension in having a transgender woman lead a predominantly gay organization. This friction handicapped her as executive director. She told me my success or failure at GLIFAA would depend on our willingness to hear each other out, to learn from each other, and work together for the common good. In short, we had to be the diplomats we were trained to be.

In this, I was as lucky as any president could be. An entirely new board had come into office with me. There were new vice presidents for State and for USAID, a new communications director, a new social director, and a new secretary/treasurer. Most importantly, Selim Ariturk came onto the GLIFAA board as policy director.

Selim and I had met briefly once before, but our relationship began for real in August 2013. On a Saturday afternoon we rented a canoe in Georgetown and paddled the Potomac for two hours, rounding Roosevelt Island. We talked of Chelsea Manning, who had that summer announced herself as transgender, Selim and I taking opposing positions on the damage she had done to U.S. security and diplomacy by leaking State Department cables. We talked about our priorities for GLIFAA. We often disagreed, but I admired the way Selim's mind worked. Over the coming year we would discuss and debate often, looking for consensus that satisfied us both and, we hoped, GLIFAA members scattered around the globe.

In September we convened a Sunday retreat of the whole board to discuss priorities and strategies. We chose three issues to top our list:

- Post-DOMA strategy and the fate of SSDP,
- *Ps & Is* for spouses and domestic partners, and

- Removal of the *transgender exclusion* from Federal Employee Health Benefit (FEHB) insurance plans.

The first issue had been a sleeper surprise. The SSDP policy enacted by Secretary Clinton in 2009 accorded family benefits to registered SSDPs, but the Defense of Marriage Act (DOMA) put limits on what SSDP could offer. Employee insurance and retirement programs still excluded same-sex partners. FSOs rotating back to Washington could not bring partners who did not have U.S. citizenship or residency.

The nationwide LGBT+ community celebrated in June 2013 when the Supreme Court overturned DOMA Section 3 in United States v. Windsor. The federal government now recognized same-sex marriage on the same basis as opposite-sex marriages.

The key word here was **married**. FSOs live and work largely overseas, often in countries that are unabashedly homophobic. What happens if an FSO finds a partner in a country that does not recognize same-sex marriage? If this couple flies to the U.S. to marry, what happens when they return to post? Could the now married partner be subject to social or legal retribution?

These were serious questions that worried gay and lesbian FSOs. The devil was in the details of how the Department of State would interpret SSDP in the post-DOMA world. Our GLIFAA board urged the State Department to go slow, to leave SSDP in place until the details could be worked out.

The second issue, *Ps & Is*, followed from the first. As far as gay and lesbian FSOs are concerned, there are three types of countries in the world:

1. Those that wonder why the U.S. had been so slow to recognize same-sex marriage;

2. Those that will never recognize same-sex marriage under any circumstances; and

3. Those that waffle in the middle, not recognizing same-sex marriage but, valuing their relationship with the U.S., are willing to grant some form of status to FSO same-sex spouses as long as it can be done quietly.

Our GLIFAA board advocated for reciprocity, a policy by which the U.S. would deny accreditation to a foreign diplomat's family member if that country had denied *Ps & Is* to the same-sex spouse of an FSO.

I personally put the *transgender exclusion* on the GLIFAA advocacy agenda. Most of my board members didn't know that an exclusionary clause dating to the 1970s denied coverage of transgender health issues to all federal employees, FSOs included. For example, in a section on *General exclusions — Things we don't cover*, one FEHB plan listed "services, drugs, or supplies related to impotency, gender reassignment, sex transformations, sexual dysfunction or sexual inadequacy." All FEHB plans included similar exclusionary clauses. Just as I was learning the issues facing my gay colleagues, they were now learning the issues facing transgender Americans.

We wrote white papers for each issue, building a lobbying blueprint for the year.[87] Lobby we did, meeting repeatedly with officials on *mahogany row,* the power corridor where the State Department's top officials have their office suites on the seventh floor of Main State. We went all the way to Secretary John Kerry's Counselor Heather Higginbottom and Chief of Staff David Wade. We met repeatedly with Undersecretary for Management Pat Kennedy and Acting Director General Hans Klemm. These were the people who had it in their power to change policy.

Selim set the agenda and tactics for each meeting. We decided early that I would advocate for the issues affecting our gay and lesbian members while Selim, State VP Christopher Hoh, and USAID VP Jay Gilliam would take the lead in advocating for removal of the *transgender exclusion.* Without even a thought to the experience at OutServe-SLDN, Selim had hit upon the strategy that cemented us as a board. The old adage is true—the best way to learn a subject is to teach a course in it.

Our results varied, but we did better than we might have expected. We slowed Pat Kennedy's rush to roll back SSDP in the post-DOMA world. He heard us even if he often did not agree with us. Like the little Dutch boy with his finger in the dike, we were able to keep the edifice of SSDP in place for another year.[88]

---

87 See Appendix 2 for an excerpt from GLIFAA's 2013 white paper on the need to eliminate the *transgender exclusion.*

88 The Department ultimately phased out SSDP in 2017. The phase-out did, however, include a grandfather clause allowing new couples to stay under the SSDP umbrella until the American FSO rotates through Washington, at which time the couple is required to marry if they wish to continue being recognized as a couple.

On *Ps & Is* we finished the year as we started. Pat Kennedy feared that reciprocity could lead to tit-for-tat visa wars. Behind-the-scenes negotiation for individual cases remained the official State position, but Pat Kennedy mandated that each post send an annual assessment of conditions for LGBT+ families. He also directed posts to advocate strongly with host governments on behalf of same-sex FSO families, and GLIFAA assisted with a number of those cases. *Ps & Is* remain a GLIFAA issue to this day.

Our most unexpected success proved to be elimination of the *transgender exclusion*. Our advocacy for *SSDP* and *Ps & Is* was inside the Department of State, but the Office of Personnel Management (OPM) administers FEHB plans. How could we influence the policies of an agency entirely outside the State Department?

Our answer was to use what leverage we did have. Both Pat Kennedy at State and his counterpart Elizabeth Kolmstetter at USAID agreed to send letters to OPM Administrator Katherine Archuleta laying out the case for removing the *transgender exclusion*. OPM could ignore GLIFAA, but it could not ignore Pat Kennedy and Elizabeth Kolmstetter. OPM wrote back that the issue was under study with no time frame for a decision. We expected this, but the letters gave us a back channel.

The American Foreign Service Protective Association (AFSPA) administers the Foreign Service Benefit Plan (FSBP), an FEHB plan tailored to overseas FSO life. We sent copies of the Pat Kennedy and Elizabeth Kolmstetter letters to AFSPA and asked that it request OPM approval to remove the *transgender exclusion* from FSBP. After all, this is our health insurance program for our Foreign Service family, and the top management officials at the State Department and USAID were asking that the *exclusion* be removed.

GLIFAA wasn't alone in pushing to eliminate the *transgender exclusion*. We reached out to LGBT+ employee associations at other federal agencies. We worked in concert with the National Center for Transgender Equality (NCTE) and with the Human Rights Campaign (HRC). We all knew we had to keep up pressure from as many directions as possible.

As winter turned to spring, we didn't know if our back-channel gambit would bear fruit. Time was running out. The annual commemoration of Pride was coming soon, and Secretary John Kerry would be our guest of honor for this well-attended event that includes the press. As GLIFAA president, I would introduce the secretary, and that introduction gave me leverage. I allowed word to seep out that if there was no progress on the *transgender exclusion* before Pride, I would denounce this discriminatory clause—in the presence of the secretary and the press.

The gambit worked. Less than a week before Pride, NCTE's Mara Keisling convened a conference call. OPM had relented. It would allow individual FEHB plans to drop the *exclusion* on the condition of no publicity. Mara said it was GLIFAA's advocacy that had made the difference. Instead of denouncing OPM at Pride, I thanked AFSPA for its unfailing support of the Foreign Service family.

· · · · · · · · · · · · · · · ·

Summer 2014. My year in Washington was coming to an end, and my thoughts were turning to pack-out and reporting to my next post in Kazakhstan. How could an entire year have passed so quickly? Surprised and somewhat in shock, I knew the time had come to say goodbye.

But instead of moving on quietly, I was on the verge of resigning as GLIFAA president, my letter of resignation already written and ready to send.

Why? In September 2013, I told my GLIFAA board that we needed to do something about GLIFAA's name. I was now president of an association with *Gays and Lesbians* in its name – but I did not see myself as either gay or lesbian. If I felt that way, why would anyone else who is transgender or gender non-conforming want to join GLIFAA?

For months it was a back burner issue; we had bigger battles to fight. We tossed around a number of ideas, but our minds were elsewhere. In the end we decided to retain the name GLIFAA but omit the *spelling out*. The association's logo and tagline would now be *glifaa, lgbt+ pride in foreign affairs agencies*. Glifaa would no longer be an acronym, but the well-known brand with a proud history would remain.

We liked this approach, but implementing it required a membership vote. Modifying the name meant minor modifications to the association's by-laws, and by-law changes require two thirds majority member vote approval. Busy with our priority issues, we neglected to explain the change adequately to our far-flung membership. When we tallied the vote, the change had failed by a single vote. I was devastated. After a year leading GLIFAA, I felt the association had not only turned its back but had actually rejected me.

Glifaa board with Secretary John Kerry in June 2014.
Third from right in front row is our invited speaker, Masha Gessen.

It was Selim who stopped me from resigning. In the same membership vote, Selim had been elected president for 2014–15. He assured me he would repeat the vote, first running a full-up communication campaign to the membership. If it failed on a new vote, he said he would join me in resigning. I put my letter away. Selim was true to his word. The second vote the following winter succeeded. *GLIFAA* is now *glifaa* in all its literature, on its web site, and in its by-laws.[89]

. . . .

My Washington year came to its end. I worked my last shift at the NRRC. We had our last glifaa meeting with me in the chair as president. Pack-out did come. No longer would I hear the sound of freight trains storming past my bedroom window at night. By now I was getting used to being a БОМЖ – *BOMZh*—the Russian acronym for a homeless person that translates literally as "without defined place of residence." That didn't make the goodbyes any easier.

The hardest goodbye was to my steady boyfriend John. For all his Irish up-bringing, tears came into his eyes the closer we got to my departure date.

---

89   This is also how I will refer to the organization from this point forward.

John said he couldn't face saying goodbye at the airport, so we had our own private goodbye several days before that. It's a truism in the Foreign Service that our careers are hard on relationships. In August 2014, I got to experience that firsthand as John and I shared our last kiss and hug. He had his career, and I had mine. Both of us had financial obligations and commitments. For now, at least, ours would be a long-distance relationship until I came back to the U.S. or he was able to visit me.

I will always look back at my Washington year with pride. Glifaa succeeded where OutServe-SLDN and other groups had failed. We showed that as different as sexual orientation and gender identity are, we can work together for a common cause. What we achieved that year, we achieved together.

PART 6

The Heart of Central Asia (2014–17)

The most difficult periods in my life have often come in the aftermath of success. My collapse in 1990 came right after the launch of Hubble and the culmination of my six years researching the purge of Soviet astronomers. My gender identity crisis in 2000–02 followed our successful redesign of pointing control systems on Hubble. Now, in 2014, I had finished one of my most successful years.

Only five years remained until I faced the mandatory 65-year-old FSO retirement age, but five years are five years. Seven years after departing Tashkent, I was going back to the heart of Central Asia. The pattern of my life would repeat. This would be no glide path to retirement. I would learn that Kazakhstan could bring new challenges, consternation, success, failure, the greatest of joys, and the greatest of heartbreaks.

1. Istanbul Gateway

> *Istanbul was Constantinople*
>
> *Now it's Istanbul, not Constantinople*
>
> *Been a long time gone, Constantinople*
>
> *Now it's Turkish delight on a moonlit night.*[90]

NOTE: This article appeared in my web journal Alice in State (https://attitude-maneuver.blogspot.com/) on September 27, 2014. I wrote it while in transit to my new home in Astana, Kazakhstan, and it captures my feelings of uncertainty and anticipation as I felt them in the moment.

Istanbul again. The last time I passed through here was in spring 2010 on my way home from Tashkent *en route* to a divorce settlement and an un-

---

90 Kennedy, Jimmy, as recorded by The Four Lads. "Istanbul (Not Constantinople)." Genius. Accessed September 10, 2023. https://genius.com/The-four-lads-istanbul-not-constantinople-lyrics.

certain future. It was a different life; I was a different person. Istanbul was the gateway.

There are several transfer points going from the East Coast of the U.S. to Central Asia. During my years in Tashkent, I went via both Frankfurt and Moscow, but I settled on Istanbul as my favored transit point. As it has been since the times of Imperial Rome, Constantinople—later renamed Istanbul—has been where East and West meet and mix. For an American going east, it is where one first feels that one has left the U.S. behind. On one's return, it is where one first feels the glimmer of home beckoning. It became a tradition for those of us at Embassy Tashkent to have that last or first Starbucks coffee or that first or last Western beer while passing through Ataturk Airport. There one could observe travelers at once so different from passengers in a U.S. airport, but different as well from those one sees in Tashkent.

I'm on my way back to Central Asia, this time to a regional position based in Astana, Kazakhstan. My journey began at 7:30 a.m. on Wednesday morning from my little Maine home. In Bangor, I gave Hillary, my 1991 station wagon, over to friends who put me on the Concord bus for the first leg of my journey to Boston. British Air took me to London and then to Istanbul. It was 6:00 p.m. local time when we landed on the Bosporus. By then I had been awake for over twenty-seven hours, not counting a few snatched minutes of sleep in economy seats.

I lost the knack of international travel during my fifteen months in the U.S. My attempt to be a smart traveler by taking the bus into the city failed totally; I missed my stop and then had to take a taxi back to my hotel in Old Town. Two drivers started fighting over me. I knew then I was in the hands of the taxi mafia and about to be fleeced, but I was too exhausted to care. I ended up paying as much as I would have for a taxi all the way from the airport.

Once checked in, I gathered enough strength to search for dinner. I was quickly reminded that I was not in Maine or Washington. The sidewalks were delightfully full of people, but these pedestrians did not move like pedestrians in American cities, dutifully passing on the right. I had several near collisions. It took me a few minutes to re-acculturate to the fact that our subconscious American rules on how to move in a crowd don't apply in much of the world.

As a single, unaccompanied woman, I stood out. All other women were with a man, with a friend, or in a group. Only I was alone. Hawkers tried to tempt me into clothing stores or cafes at every step. English was scarce, but to my surprise I heard much Russian and saw signs in Russian. Could Russia be realizing its age-old dream of taking Constantinople, if not militarily and politically, then through its tourists, traders, and guest workers?

Back in my room, I dined, called Olympia, showered, and collapsed. I had been up for 33 hours. I slept soundly for the next nine.

Today my travel instincts returned. Refreshed by sleep and a quick workout in the hotel fitness room, I headed back into the city. I ate brunch at a corner cafe, in the process exchanging names and phone numbers with the waitress from Turkmenistan. Then I walked through Old Town in the direction of the Blue Mosque and Santa Sophia not so much as a tourist but as a world traveler at the beginning of a new journey.

By 4:00 p.m. I was back at the airport via the Istanbul metro. For the price of yesterday's bus/taxi ride to the hotel, I had eaten brunch, bought a skirt and blouse at a side street shop, and arrived at the airport in comfort. My traveler's legs had returned. Istanbul had again been my gateway.

It is now 8:00 p.m. The Turkish Air flight is somewhere over Anatolia or the Black Sea, headed eastward into the night. In four hours, I will be in Astana, my home for the next three years. I am filled with longing for the people I have left behind and with nostalgia for the lives I have lived in Washington, Bucharest, Moscow, and Tashkent. When the wheels touch down, I start anew. For that's the way it is in the Foreign Service. For the good of our country and for ourselves as human beings, we are forever reinventing ourselves.

I both smile and cringe inwardly. A new phase is beginning. What will it bring?

2. Hubster

I landed in Astana at 2:30 a.m. on the last Saturday of September 2014. A social sponsor met me at the airport and took me to what would be my home for the next three years, an apartment in a new complex called High-Vill. She gave me the keys, showed me around the apartment, and bid me goodnight. I walked onto my balcony and looked out on Presidential Park and the Esil' River. On the other side I could see Akorda, the presidential palace. Beyond it I saw the futuristic government buildings at the center of this new city on the steppe, capital of Kazakhstan since 1997. I saw all of this and could only think, "OMG, how am I going to make it through three years here?" I crawled into bed at 6:30 a.m.

I didn't have long to dwell on the negative. Work provided an immediate distraction. My life as *The Environment, Science, Technology, and Health (ESTH) Hubster* had begun.

I was no stranger to the *Hub*. I had worked with the *Hub's* Scientific Affairs Specialist Bakhtiyor Mukhamadiev in Tashkent in 2008–10. I had now moved into the position occupied then by Bakhtiyor's Astana-based supervisor. My portfolio covered everything under the ESTH sun in all five Central Asian countries that had once been part of the Soviet Union: Kazakhstan, Kyrgyzstan, Tajikistan, Turkmenistan, and Uzbekistan. Eleven other *Hubsters* do the same for similarly broad geographic areas sprinkled around the globe.

My official title was *Central Asia Regional Representative for Environment, Science, Technology, and Health.* Think of it. The State Department had handed me responsibility for *everything* that could be characterized as coming under environment, science, technology, and health in five countries. Sounds like a pretty responsible position, doesn't it?

Wry FSO wisdom holds that the longer the title, the less important the person holding it. The shortest title for anyone in the Department of State is, simply, *S,* a single letter that stands for the Secretary of State. No one has more authority than *S.* Other single letters such as *P* and *M* denote undersecretaries for political affairs and for management. The lower one gets in the hierarchy, the more letters that are needed to designate the position.

Let's face it—I had a very long title. That pretty much pegs where an *ESTH Hubster* fits in the State Department's food chain. Administratively, my position was funded by the Bureau of Oceans and International Environmental and Scientific Affairs (OES) in Washington. It's a *functional* bureau staffed largely with civil servants, many of them with PhD degrees. Another Foreign Service truism holds that the way to the top is through *regional* bureaus that are on the front lines of diplomatic relations. Being a *Hubster* for two to three years does not contribute to upward mobility. The Bureau of South and Central Asia (SCA) was the *regional* bureau in charge in the part of the world I now called home.

But I couldn't care less about truisms. Being *Hubster* is where I wanted to be. The reason is obvious: my background in science, in science history, and in Soviet/post-Soviet affairs. I would be advocating for the Paris Agreement on Climate Change; I would be reporting on the environmental catastrophe left in the wake of the dying Aral Sea; and I would write about the long-term health effects of Soviet nuclear testing in Semipalatinsk. I cared about these issues. I knew this would be my last significant overseas posting before retirement, and spending three years as Central Asia *Hubster* was just what I wanted.

Being *Hubster* also meant independence. I was head of my own office, answering directly to the DCM rather than to the political or economic section chiefs. I sat at the ambassador's country team meetings as a head of section. I had my own small but independent budget with considerable freedom on how to use it for travel, for funding small grants, or for bringing speakers or specialists to the region.

What did I do on-the-job? I took particular interest in Gharysh Sapary, Kazakhstan's space agency that wants to be the dominant regional center for space research. I wrote the speech on climate change that Ambassador George Krol delivered at the Astana Economic Forum in 2016. I oversaw the agreement that moved the International Science and Technology Center (ISTC) from Moscow to Astana. I traveled to and reported on the national parks, and I stood on the shores of the Great Golden Age Lake, Turkmenistan's misguided plan to build a lake in the middle of a desert. A town in Kazakhstan named a hiking trail for me after I rode over one hundred kilometers by bicycle to deliver a talk there at an ecotourism conference. I joined forces with a colleague from the U.S. Geological Survey (USGS), and together we created a Central Asia and Afghanistan Women and Water Network, convincing Chevron to fund it out of its social responsibility fund. No one asked us to do it. We did it because we saw the need and cared.

I could list all my *Hubster* cables and reports, but that's not the story I want to tell here. The real story is in my unwritten and often unanticipated struggles, failures, and successes. Most of all, the story is in the people who came into my life and who, in many ways, will remain with me to the end of my days.

3. If It's Tuesday, This Must Be Urgench

Come watch the no colors fade blazin'
Into petal sprays of violets of dawn.[91]

As *Hubster*, I became a perpetual motion machine with a suitcase that rarely sat in the closet.

My first big travel week began on a Sunday morning in late October when my telephone alarm woke me to the tune of *Violets of Dawn* at 7:30 a.m. My assistant Marzhan was to pick me up at 9:30 a.m. to catch our flight to Almaty, Kazakhstan's large southern city and former capital. As I poured my first cup of coffee, I did a double take. My kitchen clock said 9:00 a.m. I checked my Astana cell phone. It also said 9:00 a.m. I had only 30 minutes to get dressed and throw clothes into my suitcase.

What had gone wrong? The telephone I used as my alarm came from Bucharest, and out of nostalgia I had left it on Bucharest time all through my year in Washington. After all, I knew the time difference.

I checked my Bucharest phone again. It showed the time difference from Bucharest to Astana to be +4 hours, not +3 as it had been on Saturday. Romania had gone from daylight time to standard time that Saturday-Sunday night, and my phone had automatically adjusted.

So there I was, foiled by what I thought was my good sense of time zones. I rushed downstairs as Marzhan arrived in the embassy car. When we got to the airport, we learned that our flight was delayed. If I had known, I could have stayed on Bucharest time for the morning.

By mid-afternoon we were in Almaty. Astana was already snowbound, but in Almaty it was so warm that I could walk around with my jacket unzipped. The air pollution was palpable, reminding me of New York City in the 1960s, but the Tien Shan Mountains could still be seen through the smog. We checked into our hotel and found our USGS colleagues who had come from Washington for a seismology workshop. We spent the rest of the afternoon going over plans for the first session the next morning. Our consul general was to deliver opening remarks that I had drafted.

---

91   Andersen, Eric. "Violets of Dawn." Genius. Accessed September 10, 2023. https://genius.com/Eric-andersen-violets-of-dawn-lyrics.

Back in my room, I discovered I had forgotten to bring pantyhose. I had to get a pair quickly or risk wearing jeans instead of a business suit in the morning. The hotel desk gave me directions to a nearby mall where I bought the most expensive hose of my life, $90 for three pairs. The extra hour time difference between Kazakhstan and Romania had acquired a monetary value.

Almaty changed dramatically overnight. Snow covered the ground and continued to fall all Monday morning. Marzhan and I joked that we must have brought Astana winter with us.

The seismology workshop had its formal opening. With everything going smoothly, I left our USGS friends in Marzhan's hands and headed back to the airport. I had a plane to catch to Tashkent, the city I had last seen four years, but also seemingly a lifetime, ago.

The flight took an hour and a half, but by my watch it was only thirty minutes. Crossing into Uzbek airspace, we had moved one time zone further west. The plane rolled to a stop, and I headed for the exit door. Before I could get there, a flight attendant's voice came over the PA system and announced, "Robyn McCutcheon, the VIP bus is waiting for you." In all of my flights in and out of Uzbekistan in 2008–10, I had never been treated as a VIP. I didn't want to start now. I was tired and wished for nothing more than to get to my hotel and rest.

I also felt my stomach drop as I boarded the bus. It dawned on me as we approached the terminal that an event of transgender significance might be about to take place. Who would be waiting for me in the VIP lounge? More to the point, who were they expecting to see get off the VIP bus?

I had come to Uzbekistan as a U.S. representative to a donors' conference organized by the International Fund for Saving the Aral Sea. The government of Uzbekistan had asked for me specifically. In a chain of emails forwarded with the invitation, I had seen the name of a diplomat I had met with frequently at the Uzbek MFA in 2008–10. That diplomat was now at the Uzbek Embassy in Washington, and the invitation had originated with him. He had little reason to know I had transitioned gender. My initials *RAM* had not changed, and neither had my State Department email address. He likely didn't recall my first name in any case, and as an Uzbek he may not have been aware that *Robyn* is usually a woman's name.

When I walked into the VIP lounge, I recognized a vice president of the Uzbek Academy of Sciences with whom I had met several times when I was at Embassy Tashkent. He, obviously, was the person who had come to meet the American VIP. He looked right through me as I approached. Sure enough, I was not the person he had expected to see.

In the freshest and most official voice I could muster, I introduced myself. I saw confusion in his face, but he recovered quickly. We settled into diplomatic talk about the Aral Sea conference I would be attending. The quiet diplomacy of nurturing contacts is important no matter how much I yearned for a bed and a good night's sleep. The VP then turned me over to a young man from the MFA who took me to my hotel in downtown Tashkent. I was back in surroundings that felt familiar to me from 2010.

On Tuesday, I boarded my third flight in as many days—a charter flight filled with diplomats, international aid workers, water management specialists, ecologists, and journalists. Two hours later we touched down in the Khorezm region of Uzbekistan, where the ground was frosted with patches of white. It looked like snow, but in fact it was salt. We were in Urgench.

As we pulled up to the terminal, I could see men and women in traditional Uzbek clothes waiting to greet us. The women were holding round loaves of Uzbek flatbread, and everywhere there were TV cameras, microphones, and reporters with notebooks. There were at least as many of them as there were of us. It would prove to be that way for the next two days. We, the diplomats and international aid workers, found ourselves cast as unwitting actors in a show choreographed by the Uzbek government.

As we descended the stairs to the tarmac, enthusiastic young greeters waited to sort us onto buses by language. The route from the airport took us down the main streets of Urgench past gleaming white buildings and green parks. Everything had a proud air of newness, but I wondered if this was the reality. There was a long Soviet tradition of *pokazukha*—doing things for show—and *potemkin villages* had been in Russia's blood since the time of Catherine the Great.

After a quick stop at our hotel, we were on our way again, first to an oncology center and then to a urology clinic. Both were so new that one could still smell fresh paint. The disappearance of the southern portion of the Aral Sea—the portion on Uzbek territory—has had huge health consequences for people living in the region. The salt we had seen at the airport was blown there from the dry seabed by dust storms that carry salt and agricultural chemical runoff hundreds of miles. An island in the middle of the Aral Sea had served as the site for Soviet biological weapon testing. Soviet mismanagement led to this disaster that has seen one of the world's largest inland seas nearly disappear from the planet.[92]

We next stopped outside the city where dozens of young volunteers stood holding trees next to pre-dug holes. Our task was to put the trees in the holes, shovel dirt over the roots, and water them with pre-filled buckets. Cameras clicked as we, the diplomats, starred in an Uzbek showtime version of Arbor Day.

The conference opened on Wednesday. When I entered the hall, an escort led me to my place at the table. The name tent at my seat confirmed my suspicions. It read **Mr.** *McCutcheon, United States.* I showed it to my escort and said, "I think someone made a tiny mistake?" The escort actually blushed. Within minutes he returned with a new name tent that proclaimed **Ms.** *Robyn McCutcheon, United States.*

The conference took the full day. As I listened to one presentation after another, I couldn't help but think how little had changed since I left Uzbekistan in 2010. The Aral Sea disaster was proving more dire in its consequences with each passing year, but what the Uzbek government wanted out of this event was a big show followed, of course, by large donations. How those donations would be used was a different question.

Late Wednesday evening, after a ceremonial dinner featuring stars of the Uzbek operatic stage, we weary diplomats and aid workers rode a red-eye special charter back to Tashkent. My hotel telephone woke me early Thursday morning. The Academy of Sciences VP was waiting in the lobby. I dressed and packed quickly and went downstairs. We talked about the conference in Urgench and also about next steps in the U.S.-Uzbekistan

---

92 The ostensible purpose of the donors' conference I was to attend was to collect donations for the Third Aral Sea Basin Program to ameliorate some of the worst consequences of this ecological disaster. I, however, saw crocodile tears. Exploration hinted there could be natural gas deposits beneath the now dry seabed of the southern Aral Sea. I suspected the Uzbek government was more interested in the gas than in restoring the sea. Most of the work carried out through IFAS was directed at amelioration, not restoration. In contrast, the Government of Kazakhstan with help from the World Bank erected a large dike that has been remarkably successful at restoring the smaller northern portion of the Aral Sea that lies on its territory.

agreement on cooperation in science and technology. Then the VP turned me over to his young MFA colleague who would take me to the airport.

Planting a tree outside Urgench

I arrived back at the seismology conference in Almaty barely in time to deliver closing remarks. The loop back to Astana closed Friday morning, but the week was not yet over for Marzhan and me. From morning to evening on Friday, we escorted Ingrid Verstraeten from USGS through official meetings. When we waved goodbye to her at the airport at 8:00 p.m., our grueling week was over. Well, not really over. I spent all Saturday writing my reports.

But the most significant part of this week that took me from Astana to Almaty to Tashkent to Urgench and back again had nothing to do with the workshop, the conference, or the official meetings along the way. The meaningful part lasted no more than fifteen minutes in the car that took me from the hotel to the airport in Tashkent on Thursday. When we settled into the back seat, the young man from the MFA switched from Russian to English, making it clear that he did not want the driver to understand.

He asked, "Is it true that you are an LGBT+ activist?" He told me that while I had been in Urgench, he had searched the Internet to see what he could learn about me.

I nodded my head. He responded, "Thank you for that. One day I hope everyone in my country can enjoy the rights that you enjoy in America."

I had no illusions about Uzbekistan. It was as authoritarian in 2014 as I had known it in 2008–10, but my young MFA companion represented the future. He could scarcely have been thirty years old. Meeting a transgender American for the first time—a diplomat at that—had meant something to him.

My week had been one of exhausting diplomatic spectacle, but when I looked back on Sunday, I thought that maybe, just maybe, my trip had made a difference—not in the formal conference rooms, but in the impression I made on this one young man. If so, Urgench had been worth the trip.

4. The Full Alice

So far as official Washington was concerned, it had been to all intents and purposes like talking to a stone.[93]

What I did not know about the *Hub* when I arrived in 2014 was that I would soon descend into a deep administrative rabbit hole. The Department of State was about to give me the fullest *Alice in Wonderland* experience I was to have as an FSO, an experience I have come to call *The Full Alice*.

It began simply enough. Two local employees answered to me. In Astana, Marzhan was my scientific affairs assistant (SAA) and helped with my portfolio and internal travel within Kazakhstan. A higher-ranking scientific affairs specialist (SAS) in Tashkent would help develop portfolio priorities and travel with me outside of Kazakhstan. I knew this structure from my time in Tashkent, but one important thing had changed. Bakhtiyor, the long-serving SAS in Tashkent, had emigrated with his family to Canada in early 2014.

Losing Bakhtiyor was a blow. So competent and dedicated to his job, he was the LES an FSO could die for. In 2008–10 I sometimes mused that Bakhtiyor would continue doing his job even if the U.S. cut relations with

93   Kennan, *Memoirs 1925-1950*, p. 293.

Uzbekistan, but given economic hardship and authoritarian conditions, I understood why he wanted a better future elsewhere. My *Hubster* predecessor, who overlapped with me in my first weeks in Astana, had interviewed and hired a replacement in Tashkent. Guzal, a PhD biologist and specialist in biodiversity issues, had started in her position a scant few weeks before my arrival.

If Bakhtiyor had still been in Tashkent, I likely would have flown there in my first weeks as *Hubster*. Instead, I settled into Astana, getting to know Marzhan and reviewing the papers left by my predecessor. Guzal and I corresponded by email, but I didn't meet her until December when I went to Tashkent for U.S.-Uzbekistan Annual Bilateral Consultations (ABC). My role at the ABC was to listen and learn, to bring myself up to date on how relations had evolved since I served in Tashkent. In short, I was to be a wallflower. Not content with that role, I asked Guzal to set up meetings with organizations and officials on issues ranging from biodiversity to water resource management.[94]

Guzal was not Bakhtiyor, at least not yet. She did not have Bakhtiyor's depth and years of experience. She was new to her role, but I seized on that as an opportunity. Together we would reconstitute the *Hub* as it had been prior to the breakdown in U.S.-Uzbek relations in 2005.

Back in Astana, I set to work. Guzal and I drafted cables on our Tashkent meetings, and I tasked her with writing a cable on the state of biodiversity in Uzbekistan. Together we revived the long-dormant *Hub* newsletter that had not been published in a decade. The future looked bright. With Marzhan in Astana and Guzal in Tashkent, I had everyone I needed.

It took a regional visit to Kyrgyzstan to alert me something wasn't right. On the plane from Almaty I ran into Caroline Milow, a colleague from the German Agency for International Cooperation (GIZ) whom I had known during my Tashkent years. The next night we met for dinner in Bishkek. We were on our second beers when Caroline abruptly asked, "Robyn, what is going on at your embassy in Tashkent?"

Startled, I asked, "What do you mean?"

"I mean, it's the way Guzal's supervisor treats her. Even I'm uncomfortable

---

94 Integrated water resource management is the perpetual issue affecting Central Asia, a region suffering the consequences of Soviet mismanagement and ongoing climate change.

visiting the embassy when he's present."

That's how it started. Just as I had been a local supervisor for Bakhtiyor, Guzal had a local American FSO supervisor in Tashkent. He was an entry-level FSO on his first overseas tour working in the pol/econ section much as I had in 2008–10. As I understood from Caroline, he was treating Guzal as someone akin to a secretary, a *go-to girl*—ordering her about to handle the minutiae of daily life and demeaning her in the presence of others.

I was in shock. I had had no idea, but then I thought again. Embassy Tashkent was dragging its heels on releasing Guzal's biodiversity cable. Guzal was having trouble finding time to work on the *Hub* newsletter let alone implement my plan to revive a weekly Central Asia ESTH news summary. Caroline made me realize that something was very wrong.

I expected Guzal would be reluctant to talk, but I needed to hear from her directly. In June, I would be going to Tajikistan for a UN conference on water resources, and I expected Guzal to be there. Getting back to Astana, I reminded Guzal and her local FSO supervisor that she needed to arrange her travel to Dushanbe.

Tashkent did not respond. When I arrived in Dushanbe on the Sunday before the conference, Guzal was not there, and I couldn't reach her or anyone at Embassy Tashkent by email. For the first day, I kept wondering where she might be.

She arrived the next morning. Only later did I understand that her local Tashkent supervisor had not approved her travel. Guzal had paid for the air ticket out of her own pocket and was AWOL as far as Tashkent was concerned.

Now I could ask Guzal what was going on, and she confirmed everything Caroline had told me. I said I would take this up with Tashkent, but Guzal asked me not to. She saw her first-tour FSO supervisor as an annoyance who would be there for only one more year. She could survive him. We left it at that. We attended the conference, drafted our reporting cable, and accompanied a visiting deputy assistant secretary on a trip that took us across the Pamir Mountains to the Panzh River and the border with Afghanistan.[95]

---

95   The purpose of the trip was to visit a preserve for a rare breed of sheep nestled on Tajikistan's southern border.

With Guzal (center) at the Nurek Dam outside Dushanbe, Tajikistan

While we were in Tajikistan, the storm clouds thickened in Tashkent. No sooner did Guzal arrive back than her FSO supervisor summoned her into the office of the management counselor and accused her of insubordination. He handed her a new work requirements statement (WRS) that effectively removed her from the *Hub* and placed her directly under his sole supervision. He insisted that she sign then and there. Guzal had finally had enough and gave him an unvarnished piece of her mind. In the weeks to come, the management counselor cited this explosion as proof of Guzal's insubordination. Tashkent insisted that Guzal, not her FSO supervisor, was the problem.

As diplomatically as I could, I exploded. I wrote to the chief of the pol/ econ section in Tashkent and complained of the harassment of my SAS. Our acting DCM in Astana took the issue up with the management counselor in Tashkent. If ever emails could be described as *shouting*, these emails were *shouting* at each other. As far as Tashkent was concerned, I was an insolent outsider who had tried to manage *their* LES. We presented

Tashkent with the work requirements statement for the SAS position, but Tashkent responded that they had decided to re-write the WRS as they wished. I contacted the OES Bureau in Washington. OES dredged up the original paperwork showing that the Tashkent position answers to OES and the *Hub*, not Embassy Tashkent, and is funded by OES, not the SCA functional bureau.

Embassy Tashkent could not have cared less. The view there seemed to be that the *Hub* could be ignored, that OES could be ignored. Ten time zones removed from Washington, Tashkent decided it could do whatever it wanted.

Guzal and I began talking at night by Skype when she was outside embassy walls. She lived at home with her mother, and I told Guzal's mom that we would fight and win. I told her there would be justice, but *The Full Alice* was only beginning.

Insomnia set in. If the OES Bureau could not shake up Embassy Tashkent, what could I do? On one of those sleepless nights, it came to me that I had one ace up my sleeve—Ambassador Richard Hoagland, the principal deputy assistant secretary (PDAS) for SCA Bureau. Ambassador Hoagland had been a founding member of glifaa, and we had met when I was its president.

I wrote to Ambassador Hoagland by personal email, explaining the impasse. Without putting him in the middle of it, I asked that he make the responsible offices in Washington sit around a table and resolve the dispute. Ambassador Hoagland wrote back within an hour. A few days later the new, incoming DCMs for Embassies Astana and Tashkent sat at a table with an OES representative in Washington. By the time the meeting was done, all agreed that the SAS position belongs to the *Hub*. Case closed.

Except that it wasn't. The Washington meeting further decided that the time had come to accept the reality that the *Hub* would not be returning to Tashkent. The SAS position, consequently, should move from Tashkent to Astana.

From an administrative point of view, the Washington decision made perfect sense. It was time to bite the bullet and unite all *Hub* staff under one roof. The decision should have come years earlier when it became clear the *Hub*'s exile from Tashkent was not a temporary state of affairs but a permanent new reality.

From the human point of view, however, the decision was cruel. I had warned Guzal in advance that Washington might decide to move her position to Astana, and I had asked her if she was prepared to move to Kazakhstan. She was.

Ambassador George Krol put a quick end to that idea. He would not permit a third country national to work in Astana. Embassy Tashkent, for its part, no longer wanted Guzal within its walls and informed me it intended to give her a few weeks' severance pay and send her packing. When I got this news, Guzal was sick at home with the flu, and Tashkent wanted to know when she would be coming back to work.

I would not let it happen that way. The bad news had to come directly from me. I called Guzal at home and told her I had lost the battle to protect her position. Too proud to let Tashkent fire her, Guzal marched into the HR office the next day and resigned, refusing the severance pay. Within days she had a new position with GIZ. To her credit, she continued to work for me unofficially, answering questions and setting up meetings for me for the remainder of my time in Central Asia. Like Bakhtiyor, she cared—even after Embassy Tashkent had ground its administrative heel into her face.

Here I was, a full year into my three-year assignment and now without a SAS. Surely we could announce the job opening in Astana and start interviewing immediately?

Of course not. State is a large government bureaucracy, and Embassy Astana comes under the Regional Human Resources office in Frankfurt, Germany. Regional HR would not permit moving the SAS position to Astana without a complete review of the *Hub's* workload with staffing determined in light of work requirements. It took the better part of a year for Regional HR to give its OK.

Even then there was a catch. Regional HR would allow a SAS in Astana only after downgrading Marzhan by a full grade. In Guzal's absence I had come to rely on Marzhan to take up the slack. Her background was not in science, but she had been the *Hub's* assistant for six years. She was highly intelligent and knew the issues. Couldn't we move Marzhan to the SAS position and hire a new assistant to replace Marzhan?

Foiled again. The SAS position description specified an MS or PhD in science or engineering. On-the-job experience did not count.

I continued to fight. The best I could get Regional HR to agree to was to preserve Marzhan in her grade with the stipulation that future salary increases would be reduced, in effect downgrading Marzhan over time. Breaking the news to Marzhan was no easier than it had been with Guzal. The State Department's thanks to Marzhan for taking on extra work was to slap her in the face, and I was the one who had to deliver the slap in person.

With Marzhan outside a hydroelectric power plant
near Ust'-Kamenogorsk, Kazakhstan

We began interviewing for a SAS. Given that my time in Astana was growing short, the incoming *Hubster* participated by video from Washington. We settled on a candidate who started on the job the day I turned over my duties to my successor in August 2017.

That's *The Full Alice*: three years of falling down State's HR rabbit hole and fighting a bureaucracy that did not care. I yearned for the simplicity of NASA mission support. Corporate America seemed to have more heart. I don't delude myself that corporate America can't also be exceedingly cruel, but there is usually a rationale behind personnel decisions based on engineering considerations or, to be crude, the bottom line. The years since have not softened my view that the State Department treated both Guzal and Marzhan shabbily.

The Full Alice also showed me that State Department bureaucracy did not care about me or the *Hub*. The impotence of a long job title is more than an anecdote. For me it had become a fact, proven by events.

It was only a rear-guard action, but I resolved that *The Full Alice* would not end without some measure of justice. I pursued an equal employment opportunity (EEO) action against the first tour FSO in Tashkent who had abused Guzal. The grounds? Discrimination based on gender by a man who wanted to put a woman with a PhD in her place. I knew I would lose the case. This was not sexual harassment, a rape with witnesses. It was sublime justice, however, to know that the FSO in question would have to spend months writing responses to interrogatories. The remainder of his time in Tashkent would not go by easily.

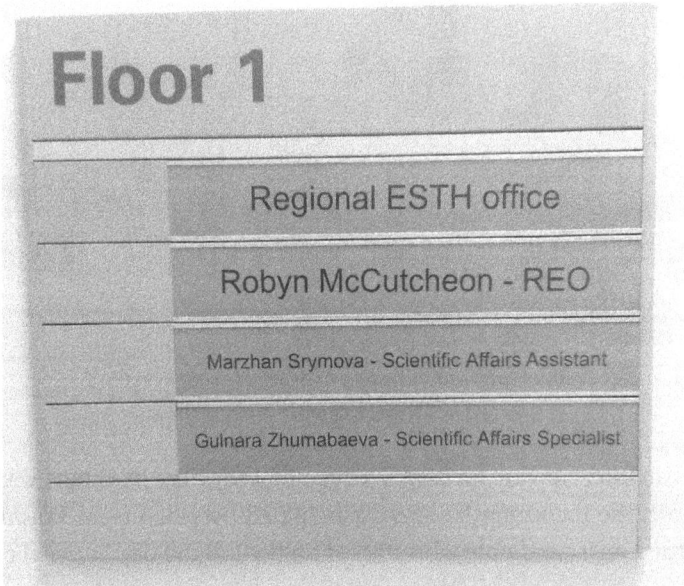

Floor 1

Regional ESTH office

Robyn McCutcheon - REO

Marzhan Srymova - Scientific Affairs Assistant

Gulnara Zhumabaeva - Scientific Affairs Specialist

The new Hub office in Astana

The Washington compromise on the SAS position did have one positive effect. During its time in Tashkent, the *Hub* had its own small office suite. Under the ostensibly temporary circumstances in Astana, I sat with the political/economic FSOs in what is known as the controlled access area (CAA) where there is heightened security. Marzhan sat with the LE staff outside the CAA. We talked by phone through the day, meeting in the hallway outside the CAA when we needed to. Given that the *Hub* was now to be reconstituted under one roof in Astana, I convinced Washington and Ambassador Krol that the *Hub* needed an office suite like the one it once had in Tashkent. It took time, but space was found. Marzhan and I moved into our new office suite the month before I left Astana.

What I did not suspect when I landed in Astana in September 2014 was that my greatest legacy to the *Hub* would have nothing to do with the Paris Agreement or any of the issues we covered. Rather, it would be the legacy of reconstituting the *Hub* with full staff and its own office in one location. That is the legacy of *The Full Alice*.

5. The Flower

"M-e-r-u-e-r-t."

The young woman at the shop counter in the Evraziya mall pronounced her name slowly, phonetically. She had long black hair and the soft, rounded face of a Kazakh, and she laughed as she tried to explain the pronunciation.

"But you can call me M-e-r-u if that's easier. Lots of my Russian speaking friends have a hard time with M-e-r-u-e-r-t. Where are you from?"

It was my first weekend in Astana, and I had gone exploring on a cold, wet Saturday. The snow that had fallen in my first week had turned to freezing rain. Winter comes early in Astana.

"I'm American." We exchanged a few pleasantries, and I went on my way, exploring this Soviet-style shopping center with its small shops.

Some time later I saw a cafeteria, went in, and took a tray. Then I saw her ahead of me in the line. Meruert is tall and stands out in a crowd. She turned and smiled, no doubt feeling my eyes on her. We had lunch together and afterward went back to her shop. It was a slow day for her, so she entertained me by singing her favorite Kazakh songs. I had caught a chill, and Meruert must have noticed I wasn't feeling well. She led me by the hand to the bus stop so that I would get on the right bus back to HighVill.

Yet another American had met yet another young local woman. A brief intercultural encounter had taken place. It likely would have ended there, an exchange of pleasantries and a chance afternoon together.

A month went by. I was living out of my suitcases, wearing warm clothes loaned by other women at the embassy. I had been very busy getting started as *Hubster*. Then I got the phone call that every FSO arriving at post waits for: my HHE, the trappings that make an apartment a home, had arrived. The movers delivered it to my apartment a few days later. At last, I would have my own warm clothes and my own kitchen pots and pans.

I was drowning in work and had no time to unpack the seventy-five boxes. I knew the embassy maintains a list of local help for hire, and I was about to ask for names. That's when I remembered the scrap of paper on which Meruert had written her number. I called.

"Might you have some time in the evenings to help me unpack? I'll make dinner."

Meruert came each night that November and helped me make quick work of setting up household. As we unpacked, I got to know her story. Meruert is an *oralman,* a *returnee,* an ethnic Kazakh born across the border in western China. When she was eleven years old, her parents decided to take advantage of the government program encouraging the Kazakh diaspora to come home to Kazakhstan.

That explained why my Russian was better grammatically than Meruert's. She hadn't spoken a word of Russian until her family moved to Kazakhstan. All school instruction in China had been in Kazakh using an Arabic alphabet, not Cyrillic as in Kazakhstan. When Meruert began school in Kazakhstan, she could barely speak or write Russian, and her classmates treated her as the class dunce. Despite all the changes and increasing nationalism in post-Soviet Central Asia, Russian was still the required language for anyone hoping to move up in the world.

In time Meruert showed them all. She became the star student in her school and received a scholarship to attend university in Astana. She was in her final year when I met her, sharing a small apartment with several other young women.

Meruert asked first. "You have such a large apartment. Could I live in your second bedroom?"

We had clicked during our month of unpacking. Meruert might have asked first, but I had already resolved to offer her the second bedroom. I really did not want to live alone in this large apartment. But first she would have to be interviewed at the embassy and registered as my official MOH.

I filed the paperwork, and Meruert went for her interview with our assistant regional security officer. The A/RSO came to me afterward, red in the face. Washington had written the questions he was required to ask. They were designed for couples, both straight and gay, who intend to co-habitate, usually as a first step toward marriage. They included questions on when sexual relations had started. Washington did not have the imagination to cover a sixty-plus-year-old woman planning to emotionally adopt a daughter.

Everything was set for Meruert to move in at Thanksgiving, but I did have a worry. I had arrived in Astana with the idea that I had put LGBT+ activism behind me. As far as anyone outside my *zone of intimacy* was concerned, there was no more need to know of my transgender heritage than there was to know of my Scot-Irish family background. People might pick up on this, but who cares? Weren't we all there to do our jobs?

With Meruert it would be different. Someone living under my roof would be inside my *zone of intimacy*. She would find out sometime in the coming three years. It was unavoidable. Between conversations about my family and the fact that I needed to dilate at least weekly, there was no way she would not find out.

On November 20, I invited Meruert for a special dinner. I lit a candle and said I had something important to tell her. It was Transgender Day of Remembrance, and I chose this day to explain my story to Meruert. She said little that night.

The next night she returned and told me she had been stunned. She had never heard the word transgender before. She spent the day searching the Internet and said she had read enough to have some understanding. But then she said she had a better idea. "You are the nice American woman I have known since the day we met. Can't we leave it at that?"

And so, we did. For the next three years I became Meruert's surrogate family. I met her brother when he passed through Astana. Her mom and dad live in a small village near Ust' Kamenogorsk. I met them via Skype. When Meruert went home for holidays, her job was to milk the cows. I would often joke about my job that, "There is work; there will always be work." Meruert would smile back and say, "There are cows; there will always be cows."

Meruert felt lost and was looking for direction. She had excelled in high school. That is how she got her scholarship to study in the capital, but her problem was the subject. Students in Kazakhstan have little say in what they will study. Someone along the way had decided Meruert should study nuclear physics.

It didn't take me long to recognize that nuclear physics and Meruert did not go together. She was having trouble with her courses. No adviser had shown the kind good sense to suggest that she transfer to a different major. Rather, year after year professors had done her no favor by passing her with C grades. She was now in the last year of a five-year program, set to graduate in the spring with no prospects for going further.

Meruert is a walker. We took long winter evening walks in the snow. Once we crossed the frozen Esil' River on the ice rather than taking the bridge. We flopped in the snow and made snow angels on New Year's Day. We talked about life and what she might do. I had no answers. At home I listened as Kazakh and Russian songs drifted from her room. Meruert has a beautiful singing voice.

Through Meruert I met many of the young women in the nuclear physics program. One of them, Akerke, became a regular visitor. Unlike Meruert, she loved nuclear physics and planned to go on for an MS degree. During my last year in Astana, Akerke taught a course on vector analysis as a graduate assistant, and for a time she took up residence on the living room couch while preparing for exams. Akerke has a passion for science fiction, and we talked about our favorite novels and movies. As my days in Astana slipped to their close, I gave Akerke my Mom and Dad's bedroom set that had traveled around the world with me. I would have no place for it in Maine but could not just dispose of it; the emotional attachment was too strong. It had to go to someone I cared about. Akerke was engaged, and this was to be my wedding gift.

I stood in for Meruert's family on her graduation day. For the coming year Meruert tried several jobs, searching for herself. Nothing seemed to fit. Then I had an idea.

"Why not come to the U.S. with me for a month?" I suggested. I was planning to go home for a month in the summer of 2016. I remembered my own travel to the Soviet Union in 1978 when I felt without direction. That summer had given me a renewed sense of purpose, and perhaps a month in the U.S. would do the same for Meruert.

I knew the odds of Meruert getting a tourist visa were minuscule. As a young, unmarried, unemployed woman, she was the very picture of a visa applicant who would be refused. All I could do was hope. I wrote a letter "to the interviewing consul" when Meruert went for her interview. In the letter I explained Meruert's status as my MOH, that she was "linked to me at the hip," that she would be on the plane with me to the U.S., would be with me every minute while we were in the U.S., and would be on the plane with me back to Astana.

Hiking with Meruert in Baxter State Park, Maine

The consul who interviewed Meruert could have ignored my letter. Most consuls do ignore letters like this. I knew it from my own year doing visa interviews in Moscow. But the consul in Astana read it and took me at my word. He approved the visa.

We landed in the U.S. in mid-August. To reduce the culture shock, I took Meruert first to my favorite cabin in Little Orleans. We slept, recovered from jet lag, and walked along the C&O Canal. The next day we drove to Washington, where Meruert met my son Matt and his family that now included my two-year-old granddaughter. We took a long train trip to Maine, stopping for two days in New York City and another day in Boston. In Maine we backpacked in Baxter State Park. This young woman who had never learned to swim fell in love with kayaking. My sisters met her when they came to Maine for a week. Meruert had become a part of the family.

The month went by quickly, but in that time, something changed for Meruert. Her English had been minimal, but coming to the U.S. made her realize there are countries where no one speaks Russian or Kazakh. When we returned to Kazakhstan, she started private classes and took the language exam given through the International English Language Testing System (IELTS). Today she is in graduate school in Ust' Kamenogorsk. Whenever a visiting professor comes, Meruert is the interpreter. She is the best English speaker in her department.

In the summer of 2017, the time had come to say goodbye. For our final lunch together, we went to the same cafeteria where we had first shared a meal in 2014. I went with her to the train station and watched as she boarded the train, found her compartment, and put her hand on the window. Like in an old movie, I put my hand on the window from the outside and walked along until the train picked up speed and pulled away.

Meruert had implored me not to make a scene, but I had tears in my eyes as the train faded from sight. A passerby asked if I was OK. "Everything's fine," I replied even as my tears flowed. They were tears of sadness at saying goodbye to someone who had become a daughter, but they were also tears of joy. Meruert had found herself.

Today, as I sit in Maine on a late February day and look out at the falling snow, I think back on my long winter walks with Meruert in Astana. I look at her picture both on my wall and on the coffee mug I am drinking from. The mug bears the inscription, "You are our flower." Meruert was mine, the flower that sweetened my life through the long winters on the Kazakhstan steppe.

6. *The Smile*

You've got a friend in me
You've got a friend in me
You got troubles, and I got 'em too
There isn't anything I wouldn't do for you
We stick together and we see it through
'Cause you've got a friend in me
You've got a friend in me.[96]

The warmest smile I have ever known belonged to Dima Tereshkevich; it could have launched a thousand ships in a landlocked country with no navy.

Ours was a platonic love affair. I was in love with a man only five years older than my own son Matt, but I was not alone. All of us were in love with this PhD ecologist, director of the Institute of Environmental and Social Health (IESH), and one-time president of the Astana Civic Alliance.[97] I came to idolize him in the way I idolized JFK and RFK in my youth. All he had to do was smile, and we would have followed him anywhere.

I found him on Facebook. Two weeks after arriving in Astana, I sat alone in my empty apartment on a Friday evening. I didn't even have a respectable notebook computer, only an antediluvian netbook. It was a painfully slow way to look at Facebook. I wondered if, perhaps, I already *knew* anyone in Astana outside embassy walls. I searched my Facebook friends. One name popped up: Dmitriy Tereshkevich.

He was online. We started chatting through Facebook messenger, and we agreed to meet the next day at a cafe called *The Hungry Rabbit.*

It was an October Saturday. Indian Summer or, as they say in Russian, Butterfly Summer, had come back. Under a warm sun in a clear sky, it took time for me to find the cafe we had agreed on. The city was still unfamiliar, and I got lost easily. I arrived late, and there was no Dr. Tereshkevich in sight. I sent a text message.

---

96 Newman, Randy. "You've Got a Friend in Me." Genius. Accessed September 10, 2023. https://genius.com/Randy-newman-youve-got-a-friend-in-me-lyrics.

97 To deflect public spotlight and to give a veneer of anonymity, I have changed the name of the institute.

He walked through the cafe door fifteen minutes later. Young, tall, and fit with a handsome Russian face, he had the twinkle of good mischief in his eye. Both serious and goofy at the same time, he made me think of Woody in the movie *Toy Story*. He carried himself in a way that said *nothing is impossible* but also that *everything should be fun*. By the time we parted, Dr. Tereshkevich had become *Dima*. His smile that radiated boundless hope and promise had captured my imagination and my heart.

Before the month was out, Dima and I crossed paths so many times that I lost count. Marzhan and I would go to a meeting or event, and invariably Dima was there. I remember taking my seat at one roundtable, familiarizing myself with the agenda, and then looking up to see Dima smiling at me from the other side of the circle.

Dima with Ingrid Verstraeten from USGS on Earth Day 2015

It made sense that our paths would cross. IESH focused on environmental contamination and its effects on human health, some of the same issues I covered. The Kazakh Soviet Socialist Republic had served as the Soviet Union's test site for everything from nuclear to chemical to biological weapons, not to mention dumping ground for lower missile and rocket stages from Baikonur Cosmodrome.[98] NKVD chief Beria is reputed once to have said that no one lives in Kazakhstan, so why not make it the Soviet Union's proving ground for weapons of all types? The health consequences of that decision persist to this day.

Not only an environmentalist, Dima engaged in civic activism through the Astana Civic Alliance. He knew how to navigate foreign donor grant processes, and he taught others to be experts on grant activities. Whether for an Earth Day event or for a civic action supporting bicyclist rights on Astana city streets, Dima was always there.

Within a month, Dima had become my closest colleague, someone I had come to depend on. Whenever a new tasker arrived from Washington, I asked Dima to give me a quick education on the treaty or compact in question. He always knew the relevant government officials. The same smile that won my heart worked in the government; doors opened to him. He was a natural-born diplomat who knew how to get things done.

Over the months Dima also became my closest friend. I experienced my first winter picnic with him at Borovoye, Kazakhstan's northern national park. I missed my kayak from Maine and coerced Dima into joining me for a chilly September day on the Esil' River in an inflatable kayak loaned by an embassy friend. We pushed off from the park immediately across from the Akorda palace. When Dima protested that security guards might not like us opposite the presidential palace, I told him not to worry, I have diplomatic immunity. Dima protested, "That's well enough for you Robyn, but what about me?" Meruert walked along the riverbank that day, taking pictures of these two crazy environmentalists. By the end, we were both soaked and chilled to the bone. We returned to my HighVill apartment for tea and something a bit stronger. Dima sat there in my bathrobe as we washed and dried his clothes.

Dima picked me up when I was down. Frustrated with our long-distance relationship, John told me in 2015 that he was moving on. I was crushed and found a rebound relationship with a man I had met in Maine while on R&R vacation that summer.[99] I thought there was something there, but in

---

98   This continues to be an issue. Baikonur is located on the territory of Kazakhstan, which leases it back to Russia. Lower stages regularly fall back to earth on the Kazakh steppe. Cosmonauts and American astronauts returning from the International Space Station in Russian Soyuz capsules land in Kazakhstan not far from Karaganda.

99   The State Department authorizes and pays airfare for FSOs posted overseas to take an

January 2016, he told me he had reconciled with his ex. They were going to re-marry. It was a Friday night, and I spent the rest of the night in tears. Meruert found me in the morning on the living room couch with used tissue scattered about. She pumped me with strong coffee and took me out into the -30°C winter day to march me at a quick pace through Presidential Park. Caffeine and arctic cold helped, but Meruert had had enough. She called Dima. "She's yours now," she said.

Sure enough, Dima appeared within the hour. He was scheduled to speak that night at an event for an association supporting handicapped children. He ordered me to put on my best work suit and then marched me across the Esil' River at as quick a pace as Meruert had walked me through Presidential Park. He assigned me the task of speaking about the Americans with Disabilities Act. He made me get out of myself by making me work.

The event over, Dima said, "Enough. Now let's go somewhere noisy and drink." We went to a club and were joined soon by Dima's friends. Into the haze of vodka and a crowded dance floor I went. When we left, a soft snow was falling. I no longer had the urge to cry. Dima had pulled me through.

I will have more to say about Dima. This is only an introduction. Just as I can look around my home in Maine today and see photos of Meruert, Dima also smiles at me from more than one photo. His smile cannot help but make me smile back.

7. The Metrology of Sex

Sex. Hot and steamy, albeit fleeting. I owe it all to metrology.

Working from the assumption that most readers know what sex is but may be scratching their heads over metrology, let me explain. Metrology is the science of measurement. Its roots date to the Magna Carta that enshrined the principal of a regulated, uniform system of weights and measures:

> One measure of Wine shall be through our Realm, and
> one measure of Ale, and one measure of Corn ... and it
> shall be of Weights as it is of Measures.

The nobles who forced King John to sign the Magna Carta in 1215 recognized that uniform weights and measures are keys to an ordered system of

---

annual "rest and relaxation" (R&R) trip home to the U.S.

commerce. The same principle is to be found in Article I, Section 8, of the U.S. Constitution: "The Congress shall have Power ... to fix the Standard of Weights and Measures." Like the water that is supposed to flow when we turn the kitchen tap, metrology is the underpinning of our daily lives, unknown to most because, like water, it is simply supposed to be there.

So let me get to the sex part. John had set me free, and my brief flirtation with a man in Maine had ended in tears and crumpled tissue. As usual, I found release in work. I had a particular interest in what the international community planned to do with leap seconds. In 1972, when it was decided that Coordinated Universal Time (UTC) would be based on the atomic clock second, the leap second was introduced to keep UTC within one second of time as determined by the earth's rotation. When needed, leap seconds are added at midnight on June 30 or December 31, thereby making the last minute of those months 61 seconds in length instead of 60.

Bear with me. The sex is coming.

In 1972, no one was thinking about smartphones, GPS, and the twenty-first century Internet world. As those technologies developed, programmers came to hate leap seconds. Software loves predictability, and leap seconds are anything but. Programmers want them gone. Astronomers want to keep them, and they find support among those who think that, ultimately, time should be tied to the rising and setting of the sun. Without leap seconds, over many centuries UTC will get noticeably out of whack with human-based lives.

I promise, it's coming. Really it is.

This is where metrology comes in. The International Bureau of Weights and Measures (BIPM) is charged with maintaining the International System of Units (SI), and that includes the definition of the second. Most countries have a national metrology institute (NMI), and BIPM provides the framework that links these institutes and integrates their work to propagate and improve SI units. The International Organization of Legal Metrology (OIML) promotes the international legal aspects of laws and statutes resulting from metrology.

Many of the NMIs are linked regionally. In 2015, I learned that COOMET, the network of metrology institutes for the former Soviet Union, would meet in Tajikistan. I decided I should attend.

Almost there.

COOMET, as it turns out, is still a largely Russian organization. The organizing committee in Tajikistan invited me, but COOMET's Russian chair was decidedly unhappy to see me. When I introduced myself and extended my arm to shake his hand, he took it grudgingly, commenting as he did about *the long arm of Washington.*

We've made it. Here comes the sex part.

The Russian chair told me that many of the afternoon sessions on the first day were closed to outside observers. I would have time on my hands. The conference took place at a Soviet-era resort on a reservoir outside Khujand. It was a beautiful day, and I had been handed some unexpected time off.

As a delegate to the metrology conference in Tajikistan

After tramping around the resort grounds, I found a beautiful patch of green and decided to rest. I lay down, put my straw hat over my face, and drifted into fantasy, imagining myself as a coed lying on The Lawn at UVa in the 1970s. I had always wondered what it would have been like to be a coed on a quiet Saturday on The Lawn, perhaps with a boyfriend sitting next to me, strumming on a guitar.

"You are the most beautiful woman I have ever seen," I heard a voice say. I was loving this fantasy.

"Are you OK? Would you like some water?" The voice was speaking in Russian. I moved my straw hat aside and saw a young Tajik man leaning over me. I could hardly make out his face against the bright sky, but he was real, not a fantasy.

He got down on his knees and repeated, "You are the most beautiful woman I have ever seen." On this warm, sunny day in Tajikistan, I was hearing words I thought I would never hear in my life. He asked where I was from, why I was in Khujand. We chatted lazily, and then he proposed going somewhere for a drink. He helped me up, and I got a better look at him. Definitely cute, he was at least a head shorter than me. I was about to go with this short, cute Tajik, but then visions of a set-up entered my head. Was this being filmed? I felt a cold shiver go down my back, made an excuse, and walked quickly away.

The next day was taken up by the meat of the conference. I sat with two BIPM representatives who, with me, constituted the international component of the event. They were happy to see U.S. interest and to know that I would send my report to the State Department with a copy to NIST, the National Institute of Standards and Technology. I learned a great deal that day about philosophical East-West differences on metrology. COOMET still saw it through a Soviet lens.

The work of the conference done, I had several hours to kill before the evening's ceremonial dinner. This being a Russian-dominated event, I knew that all the women would be expected to come with their best dresses and dancing shoes. Russian men never tire of saying how their women scientists and engineers are *real women* who step into their ball gowns and feminine roles when the men click their fingers. I, too, had made sure to pack an appropriate dress.

I saw him as I walked back from the conference hall. My little Tajik was sitting on a bench on the path leading to the hotel. He stood. "Won't you please have a drink with me?" he asked. He said he had been sitting on the bench for hours in the hope that he might see me again.

That got to me. He had been sitting there for hours, not knowing if I would come that way or not. This U.S. representative to the regional metrology conference knew she should send him away, but something about this swarthy little Tajik screamed, "Let's go!" Passion ruled. I took him up to my room and didn't care if there might be hidden cameras rolling.

For the next two hours, we were two naked, sweaty bodies taking our turns on top and on bottom, groping and fondling all that our arms could reach. I felt the sexual power of being a woman, the possible danger of the tryst adding to the passion.

By the time we were done, I had no more than a half hour to get ready for the ceremonial dinner. I would be sitting at the head table and knew from experience that I would be expected to say a few words as the sole U.S. representative. I rushed to the shower, my Tajik following me to the door. He wanted more, but I was already cooling my passion under a cold shower stream.

"I know why you stopped," he said. "You don't want to get pregnant."

Oh, you sweet thing. He had no idea that I was over sixty years-old and trans to boot. Those words were almost as endearing as his first words telling me I was the most beautiful thing he had ever seen. I pushed my Tajik out the door as I made quick work of hair and makeup. He insisted we'd meet again in the morning and that he wouldn't let me go.

I wasn't as well dressed as the other women at the ceremonial dinner, and I had to endure the Russian chair as he repeated his comment about *the long arm of Washington*. Still, when I danced, I had an extra spring in my step and a smile on my lips.

The diplomat in me knew enough to be up and gone at the crack of dawn. Who knows what my Tajik might have said or done if he had gotten to the lobby before I checked out? The last thing I needed was a scene, a scandal with potential for becoming an indelicate diplomatic incident.

I later wrote and sent my report that was met with "that peculiar and profound sort of silence which is made only by the noise of diplomatic dispatch hitting the State Department's files."[100] I learned much in those two days about metrology in the former Soviet Union, and I maintain that the U.S. should take a greater interest.

But most of all, metrology had given me two hours of hot, steamy sex that were the opposite of a *peculiar and profound sort of silence*. The trip to Khujand had been more than worth it.

8. *My odno tseloe*—We Belong

And when the same old voices say

That we'd be better off running away,

We belong, We belong anyway.[101]

I was done as an activist, now intent on living my life and doing my job, nothing more. Or so I thought. Two things changed my mind.

In December 2014 I traveled again to Almaty. Air Astana has so many flights between Astana and Almaty that it feels like the Washington–NYC air shuttle, and I was a frequent passenger. Sometimes I would even go only for a day, flying down in the morning and back at night.

On this visit I planned to meet Kate, a science fellow from the American Association for the Advancement of Science (AAAS). The AAAS has a program that sends young scientists to diplomatic missions to gain experience in diplomacy and in regional issues. Kate worked on water management issues at the USAID Regional Office in Almaty. We had chatted by telephone and email, but this was the first time we would meet face-to-face. We had a meeting scheduled together with the consul general.

Kate met me in the lobby at the consulate, and we got on the elevator alone. When the door closed, she asked, "What pronouns should I use for you?"

The question startled me. It's appropriate when meeting a transgender or

---

100 George F. Kennan lecture at the National War College as quoted in John Lewis Gaddis, ibid., p. 160.

101 Brennet, Namoli. "We Belong." Songlyrics. Accessed September 10, 2023. https://www.songlyrics.com/namoli-brennet/we-belong-lyrics/.

gender fluid person the first time, especially if that person is at an inde-terminate place on the gender spectrum. It's a way of honoring every per-son's self-identification. I, however, was wearing one of my best dress suits, appropriately attired for a meeting with the consul general and wearing subdued makeup just as Kate was. Moreover, Kate and I had already cor-responded and talked by phone.

"How did you know?" was all I could ask in response.

"Your predecessor told me all about you," Kate replied.

Back in Astana a few days later, I wrote to my predecessor and asked how many people he had told. As best he could recall, there were perhaps a half-dozen.

Diplomatic missions are like small towns where personal news travels fast. Case closed. If my predecessor told a half-dozen people, it meant everyone knew. It was pointless to pretend otherwise. I didn't need to go around ad-vertising, but from that time forward I worked from the assumption that my status was common knowledge. I wasn't yet prepared to march around with a rainbow flag, but a second event changed that as well.

"What are you doing for IDAHOT?"

The person asking was Aron le Fèvre, a young gay intern from the Embassy of The Netherlands. He addressed the question to Lynne Madnick, the human rights officer in our political section. I had offered to sit in on the meeting.

"What are you doing for IDAHOT?" Aron asked again.

IDAHOT is the International Day Against Homophobia and Transpho-bia. Commemorated annually on May 17, it is the main event in countries where LGBT+ life is underground with no possibility of Pride parades, film festivals, or other public celebrations.

Lynne answered, in effect, "Well, nothing in particular." That wasn't good enough for Aron. We had to do something.

That's how it started. Aron said he would organize a small IDAHOT com-memoration. He had a short list of gay friends and friends of gay friends to invite, and I already knew a few people in Astana's underground transgen-der community. I offered a DVD of *The Stonewall Uprising* with Russian subtitles for screening. Lynne said she could get representational funds from the political section for refreshments.

Aron le Fèvre in 2017

Between diplomatic personnel and local community members, a dozen or so gathered at the Embassy of The Netherlands. We watched the movie, talked about LGBT+ life in Kazakhstan, and enjoyed the refreshments. As far as we know, this modest event on May 17, 2015, marked the first time an IDAHOT commemoration took place in Astana.

After that, it didn't take long for me to become a focus of the local community much as I had in Romania. My list of contacts exploded. I revived my Bucharest tradition of monthly gatherings in my apartment. In Romania it had been *3rd Friday @ Robyn's* that sometimes devolved into partying and drink. To avoid that, in Astana I provided pizza, but there was to be no alcohol. I also moved the day from Friday to Thursday to encourage discussion over partying. My role, I explained, was to provide a safe space. In time, attendees ran the evenings, setting the program and discussion. I explained facetiously that my goal was to launch a *pizza revolution*, a chance for the community to come together and find its own way.[102]

---

102 In this I consciously copied the practice of Mindy Michels from Freedom House.

I added LGBT-related meetings when I traveled regionally. Unregistered, below-the-radar interest groups existed in Almaty. In Kyrgyzstan, Bishkek was home to Labrys, an official NGO and the leading organization for LGBT+ rights in Central Asia. I met with community members in Tajikistan, and in Tashkent, I met with a transgender man, an artist and actor who told me how the transgender community survived in authoritarian Uzbekistan. In Turkmenistan it was more difficult, but I did manage to meet with a woman activist in Ashgabat, the two of us going on a long evening walk in a city park until she detected that we were being followed. We separated quickly. Two women walking together in Turkmenistan were suspect by definition.

These meetings usually happened in the evenings, on the margins of my official meetings and events. I was conscious, however, that my duties as regional ESTH officer included the letter *H* for health. There was overlap. I incorporated HIV/AIDS into my reporting, meeting with state-financed HIV treatment centers when I traveled.[103]

During my final months in Astana, I found another opening. In 2017, Kazakhstan hosted an international exposition that it was counting on to put Astana *on the map*. The theme was *future energy*, a field very much within my official portfolio. For months, Ambassador Krol had been asking our cash-strapped embassy sections to bring speakers from the U.S. As *Hubster*, I had sufficient budget and knew just the person to bring—Amanda Simpson, former deputy assistant secretary of defense for operational energy during the Obama administration. Between jobs after the inauguration of President Trump, she agreed to come to Kazakhstan for a week. Amanda spoke at the expo, and I set up meetings for her with Ministry of Energy and energy-sector officials, specialists, and entrepreneurs in both Astana and Almaty. Ambassador Krol was thrilled.

During her time in Albania, Mindy hosted monthly discussion evenings she called her *lasagna revolution*. By the time Mindy left Albania, a national LGBT+ movement had risen out of her evening discussions.

103   The HIV crisis in Kazakhstan stems mainly from intravenous drug use, but the percentage stemming from sexual contact of all kinds is growing. At the HIV center in Karaganda, I asked the deputy director about the LGBT+ community. He acknowledged there is a problem that is heightened by stigma, but he said they were making some inroads in the gay community. When I asked about transgender women and men, he said there were none in his region. When I pressed, he took umbrage, saying that of course he would recognize a transgender person if he saw one.

That was during the day. At night Amanda met with LGBT+ community members. One of the first four high-level transgender appointees to the federal government, she outranked me by several levels. She is easily the most visible and influential transgender activist ever to visit Kazakhstan.

In 2016, we moved the IDAHOT commemoration to the U.S. Embassy. Some forty local community members attended. We played pre-recorded video messages from the *out* gay ambassadors appointed by President Obama, and the Dutch Embassy provided a movie.

In 2017, over seventy-five community members squeezed into the embassy's multi-purpose room. It was standing-room-only. Singer-songwriter Namoli Brennet made a special recording of her song *We Belong* with shout-outs to community organizers in Kazakhstan. Ty Cobb, head of the international division of the Human Rights Campaign in Washington, spoke and fielded questions via video link. Marzhan interpreted.[104] Ambassador Krol delivered opening remarks. Visibly impressed, he stayed for the entire evening.[105] So did the visiting Belgian ambassador and representatives of several other diplomatic missions. IDAHOT 2017 was the largest LGBT+ gathering in Astana until that time.

After Lynne's departure in 2016, Vera Partem took over the human rights portfolio and threw herself into the 2017 IDAHOT event with a passion. More than that, she continued organizing IDAHOT after I left the country. In 2018, she widened the participation and co-sponsorship of friendly diplomatic missions. Together, they found a safe meeting space outside embassy walls. More than a hundred attended. What started with a simple question from Aron le Fèvre in 2015 has become a firm tradition in Astana.

As I prepared to leave Kazakhstan in 2017, I heard I was to be given a Superior Honor Award. The award had nothing to do with my official work

---

104 Working at these events fell well outside Marzhan's official duties. I will be forever grateful to her for volunteering her time and her expertise as the embassy's best interpreter.

105 Ambassador Krol always supported my work, and he supported me personally. He was, however, cautious. In 2016, he declined my request to display the Rainbow Flag *inside* the chancery building on IDAHOT. Convincing him the following year required behind-the-scenes lobbying, a tactic that FSOs call *managing up*. I engaged the relevant bureaus in Washington and asked that language be added to the 2017 instruction cable on IDAHOT and Pride events that would explicitly give Chiefs of Mission the authority to display the Rainbow Flag. With this language added, Ambassador Krol authorized display of the flag in the chancery atrium on IDAHOT in 2017.

as *Hubster* but was, rather, for my work promoting LGBT+ rights. Superior Honor awards must be approved in Washington and signed by an assistant secretary. For me this was a big deal, the highest award I received during my State Department career. The citation read, "For exceptional dedication and creativity in advancing LGBT+ rights in Kazakhstan and making this an integral part of the Mission."

I didn't receive the award until I was back in the U.S. How I reacted and what I did with the award when it came in the mail is another story that I will tell in due time.

9. *The Round Table*

The Bureau of Democracy, Human Rights, and Labor (DRL) administers a grant program for non-governmental organizations working to advance LGBT+ rights. The grants are no more than $25,000, but they play an outsize role in supporting LGBT+ communities around the world. For many recipient countries where rights are repressed, there are no other funds to support this work. These countries also tend to have underdeveloped economies where a few thousand dollars can accomplish far more than they would in the U.S.

The annual DRL grant competition notification came in early 2015.

"Robyn, the competition this year has a special focus on transgender rights," said Lynne. "Could we do something here in Kazakhstan?"

We decided to try our luck. We reached out to community members. They told us that anything we could do to make it easier for transgender Kazakhstanis to change their passports to reflect gender identity would be a great advance.

In Kazakhstan, as in much of the world, it is exceedingly difficult to change gender in official documents. This means perpetual banishment to the edge of society. A famous quote from Mikhail Bulgakov's *Master and Margarita* holds, "Remove the document, and you have removed the person." This describes the predicament of transgender Kazakhstanis in a country where documents are everything. When presenting documents, trans people are often accused of having stolen them; years of hormones have resulted in gender presentation that no longer matches document photos. As a result, transgender Kazakhstanis are denied medical care. They are refused international travel. No one will hire them. Underpaid piecework labor or streetwise sex work are the norm. To a transgender person in Central Asia, my story of gender transition as a U.S. diplomat seems beyond fantasy.

The DRL grant process is a competition between U.S. missions. Moreover, the grant funds don't go to the mission but to a local, officially registered non-governmental organization. We knew of no NGO in Kazakhstan that would touch a project on transgender rights. Or perhaps we did?

"Let me ask Dima," I suggested to Lynne. IESH was a registered NGO. Dima and his organization were experts at grant management.

I got together with Dima the next day. I asked him. Might IESH be willing to work on a topic considered scandalous, even explosive in Kazakhstani society?

His smile never faded; he would give it a try. After all, we were only submitting to the grant competition with no guarantee of selection.

We spent the next four months developing our proposal. IESH would review Kazakhstani law and medical procedures and do a side-by-side comparison with the laws and procedures in other countries, in particular in other post-Soviet countries. There would be quiet community outreach, but it didn't end there.

Dima said he could organize a round-table including officials and community members. He was certain that he could produce people from the Ministry of Health and from the Republican Psychiatric Institute. Putting them together in a room for an organized discussion with transgender community leaders would give a rare opportunity to demonstrate how inhumane Kazakhstani laws and procedures are towards transgender people. It might not change laws tomorrow, but it could raise questions.

In September, DRL selected our proposal for funding. We were off.

Dima was as good as his word. He put together regular meetings with community members, and he put his staff to work researching laws and procedures. He began organizing the roundtable that would take place in March 2016. Dima met with Yelzhan Birtanov, deputy minister of the Ministry of Health and Social Development, and he obtained assurances that the Republican Psychiatric Institute would send representatives.

IEHS would bring leading transgender community members to Astana to speak at the roundtable.

As we got closer to March, I found I had some extra discretionary *Hub* funds. Reminding myself that the *H* in ESTH includes LGBT+ health, I invited Jamison Green, president of the World Professional Association for Transgender Health (WPATH) to come to Astana as our U.S. expert on transgender issues. When Labrys in Bishkek got wind of our plans, it sent representatives to Astana. They also invited Jamison to Bishkek for a similar roundtable in the context of Kyrgyzstan.

The roundtable took place as scheduled in March and went like clockwork. Lynne and I only had to appear at the event as embassy representatives. Dima and IESH had done it all. For a full day in a hotel conference room in Astana, the first high-level discussion of transgender rights in Kazakhstan took place. The ministry representative seemed unimpressed, but it was a different matter for the lead psychiatrist from the Republican Psychiatric Institute. As the day went on, I came to realize we were winning an ally.

That was what we had aimed for. The roundtable was a modest affair, but as with our IDAHOT commemorations, it was a start. Transgender rights in Kazakhstan had taken a step forward.

10. For a Dancer

Keep a fire burning in your eye

Pay attention to the open sky

You never know what will be coming down

I don't remember losing track of you

You were always dancing in and out of view

I must've thought you'd always be around.[106]

Life and work continued after the transgender roundtable. I went on regional travel, and Marzhan and I got ready for the kickoff meeting of the Central Asia and Afghanistan Women and Water Network in June. It was a busy time.

---

106 Browne, Jackson. "For a Dancer." Genius. Accessed September 10, 2023. https://genius.com/Jackson-browne-for-a-dancer-lyrics.

Dima was also busy. We rarely saw each other after the roundtable, but we talked often by phone. Dima would represent Kazakhstan at a conference on sustainable development that would take place in Turkmenistan at the end of May. I also hoped to go. Since there are very few direct flights between Astana and Ashgabat, we planned to travel via Istanbul. Dima and I began to talk about the good release we would have on our layover day. We could be tourists. We could have a good dinner. For one day at least, we could enjoy life with no pressure.

Dima needed a day that would just be fun. Preoccupied with other matters, I wasn't paying attention to the forces beginning to move against him and IESH. With his signature smile, Dima kept the news from me—until there was no way to hide it.

The Astana Civic Alliance, an organization once led by Dima, threw IESH and Dima personally out of the organization. It evicted IESH from office space leased to it by the Alliance at a reduced rate. Inspectors from the KNB, post-Soviet Kazakhstan's equivalent of the KGB, descended on IESH multiple times to go through financial records.

Why? On the eve of the roundtable, Dima had given a press interview in which he asked for tolerance for transgender persons in Kazakhstan. The social media response had not been kind. Dima was accused of advocating values *not comporting with traditional Kazakh values.* The KNB wanted to know where IESH had gotten its funding for the event.

Dima laughed it off. For our part, we went back to Washington and got emergency funds for IESH to find a new office location. Dima intended for the move to take place as soon as we got back from Ashgabat. Meanwhile, he split all files and computers among the apartments and cars of his IESH staff.

The government of Turkmenistan did not approve my visa to attend the conference in Ashgabat. Dima and I would not have that day together in Istanbul. He would go alone.

Saturday, June 4, 2016, brought with it a beautiful blue sky. The snow in Astana had melted at last. Dima wrote to me that morning from Istanbul, his messages full of humorous banter. The men in Istanbul are gorgeous, Dima wrote. I should look for my next boyfriend there. He would fly back to Astana on Sunday.

I headed out for my first bicycle ride of the season and spent the whole day reveling in the sun and warmth. Then something unusual happened. Thunderstorms are rare on the steppe. I had never seen one, but this day the storm clouds gathered quickly. I pedaled fast and made it to HighVill as the storm broke. I went out on my balcony to watch the lightning display, a magnificent end to a wonderful day.

A call awoke me on Sunday morning. It was my friend Tanya, sobbing. She kept repeating, "Dima myortv." She had to repeat it a half-dozen times before I could make sense of the words: "Dima is dead." He had been found dead in his hotel room in Istanbul. My closest friend had died at age thirty-three. I broke into a million emotional pieces.

Officially it was a heart attack, but I didn't believe it. Dima had always radiated good health. I didn't understand how someone so young and seemingly fit could have died of a heart attack at age thirty-three.

When Dima's family flew to Istanbul to collect his body, they found his money and computer were gone. Had he been robbed? Turkish police had no interest in investigating. Why should they care about the death of a Kazakhstani national? Turkish authorities only wanted the body out of the country.

I announced Dima's death at the country team meeting on Monday morning, falling apart as I said the words. Ambassador Krol's office management specialist, a hardened ex-Marine, took me aside and said quietly, "Ms. McCutcheon, I think you should go home."

More than 150 people attended Dima's funeral in Stepnogorsk. That included three of us from the U.S. Embassy, the Swiss ambassador, and representatives of more diplomatic missions than I can remember. Ambassador Krol sent a personal letter of condolence. Every environmental organization in Kazakhstan sent someone.

Dima's mom and dad flanked his casket. Dima had often said he wanted me to meet them, but I had never imagined it would be like this. Dima looked so much like his mom.

At the edge of the crowd of mourners stood one young man whose tears flowed most of all. He was Dima's partner. Dima was gay. He was gay in a country where gay people are victimized, sometimes murdered if their orientation becomes public. In the aftermath of his death, it is this aspect of Dima's life that all seemed most intent on forgetting.

Dima's grave in Stepnogorsk

What happened in Istanbul? There are theories. Dima and his partner had been arguing before he left. Dima's final postings on social media say he had met someone, perhaps a gay date for the night. That date, intent on robbing Dima, may have put something in his drink—and the drug killed him instead. Or he was murdered by someone who hates gays. We will never know.

Would it have been different if I had gotten my visa and gone to Ashgabat with Dima? I have wondered about this ever since. I carry the guilt of knowing that his troubles began because of his association with me, with the grant, and with the roundtable. He believed in me, and I believed in him. In a transgender world where many think gay men don't care about them, Dima had given everything.

Dima's photo smiles at me from the mantelpiece today in Maine. Before leaving Kazakhstan for good in the summer of 2017, I went with friends to visit Dima's family in Stepnogorsk and to say goodbye one last time. I collected some small stones by his graveside. Today those pebbles surround two memorial candles. They are my shrine to Dima.

There on the windswept steppe of northern Kazakhstan lies Dr. Dmitry Tereshkevich, my Dima, one of the greatest friends I will ever know.

11. Sultana

I've looked at life from both sides now

From up and down, and still somehow

It's life's illusions I recall

I really don't know life at all.[107]

"Do you have any idea what you just did?" I was red in the face, yelling loudly.

Across from me stood Sultana, shocked that her usually quiet American *little sister* had chosen this moment to explode. We were in a gully not far from Lake Issykul in Kyrgyzstan. The landscape was reminiscent of the American Southwest, and Sultana had run ahead so that we lost sight of her. Marzhan, Sultana's mom Natasha, and I were frantic. For a quarter-hour we called her name, looking for footprints. Then she appeared, waving from a hilltop several hundred feet above us, a steppe-dweller getting her first exhilaration at climbing a hill.

When she came down, I snapped. I emptied the tensions of the past year on the very person I had dedicated my life to. It was May 2017. My time in Astana was growing short, and my world seemed to be coming apart at the seams. Our family vacation at Lake Issykul had been interrupted by bad news. That morning Trump had announced the U.S. would pull out of the Paris Agreement on Climate Change, thereby casting much of my work into the waste bin. It was too much. Sultana was my unwitting target.

. . . .

---

107 Mitchell, Joni. "Both Sides Now." Genius. Accessed on September 10, 2023. https://genius.com/Joni-mitchell-both-sides-now-lyrics.

I met Sultana Kali in March 2016 at the welcome dinner I hosted on the eve of the transgender roundtable. I spotted her kneeling in front of my record collection.

"May I look at them?" she asked.

"Of course," I replied. A few moments later she exclaimed: "You have Joni Mitchell! Could we listen to Joni Mitchell?"

How was it possible that this eighteen-year-old from a provincial city in Kazakhstan knew about Joni Mitchell? I was hooked.

Sultana spoke at the roundtable the next day. With poise and dignity, she told how she had been expelled from her high school in Pavlodar in 2015 after coming out as transgender. She had been only a year away from graduation.

After the roundtable, I asked Dima if we could find a school somewhere that would accept Sultana. He was sure we could. I contacted Sultana and her mom and asked if that is what she would like. They did. Dima would explore the process over the summer. If he had gotten government officials to attend a roundtable on transgender rights, there was no question in my mind but that he would find a safe haven for Sultana in a Kazakhstani school somewhere.

But then Dima died. I was on my own. Dima knew how to work the system. I did not. Still dealing with my grief, I set to work as best I could. Most of all, I feared I would be viewed as an outsider, an American who does not respect *traditional Kazakh values.*

Through the summer I found all doors politely but firmly slammed in my face. That included the international schools and the elite Nazarbayev University. No official would admit to being transphobic. Instead, they would allude to administrative problems with admitting a transgender student. The admissions officer at Nazarbayev University recommended that Sultana study abroad. The director of an international school recommended an American community college.

Sultana and her mom Natasha moved into my apartment. Natasha kept us fed through the frigid winter. Taller than me, Sultana called me her *little sister*; to me she was my *big sister*. Together with Meruert, there were now four of us living in my Astana apartment with Akerke sometimes being a fifth.

Then the election happened. On November 9, 2016, I was in Copenhagen for a conference of regional ESTH officers, an opportunity to confer with other *Hubsters* like myself. When I woke that morning, the Trump victory was not a foregone conclusion. Hillary could still pull it out. I felt sure of it as I headed out from my hotel. But by the time I reached the conference, it was over. Embassy Copenhagen was as quiet as a tomb. Ambassador Rufus Gifford, one of the out gay ambassadors appointed by President Obama, spoke to us soothingly, but it was clear that even he was distraught. I spent the day in numbed shock, feeling I must be inside a nightmare from which I would surely wake. But there would be no waking from this nightmare.

The conference over, I remained in Copenhagen for the weekend. Olympia flew up from Bucharest in expectation of a fun weekend but found me in tears. We walked endlessly during the day and spent an evening listening to mournful jazz at a Copenhagen club. When I heard the strains of *Bridge Over Troubled Waters* drifting out of a Nyhavn club, I burst into tears again. Would the U.S. ever be the same? What would it mean for Sultana?

I flew to the U.S. in January, using my last authorized R&R trip home to be in the 2017 Women's March the day after Trump's inauguration. I needed a boost of confidence. Surely, we could resist what was to come? Surely *Project Sultana* would succeed?

In my mind, Sultana had become *Project Sultana*. My son Matt's college quest had been a breeze. He received a full scholarship from the University of Maryland, and he found part-time work as a laboratory assistant. He graduated college with money in the bank, something almost unheard of in the U.S. today. For a parent, Matt's journey had been easy.

I became for Sultana what I had never been for Matt: a driving, demanding parent, my desk calendar filled with application deadlines. There were application essays to write. There were scholarship essays. We needed to start a crowdfunding effort. When not at work, I was full time on *Project Sultana*. I began to show the same frayed edges that many American parents experience during the college application process. I had become more invested in Sultana's college future than she was herself.

That isn't to say that Sultana was not growing. She began setting the program for the monthly 3rd *Thursday @ Robyn's* discussion evenings. She appeared in Embassy Astana's Human Rights' Day video and introduced Ambassador Krol at IDAHOT 2017. She was developing into a recognized, fearless young feminist in Kazakhstan's LGBT+ community.

Sultana seemed so very American. Her English is as good and as unaccented as mine, and it was easy to forget that she had never set foot in an American city, that she had not had an American childhood. For her, Astana was already the big time.

Sultana in the winter of 2016-17

We worked through the winter. In the end, Lane Community College in Oregon accepted her. They also gave a small scholarship for her essay "I Just Want to Live an Ordinary Life— and Create a Revolution" in which she wrote about how a degree would help her improve conditions for LGBT+ persons in Kazakhstan. As the ice on the Esil' River began to melt, things were looking up. Crowdfunding had pulled in over $5,000, and I had resolved to make up any shortfall so that there would be enough to cover the first academic year in the U.S.

In May, I suggested to Sultana, Natasha, Meruert, and Marzhan that we take a break and go on a family vacation to Lake Issykul in Kyrgyzstan. In my five years in Central Asia, I had never seen Lake Issykul, one of the purest mountain lakes in the world. Even on vacation, however, I spent the week obsessing about the upcoming visa interview. It was too much: Dima's death, Trump, a grueling winter of college admissions.

After I bawled her out, it was days before Sultana would speak with me again. Over those days I forced myself to understand my *big sis*. Of course, she would run up that hill in Kyrgyzstan. She was young. She had never been in the mountains before. She didn't know the first thing about hiking safety in a group. I had failed her, allowing her to run ahead.

The morning of her visa interview, I walked Sultana through the process. Meruert shared her visa interview experience from the previous year. I gave Sultana a hug and told her she had nothing to worry about.

I came home later to find her on her bed, curled in a fetal position. After a three-minute interview, the consular section chief refused her, saying she didn't have enough money to make ends meet for four years in the U.S.

I assured Sultana that we could overcome this hurdle. Nothing in U.S. immigration law says international students must demonstrate sufficient funds to stay afloat for four years, but consuls are not required to explain their decisions. Sultana submitted a second application. This time, I filled out an *attestation of support* committing to cover expenses for all four years.

Sultana went for the second visa interview in July. Refused again. The vice-consul didn't even glance at the additional documentation. Not one to give up, Sultana tried a third time, this time after Senators Tammy Baldwin, Ben Cardin, and Susan Collins had made inquiries on her behalf. Denied again.

I despaired. There was nothing I could do internally. State Department rules forbid FSOs from intervening in visa cases. What, I wondered, had the consular officers seen in Sultana as she stood at the interview window, handing over forms, bank statements, and passport?

I remembered my own time at a visa window in Moscow. I remembered the PhD candidate who had been refused twice because she happened to be young and pretty and, therefore, *a likely sex worker*. That, at least, is what must have gone through the minds of the consuls who had refused her twice without a glance at her CV. That experience taught me that consuls do make mistakes, seeing applicants through their own cultural lens, perhaps a discriminatory lens they are not even aware of.[108]

In 2017, Sultana still carried a passport bearing a male name and gender marker. Was she rejected as an openly transgender woman, someone whom consular officers suspected would remain in the U.S. illegally, an *intending immigrant*? Under the law, that finding would make her ineligible. Since I can't ask directly, I will never know.

But I know this: Of sixteen Kazakhstani students accepted by Lane Community College between 2010 and 2016, Sultana was the first to be turned down for a visa.

It pains me to think that this type of dream-crushing, arbitrary decision-making may have come more naturally to consular officers at a time when Trump was intent on curtailing travel to the U.S. by citizens of Muslim countries. He called them inherently dangerous, and he referred to transgender troops as a *burden* America cannot afford. It pains me that there is no avenue for redress or appeal.

. . . .

This is why I wanted to tear up and burn my Superior Honor Award for LGBT+ outreach. *Project Sultana* had failed. *I* had failed. For the State Department to give me an award but deny a visa to Sultana was, in my eyes, the height of hypocrisy.

It has taken time and space for me to understand that the failure of *Project Sultana* was mine, not Sultana's. I had come to see myself as a miracle worker, and it took the reality of failure to bring me back to earth.

The movers came the day after Sultana's third visa refusal. Within hours, the Astana apartment that had become a home for me and for Meruert, Sultana, Natasha, and Akerke reverted to a cold, empty space. I wondered if the next FSO occupant would have initial misgivings. Would that FSO stand on the balcony at 3:00 a.m. and wonder, as I had in 2014, "OMG, how am I going to make it through three years here?"

---

108 For more on how a consul's cultural lens might influence visa decisions, see Robyn Mc-Cutcheon, "U.S. Consuls Already Have the Tools to Discriminate in Visa Decisions," *HuffPost,* 3/7/2018 (https://www.huffpost.com/entry/opinion-mccutcheon-visa-discrimination_n_5a9cc6e2e4b089ec353bee8d).

Now, in the aftermath of struggle, grief, loss, and failure, I faced a very different question: "How am I going to go on without my Astana family? How would I find a purpose, the will to continue?" I had two years to go until retirement in 2019. How would I find a purpose, the will to continue? I knew I had to, but how?

PART 7

In Opposition: Washington (2017–19)

My working life began in Silver Spring, Maryland, in 1978, and I lived there for twenty-six years before taking the risk and jumping to the Foreign Service in 2004. My return to the D.C. area in 2007 had meant divorce, and my return in 2010 had meant divorce mediation followed by court and post-divorce litigation. Only in 2013–14 had my life in D.C. meant success without trauma. Now I was returning for a final two years, exhausted and broken in spirit.

Planets shine most brightly when in opposition, at the points in their orbits when they are nearly opposite the Sun as seen from Earth. That's how I view my time in Washington in 2017–19. I stood ever more in opposition to the State Department and to the divisive politics descending on my own country, but my journey was not over. These two years were to bring echoes of the past, a reprise of *The Full Alice*, and friends who steered me to a safe haven in a politicized Washington I no longer understood.

1. My Long Journey . . . Home?

A day of despair, in the middle of such a horribly senseless city, and of wondering whether there were not still – somewhere in America – a place where a gravel lane, wet from the rains, led up a hill, between the yellow trees and past occasional vistas of a valley full of quiet farms and woodlands, to a house where candles and a warm hearth defied the early darkness and dampness of autumn and where human warmth and simplicity and graciousness defied the encroachments of a diseased world and of people drugged and debilitated by automobiles and advertisements and radios and moving pictures.[109]

***September 5, 2017, 10:00 p.m.; Aktau, Kazakhstan**—I was the last person to board the rusting Soviet-era ferry that will take me across the Caspian Sea to Baku ....*

---

109 George F. Kennan diary entry from October 24, 1937, as quoted in John Lewis Gaddis, ibid., p. 109.

Those were the opening, heartbreaking words of my article in the *Huff-Post*, marking the end of my life in Kazakhstan, the end of my journey with Sultana.[110] It was the beginning of a new road, destination unknown.

If all had gone according to plan, Sultana and I would have boarded a plane to the U.S. on September 1. I planned on going with her to Oregon, getting her established in her dorm. I looked forward to the traditional ritual of an older sister taking her younger sister off to college. Then I would head home to Maine and onward to my last assignment in Washington.

The final visa refusal on August 22 decreed that none of this was to be. This is the story of a solitary journey I never intended to take, a crying in the wilderness and a painful, incomplete attempt to come to terms.

The eighth pack-out of my State Department career took place on August 24. Sultana, Natasha, and other close friends saw me through that event that always makes for a traumatic day.

Three days later, on Sunday, I walked out of Embassy Astana for the last time after performing my first act of open protest in the form of a dissent cable pointing out the lack of understanding of LGBT+ issues in our consular section. Two hours later, Sultana, Natasha, and I were in a taxi for the multi-hour ride to their home in Pavlodar where I spent four days with my adopted family. We took long walks in the city and to the embankment of the Irtysh River. Sultana's granddad took us to the family dacha that was more of a small farm than garden plot.

On Friday, September 1, Sultana and I boarded a train back to Astana. I had washed my hands of the embassy and had torn up my State Department air ticket back to the U.S. Sultana and I spent the night with friends and the next day headed to Astana's new train station. We almost missed our train to Aktau when the taxi driver initially headed for the old train station on the other side of town. By the time we realized his mistake, we were running out of time. We raced to the station and ran to the platform. When we got there, the doors of the high-speed Talga train were closing. The conductor waved us off, yelling that we were too late. For the last time in Kazakhstan, I yelled back "Diplomat!" and hurled myself into the doorway, pulling Sultana behind me.

---

110 Robyn McCutcheon, "Why Is the U.S. Denying This Young Trans Woman a Student Visa?" *HuffPost*, 11/14/2017, https://www.huffpost.com/entry/trans-student-visa-kazakhstan_b_5a0a2626e4b0bc648a0d5569

The journey from Astana to Aktau takes a day and a half, crossing Kazakhstan's limitless steppe. We dozed. We talked. We drank beer and tea in the dining car. I played Arlo Guthrie's classic train song *The City of New Orleans* on my telephone.

Our hotel in Aktau did not rate even two stars, but it was a block from the sea. Sultana had never seen a true sea. We immediately set out for a long walk along the beach. After sunset we sat on rocks, dipping our hands into the Caspian and listening to the whisper of the waves.

There is a ferry from Aktau to Baku, but it is mysterious. There is no schedule, and the office and telephone number for the agent keep changing. We learned there would be no ferry on Monday and spent another day together walking through Aktau and along the Caspian.

My call on Tuesday was met with the news that there would be a ferry that evening. The agent told me where to go and to be there at 6:00 p.m.

The Caspian ferry serves freight, not people. It is used almost exclusively by truck drivers, and the port is designed with that in mind. We found the ferry office with difficulty and learned that boarding would not start for at least another two hours. We found the one cafe in the port, and there I had my last supper in Kazakhstan. Returning to the office, we found several German and Swiss tourists had joined our small passenger group. Boarding was finally announced after 9:00 p.m.

I did not want to part until the last possible moment. Sultana and I hugged each other tightly. When the final boarding call came, I walked through passport control with tears flowing, the last person to board the ferry.

The memory of Sultana's final hug stayed with me as I found a solitary place on deck. It was after 2:00 a.m. when the ferry pulled away from the dock. I remained on the deck for two hours, watching the lights of Aktau, the last lights I would see from Kazakhstan, fade into the distance. I fancied myself in a 1930s movie, in the days before air travel. My tears, anger, and hurt mixed with the dampness of the Caspian night. I knew that Sultana was watching from the shore as the mist swallowed me.

· · · · · · · · · · · · · · ·

The Caspian crossing was a time capsule. The ferry had been built in the time of Brezhnev and must have had the Soviet look of *instant aging* even when new. The cabins and food were basic. The Azeri woman responsible for the cabins spoke no languages other than Azeri and Russian, and none of the European tourists spoke either. I became her interpreter, and she repaid my service by putting me in a private cabin and treating me to tea and dates. The voyage was uneventful except for the moment when water came through my porthole and soaked my bed. Luckily, I wasn't lying there when it happened. The crew were cleaning the deck and had forgotten to tell us to close our portholes. I was not the only one whose cabin received an unexpected soaking.

I chose this way of leaving Kazakhstan to distract myself from the anguish of failure and loss. When I boarded the ferry in Aktau, I knew only that I would be going to Baku. I had no idea where I would stay there, for how long, or where I would go next. These were all things I would need to work out as I went. The mechanics of this solitary journey would occupy my brain.

But I would be haunted the entire way. Unlike Kazakhstan, few people in Baku speak Russian well. I had arrived in a different kind of nationalist post-Soviet space where all signs are in Azeri. For two hot, humid days, I took sweaty walks around Baku's old walled city. I sat on the embankment and looked eastward across the Caspian, taking a picture of my hand waving to friends on the other side. I thought of the coolness of Astana and my walks with Meruert, no matter what the weather. I had dinner at a *Traveler's Coffee* and thought back to dinners at a *Traveler's* with Sultana in July, when I was certain everything would still work out. On my last evening I found a Kentucky Fried Chicken at the train station. As I ate, I recalled how Meruert had thought the chicken at KFC in the U.S. in 2016 "just didn't taste like the real thing."

An overnight train as old as the ferry took me from Baku to Tbilisi, to a Georgia I had not visited since 1981. Somehow, I found a Russian-owned bed and breakfast, perhaps because the default setting of my smartphone from Kazakhstan is Russian. Outside the hotel, I was better off speaking English, visiting this country that had been at war with Russia. For two days the warm hospitality of the old city softened my anger. I walked everywhere and rode the funicular to the park above the city where I sat on a bench with a Russian woman from Kislovodsk. We shared ice cream and talked about the challenges of our lives.

When I boarded my next train to Poti, over a week had passed since I left Astana. Another port city, Poti made Aktau look luxurious by comparison. There were palm trees, but the reality is an unreconstructed Soviet city for port workers. I had to search for the next ferry office, this one owned by a Ukrainian line. Once again, I was told there would be no ferry that day.

I was stuck in Poti for another day. I had already walked the city through on my first day. I had watched the sun set over the Black Sea from a crumbling embankment dominated by an English lighthouse brought there in the nineteenth century. The owner of my no-star hotel took pity on me; he drove me out to another hotel he owned outside the city. For the first time since 1978, I swam in the warm, clear waters of the Black Sea. I also made my way to a national park outside Poti and rented a kayak, remembering when Dima and I had launched our inflatable kayak into the Esil' River. I ate *shashlyk* at every meal, wondering when I might ever find it on the menu again.

On the third day, the ferry office told me to come at 6:00 p.m. Aktau repeated itself. When I arrived at the office, I was told to come back in two hours, but when I did, there was still no hint of boarding. Only at 10:00 p.m. were we allowed to board the ferry. While waiting, I made friends with a young Ukrainian backpacking couple and a woman from Kyiv. They would be among my fellow passengers for the voyage to Odessa.

I breathed a sigh of relief. Unlike the Caspian ferry, this Black Sea ferry was new, clean, and modern with a cozy cafe and decent food. My cabin was almost luxurious. In the morning I watched as dolphins swam alongside.

But the calm ended abruptly with an event that underscored my place in the world as a single woman outside the diplomatic umbrella that had protected me in Astana. Having gone rogue in my journey to the U.S., I had no diplomatic status on the waters of the Black Sea.

It started innocently enough. A Georgian policeman and his friend sat down at my deck table that evening. My new friend from Kyiv was there also, and thus we were a foursome. My Georgian was overweight but handsome. The other Georgian said almost nothing. My Georgian was drinking and began hugging me and introducing me to others as his future wife. He claimed that his own wife and daughter had died a few months before in an auto accident. As he was becoming drunker, his quiet friend and I helped him back to his cabin.

I didn't recognize the danger signs. Nothing in my upbringing, my gender socialization as a child or teenager, had prepared me for this. Would a cisgender woman have entered a private cabin in the company of an intoxicated man? I doubt it. Having done just this, I was about to be taught a belated and needlessly dangerous lesson.

Now in the cabin, my Georgian drunkenly asked me to lie on the bed next to him. No sex. Only lie next to him. I felt sorry for this drunk Georgian, and several glasses of wine had fogged my reason. Crazy as it was, I lay down on the bed.

I must have fallen asleep. When I came to, I felt hands groping me. My Georgian was caressing me and telling me to have sex with his friend. We were not alone on the bed. The quiet Georgian lay there too, naked and coming into me from the rear. At first, I froze. I thought I was in danger and had better do as they asked. I climbed on top of the quiet Georgian and took his penis in my hands, starting to guide him inside me.

But then I screamed, jumped, and ran. Despite the wine, I was nowhere near as drunk as the two Georgians. Now stone sober from the adrenaline rush of fright, I ran down the hall to my own cabin and locked myself in. The Georgians followed and began pounding on my door. I ignored them. Shaking, I took a hot shower, scrubbing as hard as I could to somehow wash away what had happened. I put on headphones and listened to music and cried until dawn.

Arrival in Odessa the next day brought the relief of being in a city that felt familiar. No one here cared if I spoke Russian. I went to the store to buy toiletries, the last time I would see such bottles and packages with labels in Cyrillic.

In the afternoon, I boarded a nearly empty Bulgarian bus on which the only other passengers were three Ukrainian women going on holiday to Varna on the Bulgarian coast. We made our way westward through the rolling Ukrainian countryside, stopping at a border town where I spent my last Ukrainian grivny at a lonely kiosk. We reached the border with Moldova and passed slowly through customs and passport control. A half-hour later we were at the Romanian border.

I had passed out of post-Soviet space. If I were to speak Russian here, no one would understand me. How strange that my primary language for day-to-day life would no longer be understood. By prior agreement, Sultana and I switched languages in the daily messages we exchanged. For a year we had communicated in English to help prepare her for college in the U.S. Now I was the one who needed practice with Russian. If not with Sultana, then with whom?

At midnight the bus pulled into Constanta on the Black Sea coast. I stepped down onto the sidewalk and looked around to see Olympia walking quickly toward me. For the first time since Aktau, I was with a person I cared about. We hugged.

It was a long, tearful, but happy reunion. Our hotel room had a view of the Black Sea, and we walked for hours as we had in Bucharest. The city was little changed from the time of Ceausescu, but the sea was timeless and beautiful at sunset on the rocky jetties that dot the coast.

Three days later, we boarded a bus to the airport in Bucharest. Now I had to prepare myself for the greatest culture shock of all, a return to a country I no longer understood after the election of 2016, a country that had turned its back on me. Is America still my home?

As I boarded my flight in Bucharest, I was no longer sure. I felt my heart being tugged back to the East where my chosen family lives. Surely it is not over? Surely, I will return there and yet again make snow angels with Meruert on a New Year's morning? Surely, I will again row a kayak up the Esil' with the spirit of Dima beside me? If I had resolved anything during my long journey, it was this: I will go back. Too much of my life remains in Kazakhstan. A part of my heart is there on the cold, windswept steppe, and it calls me home.

2. Starting Over

To Everything (Turn, Turn, Turn)
There is a season (Turn, Turn, Turn)
And a time for every purpose, under Heaven.[111]

My HHE from Kazakhstan went to my home in Maine. I had not had time

---

111 Seeger, Pete. "Turn! Turn! Turn! (To Everything There Is a Season)." Genius. Accessed September 10, 2023. https://genius.com/Pete-seeger-turn-turn-turn-to-everything-there-is-a-season-lyrics.

to think where I would live for my final two years in Washington. Did it matter?

Landing at Dulles Airport, I made my way to the storage facility in Virginia where my car Hillary had been stored for three years. I put the key in the ignition and found that she still had life. No longer used to being at the wheel of a car, I drove slowly to Maine over three days, avoiding cities and taking back roads where traffic would be light, roads I could cope with until I got back the knack of driving.

I had two weeks of home leave left when I reached Maine, but I still had no idea where I would live in Washington. Then a thought hit me. I had begun my working career in a group house. Why not end it that way? I had met Dani, a young woman from USAID. at the Women's March in January. I knew that she and her fiancé Petra, both younger than my own son, were planning to buy a house. I wrote. Sure enough, they had bought a fixer-upper in NE Washington and were looking for housemates to reduce the mortgage burden.

Home leave ended. I took the train to Washington and went straight to Main State, pulling my two suitcases behind me. That evening I took the Metro to NE and found my way to the group house that I will diplomatically describe as a *1930s home with potential.* The tiny bedroom had barely enough width to change clothes, and the one functioning bathroom lurked in a dark corner of the basement. Still, at $500/month, it was the cheapest possible accommodation one could imagine in Washington, cheaper in real terms than the room I had rented in 1978.

It was good to be with Dani and Petra, young people just starting out. They knew my story, every bit of it. When Dani hugged me and sat me on the couch that first evening, I knew the warmth of this new home outweighed the physical downsides of living in a fixer-upper.

I made a quick run to Maine a couple of weeks later and brought back another suitcase of clothes. I shipped my bicycle so I would have an alternative way of getting around D.C., other than foot and Metro. I was ending my career in the same way I had begun it, in a group house with minimal possessions and a bicycle.

The sand in my career hourglass trickled to its end. I often spent weekends with my sister Irene in Gambrills, MD, and I spent time with my son and family, finally getting to know the granddaughter who was born a week before I left for Astana in 2014. I attended glifaa meetings, distressed that the new board had decided the best strategy after the Trump election was to keep a low profile. I went home to Maine every month or two to open boxes, set up housekeeping, and downsize. I had enough kitchenware for three households. It was time to consolidate, and a local thrift store became the beneficiary of my pruning. Without Meruert to help, it took me a year to go through all my boxes.

I continued to battle for Sultana. I published several pieces in the *Huff-Post*,[112] going right up to the line of accusing consular officers of inherent bias. The Kazakhstani edition of *Esquire* picked up and published an intentionally inflammatory Russian language interview I had given to journalist Botagoz Omarova before leaving Kazakhstan.[113] This forced Embassy Astana to respond, albeit with characteristically bland verbiage that privacy concerns prevented it from commenting on individual cases. The dissent cable I wrote on my last day in Astana earned me a DAS-level meeting in the Bureau of Consular Affairs.

I knew my efforts would lead nowhere. Nothing would change. I needed to fight in order to look myself in the mirror each morning and report to Main State rather than resign. I had written a resignation letter on my way back from Kazakhstan. I had nothing to lose, so why not scream my head off wherever I could? What could the State bureaucracy do anyway?

---

112 HuffPost articles: "Why Is the U.S. Denying This Young Trans Woman a Student Visa?" ibid.; "U.S. Consuls Already Have the Tools To Discriminate in Visa Decisions," ibid.; and "A Transgender American Diplomat Who Does Not Exist," 11/10/2018 (https://www.huffpost.com/entry/trans-student-visa-kazakhstan_b_5a0a2626e4b0bc648a0d5569).

113 The Kazakhstan edition of *Esquire* does not maintain an archive of older articles, but the Internet portal Vteme.kz picked up the theme in "ТРАНСнациональная трагедия [TRANS-natsional'naya tragediya]," 11/21/2017 (http://vteme.kz/publ/analitika/ehnigma/transnacionalnaja_tragedija/34-1-0-133). Video of my Russian-language interview with journalist Botagoz Omarova can be found at "Трансгендерной девушке, ЛГБТИК+ активистке, Султане Кали отказали в выдаче учебной визы в США [Transgendernoi devushke, LGBTIQ+ artivistke, Sultane Kali otkazali v vydache uchebnoi vizyv SShA]," 8/27/2017 (http://101tv.kz/video_news/723-transgendernoy-devushke-lgbtik-aktivistke-sultane-kali-otkazali-v-vydache-uchebnoy-vizy-v-ssha.html). An English-language interview with the Kazakhstani LGB organization kok.team can be found in "Robyn McCutcheon: 'The dark times ushered in by Trump will pass,'"10/9/2017 (https://www.kok.team/en/2017-10-09/robyn-mccutcheon-the-dark-times-ushered-in-by-trump-will-pass).

I was facing the mandatory retirement age. Just as with gender transition in 2010–11, I might as well go down fighting. To its credit, State cleared each of the *HuffPost* articles. They were *not of official concern* even if I did use fighting words.

I went to battle with the glifaa board, incensed that it censored my writings on glifaa's social media platforms. Selim Ariturk, my policy director in 2013-14, was not happy either. Together we drafted an amendment to the glifaa by-laws guaranteeing freedom of speech in all glifaa forums. It went to a membership vote. We won.

I started dating again, meeting and spending many a wonderful evening and night with an army linguist. John, my boyfriend from 2013–14 reappeared, slowly at first for a weekend movie, then warming to an intimacy exceeding what we had once known.

I returned to the PATC cabin in Little Orleans four times for needed solitude and reflection. A fifth visit was the opposite of solitude, a time to gather my son, family, and close friends to share my special place.

I stayed in touch with Sultana, Natasha, Meruert, and Olympia. If there is a benefit to twenty-first century technology, it is that we can communicate easily across six time zones to Romania and eleven to Kazakhstan, something inconceivable when I first went to the Soviet Union in 1978.

Finally, I did not burn the Superior Honor Award for my LGBT+ outreach in Kazakhstan. A better idea came to me. I mailed the award back to Astana to Vera Partem, our human rights officer who was continuing what Lynne and I had started. Vera took the award to every community member she could find, and they all signed it. There is scarcely a blank square centimeter on the document. Instead of a hypocritical award from the Department of State, I have a prized memento from my time in Kazakhstan: expressions of love from those whose lives I touched and whose lives touched mine.

That was my personal life in Washington for two years, living out of a suitcase with one foot still in Kazakhstan and another already in Maine. The State Department, however, was not done with me. It had one more surprise in store.

3. *Reprise of The Full Alice*

But what I can do will be known to very few people, and will be appreciated by fewer still; and the effort will probably end in personal catastrophe for myself and the family.[114]

After my experiences in Kazakhstan, I did not have much fight left in me. With two years to go until mandatory retirement, I chose to return to the NRRC, the same office where I had worked in 2013–14. It would be *good, honest operations work* at a time when it was best for a progressive liberal like me to stay away from policy—if only in the interest of staying sane.

It's the NRRC watch officers who do the lion's share of the work. They are the ones on the line processing arms control treaty notifications 24/7, doing very technical translating from Russian and other treaty languages as needed. I would not be a watch officer this time around. I was returning as senior watch officer (SWO). When I had last served in the NRRC, the SWO was little more than the first among equals on the Watch. The SWO did the same work and pulled the same rotating shifts.

Things had changed since 2014. Now, it turned out, the SWO functioned more as a supervisor. The position was almost superfluous, a buffer be-tween the Watch and front office management. The SWO frequently served as a mouthpiece for management directives while watch officers did the real work.

If there was one thing I remembered from my time on the Watch in 2013–14, it was that the work is labor intensive with lots of repetitive manual processing. It screamed out for automation. With twenty-five years of IT experience behind me on NASA projects, I envisioned software that could save a watch officer an hour or more during peak shifts. Just think of it, an entire hour that a watch officer could devote to substance rather than to repetitive manual operations akin to those on an assembly line! Now back as SWO, I decided the time had come to turn this vision into reality.

By December 2017, I had prepared design and build plans and had built a beta version. I called the project *NRRC Cable Express*, a software package that interfaces with the State Department's Messaging and Archive Re-

---

114 George F. Kennan diary entry from August 28, 1942, as quoted in John Lewis Gaddis, ibid., p. 158.

trieval Toolset (SMART) to provide the needed automation. I presented the preliminary design to the front office, which gave me the go ahead to proceed. An external review by State IT personnel would take place sometime in the spring, but in the meantime, I had a blessing to deploy *NRRC Cable Express* to those watch officers who were willing to be beta testers. Between January and April, I progressed through several beta releases, updating and distributing documentation at each step. Almost all watch officers were now clamoring to be beta testers. I stayed after hours and came in on non-workdays to push the project forward. I saw this effort as my gift to an office that had been good to me in the past and that was now giving me a haven in this difficult political time. I was repeating a pattern from my past: immersing myself in work and doing far more than was expected. I needed intense work to see me through to my retirement date.

In May 2018, I was rudely awakened from this idyllic view when I returned from two weeks' leave in Maine. I was working the evening shift on my first day back, digging out of accumulated emails. At about 8:00 p.m. I came to the message that changed my life. It was a *Mandatory Guidance* signed by the front office. It instructed watch officers to return to manual methods pending an investigation of the methods developed by SWO Robyn McCutcheon.

Stunned, I searched to see if there had been some attempt to contact me prior to issuing this *Mandatory Guidance* or to explain to me afterward why it had been issued. There was nothing, not a word of explanation. Moreover, the guidance had been issued only two workdays before my return.

I give you the reprise of *The Full Alice,* another bizarre adventure in the *Alice in Wonderland* realm of State Department bureaucracy, turf battles, and gender hierarchy.

A suspicion lurking in the back of my head jumped to the foreground. Could this be a matter of gender? There had been tense moments between supervisors and some of the female watch officers. Although the front office had given its go-ahead to my modernization effort, that approval had been lukewarm. After the initial go-ahead, front office management had always responded with "some other time" when I suggested demonstrations and follow-up design reviews. I became aware that a dispute had broken out during my absence when a female watch officer was ordered to stop using *NRRC Cable Express.* The *Mandatory Guidance* came the next day.

I took my concerns to front office management, explaining that *NRRC Cable Express* is meant to ease the burden on watch officers. Whether the Watch uses *NRRC Cable Express* or continues to process manually is akin to whether Egyptian slaves used a wheeled sledge to transport stones or instead carried them on their backs. The pyramids would be built regardless. Similarly, NRRC dissemination cables are reviewed and cleared without regard to how they are produced. Whether produced manually or with the aid of *NRRC Cable Express*, it's the end product that counts.

The front office response stunned me yet again. Management cast me as a troublemaker and ordered me to forget automation, do my job, and not contest the *Mandatory Guidance*. I responded that under those circumstances, I no longer wished to work in the NRRC. Once named *NRRC Watch Officer of the Year* and recipient of a NRRC *Meritorious Honor Award*, I tore off my smiley face and reached inside to find my *inner bitch*. During my Hubble years I was used to respect, but could that have been due in part to my gender, my male privilege? With that privilege stripped away, had I become the woman in the room who could be ignored? I opened an EEO case, all the while knowing that the complaint would go nowhere. It would be no different from my EEO battle for Guzal in Tashkent. I would be told that my gender had nothing to do with the crafting of the *Mandatory Guidance*.

As the front office started talking about disciplinary action, I dusted off my resignation letter and very nearly sent it, but a wise FSO friend stopped me. Following his good guidance, I found a therapist who supported my application to use Family Medical Leave Act (FMLA) to get out of a tense office situation. This gave me the time I needed to plan my future calmly. I broadcast an SOS message to FSO friends, asking for word of an office with an immediate need. I found such an office. The Office of Global Programs in the Bureau of Democracy, Human Rights, and Labor (DRL/GP) needed a contracting officer's representative (COR) to oversee contracts for the coming year. I was desperate. They were desperate. We shook hands on the deal.

Still, nothing is automatic in the Foreign Service. To get out of the NRRC, I had to submit a request that would be reviewed by a *curtailment panel*, and I knew the NRRC front office would oppose the curtailment. The odds were not in my favor. I had my resignation letter ready to go just in case, and the same wise FSO friend used a back channel to let the *curtail-*

ment panel know I wasn't kidding. The panel met at the end of June and approved my request. By mid-July I had moved to DRL/GP.

This Washington reprise of *The Full Alice* was shorter in duration than the Central Asia version, but what it lacked in length, it made up for in intensity. What do I take away from the reprise?

First, being taken seriously as an intelligent, capable woman at State is as difficult as being taken seriously as a woman anywhere. I don't think anyone in the front office had bothered to read the regular stream of design and user documentation I had been issuing for months. The only people who cared were the watch officers, the ones with the most to gain. Faced with this, I recalled the many talented women engineers and managers I had worked with during my NASA years at CSC. I now have a deeper understanding of the battles they had to fight to rise to leading positions in a male-dominated field.

Second, after my near-rape experience on the ferry in 2017, I realize I am thin-skinned, to put it mildly, when my fate is being decided by men who treat me shabbily, as though I'm not there.

Third, I may not have the fight left to go against an entire bureau that has decided I'm a troublemaker, but I do have the strength to make principled demands. If they are not met, I will not compromise. In this case I had demanded the rolling back or revision of the *Mandatory Guidance*. When it became clear this was not going to happen, I made the decision to leave. With support from colleagues and friends, I did this without resigning outright.

Lastly, living by one's principles does have a price. In my case it was a month of leave without pay while on FMLA. Also, my position in DRL/GP came with a lower salary, but it was lower for a good reason: no 24/7 shift work, 365 days of the year.

Emerging from *The Full Alice*, I left the NRRC with my dignity intact and, I hope, set an example for other women at the State Department. There are times one must stand on principle no matter what the career consequences.

4. Rolling Home

True to the maxim that an FSO generalist can do any job the State Department demands, I had my COR certification within weeks of starting work in DRL/GP. It was not a demanding job, but I threw myself into it. GP is an office of young people, most of them contractors. My job was to make sure their contracts were in order, exercising option years and setting up re-competes as needed. In other words, my job was to see to it they can do their jobs.

Moreover, they all have that *look in their eyes*. They have a passion for defending human rights in all its forms. Trump in the White House or not, they are out to make the world a better place. It is this office that had given the small grant for our transgender roundtable in Astana in 2016.

I automated much of the mechanical aspects of COR work. I had never before programmed in Visual Basic for Applications (VBA), but software is software. VBA is not much different from any other procedural language I had ever programmed in. It felt strangely comforting to finish a career much as I had started, writing software.

I also finished the NRRC automation effort. I hate leaving any project half done. I often stayed late in DRL/GP and came in on weekends. I delivered the final version of *NRRC Cable Express* with full documentation in spring 2019. The new SWO was a watch officer who had been promoted up to the position, and he understood what *NRRC Cable Express* had accomplished even in its beta form. As I approached my final day as an FSO in August 2019, I received many expressions of thanks from watch officers, and that was all the recognition I needed.

On August 31, 2019, on a bicycle loaded with a tent, sleeping bag, and supplies, I rolled out of Washington, D.C., for the last time. My route took me west for a goodbye sojourn at Little Orleans and then onward to Cumberland. Northward I went through Pittsburgh to Lake Erie and onward to Niagara Falls, the Adirondacks of New York, the Green Mountains of Vermont, and the Whites of New Hampshire. On October 2, I rolled into my own driveway in rural Penobscot County, Maine, in time to watch my maple tree turn to full fall colors. On October 19, I sat and watched as the sun and its last rays slipped below the horizon, leaving behind patterns of red between tree leaves and branches, suggestive of Japanese lanterns marking day's end. As I watched, I saw them as the lanterns that have illuminated my life ... and decided there was a story to be told.

Arrival home to Maine

Afterword: Queer Diplomacy

I began this memoir by stating a simple purpose: *to inspire other transgender Americans who wish to serve their country in diplomacy.* If my personal story has convinced even one transgender or gender-conforming American to pursue a life in foreign affairs, I have succeeded.

I also posed three questions:

1. How does a transgender person represent the U.S. government in the countries where she/he/they is/are posted?

2. Is a gender non-conforming person able to influence U.S. policy in ways that a cisgender person is not?

3. How does being a diplomat affect the personal life of someone who is gender non-conforming?

On the surface, the answer to the first question is simple. A mid-level transgender FSO represents the U.S. no differently than any other mid-level FSO. We are diplomatic foot soldiers whose job is to advance and implement policies that have been developed in Washington.

Below the surface, however, there is nuance to this answer. If the FSO is openly *out* as transgender, there is value added. The transgender communities in the countries where I was posted are repressed. They are largely underground, deprived of education and work, and they are presented as lewd caricatures in the popular culture. An openly transgender FSO advances transgender rights by the simple fact of existing. That was brought home to me most vividly in my encounter with the young Uzbek MFA official during my travel to the Aral Sea water conference in 2014. In all of my meetings with host government officials, my very existence may have been a first step in dispelling stereotypes.

How about influencing U.S. policy? Again, the surface answer is simple. Mid-level diplomatic foot soldiers may influence U.S. policy through their reporting, but they do not have a direct say in formulating policy. During my years in the Foreign Service, I came to understand that one has to rise to the level of ambassador to get an entry-level seat at the policy-formulation table.

Again, however, the answer has nuance for a transgender FSO. Even among the local LES staff at our embassies, there sometimes is the sense that the U.S. spouts beautiful words about human rights but that these are only words, not something truly to be believed. The very existence of a transgender FSO proves that the U.S. not only *talks the talk*. It also *walks the walk*. When a transgender FSO is advancing a Washington issue or policy, there is value added in that the FSO is, in effect, carrying an unspoken but perceptible transgender flag.

The first two questions are not unique to transgender FSOs. They have applied and continue to apply to all visible minority groups in an organization historically derided as *pale, male, and Yale*. When I joined the Foreign Service in 2004, all three of those adjectives applied to me. In the years following my transition, the second adjective flipped to *female*, and I got a sense of what it is to be discounted because of my gender. Although I continued to serve in responsible positions after transition, I am fully conscious that my rapid advancement in 2004–07 might have been due not only to my proven capabilities and achievements. The privilege that comes with being *pale, male, and Yale* may have played an unspoken role. I did not know I had that privilege until it was, in part, stripped away. In its place I now have the greater privilege of understanding what Black, women, and other minority FSOs have known throughout their careers.

How about my final question? How does being a diplomat affect the personal life of someone who is gender non-conforming? Here my answer, like the question, is deeply personal based on my own circumstances as a transgender woman who transitioned later in life. I believe my lifestyle post-transition sets me apart.

In short, *I went native*. Olympia in Romania and Meruert, Natasha, and Sultana in Kazakhstan are my emotionally adopted daughters. These relationships are for the long term, not just for my time overseas. I may have opened my door to them in the literal sense of bringing them under my roof, but they opened the door into their lives. That comes with a responsibility that I do not take lightly. Also, I have not forgotten Sophia and Tamara in Uzbekistan. They may be on the other side of the world from me today, but I feel that they are all in the next room. We will be in each other's lives until the end of my days.

It is with my overseas family that I end my story. During my years in the

Foreign Service, I had a wild ride—and the privilege—of representing my government on issues as varied as nuclear energy, climate change, and human rights. Yet in the end, this is not where I had my greatest influence. That came not in carrying forward the policies of official Washington. It came in the personal. As Sultana has reminded me again and again, I did not fail her in 2017. Rather, she says, I changed her life in ways she never could have imagined before she met me.

To all my readers, in particular to other transgender Americans, that is my closing message. The greatest influence you will have in the Foreign Service is not in official acts but in the lives of the people who enter your life and allow you into theirs. You may not always know how you have touched the lives of others, but act always with love and caring. Do this and you may be enriched in ways no government award will ever be able to capture.

Burlington, Maine
March 2020

Epilogue—Where Are They Today?

I finished the first draft of this memoir in early 2020, and some readers may wonder what has happened since then in my life and in the lives of the people who have played a big role in my story. I will oblige with a brief update.

The world has not been a calm place since I retired in 2019. First there was the worldwide COVID-19 pandemic. I had planned to go back to Romania and Kazakhstan in the first half of 2020, but the pandemic made that impossible. 2021 came, and still there could be no thought of international travel.

Instead, I became a long-distance bike-packer. After all, what could be more socially distant than riding a bicycle six or more hours each day and then camping? Also, my life path was such that I had seen more geographically in the former Soviet Union than I had in my own country. It was time to discover North America.

I have now crossed the country twice, from Maine to Washington state in 2020 and from Virginia to Oregon in 2021. In 2022 I flew with my bicycle to Deadhorse on the Arctic Ocean in Alaska. From there I made my way south on the Dalton Highway to Fairbanks and then onward through Canada to an end point in Montana. My motto at age sixty-eight is that the more I move, the longer I'll keep moving.[115]

I am also out and involved as a volunteer. I serve on the advisory committee for Equality Maine's network for older LGBT+ adults, and I am on the board for an environmental NGO headed by a colleague I worked with in Kazakhstan.

All four of my sisters are still living, although two of them have been stricken by Parkinson's disease. My sister Irene is still my closest confidante and, at age 82, is socially and physically active, the epitome of health that I aspire to be at her age.

John and I are still together. It's a long-distance relationship, but we see each other frequently. He's my younger guy and has a year to go before he

---

115 See my web journal *Alice in and out of State* (https://attitude-maneuver.blogspot.com) for more on my bike-packing adventures.

retires. He has become a regular at the family reunions with my sisters, and we spent Christmas Eve 2022 with his family, an evening that included his ex-wife and her partner. Alas, Helena has refused all contact from me, but Matt maintains good relations with both of us. My granddaughter is now eight years old, and I'm her *grandma Robyn*.

Approaching the Brooks Range in Alaska, June 2022

With John on Maryland Heights in October 2022

Olympia has had the hardest time. No longer able to make ends meet on her dwindling income as an online sex performer, she had to leave Bucharest. She now lives with her parents, who are paying for her to attend nursing school. This help came with a condition: she must become Octavian again. She dreams of the day when she can go to western Europe with a nursing certificate and live her life as herself.

Meruert is now working on her PhD in tribology, an engineering discipline that I have gotten a sense of by proofreading her English-language articles for international journals.

With Meruert in December 2022

Natasha continues to live in Pavlodar where she cares for her father and is starting a catering business. She instructs me by video on kitchen recipes and, most recently, on the fine art of coloring my hair with henna at home.

Sultana moved to Almaty where she has been working as a researcher in several different projects related to diversity and LGBT+ issues. In these she has worked closely with project organizers at Columbia University and in the German Goethe Institute. Now an international traveler, she has represented Kazakhstan at conferences in Estonia and Armenia. In late 2017, she was able to change the gender marker in her passport, one of the few transgender persons who has successfully gone through this laborious process in Kazakhstan. She also has a sideline doing video voice-overs in English and Russian. I think her English may be better than mine.

The pandemic meant that throughout 2020 and 2021, my communication with Sultana, Natasha, Meruert, and Olympia could only be on Zoom, WhatsApp, and Telegram. When 2022 dawned, I thought I could travel to see them in person at last. Street disorders in Kazakhstan that January put off travel yet again. Sultana and I thought we might instead meet in a third country where both she and I could travel without visas. We chose Ukraine and started planning to meet in Kyiv in March. Russia's invasion put an end to that idea.

So much of my life has revolved around Russia, and now I wonder if I will ever be able to return there in the years left to me. After the invasion, I worked with an on-line volunteer group assisting Ukrainian refugees. When I bike-packed from Alaska to Montana in summer 2022, I collected donations for the independent Russian journalists at *ТВ Дождь (TV Rain)*. Despite my horror over Russia's war and the atrocities it has committed in Ukraine, my love affair with the language and culture continues. I stream independent Russian-language radio, videos, and podcasts—often shadowing the words out loud to keep the linguistic brain-mouth connection intact.

In December 2022, I was finally able to fly back to Romania and to Kazakhstan with a quick side trip to Uzbekistan. After more than three years of COVID, street disorders, and war, I went home. Sultana was there waiting for me when I passed through passport control in Almaty. Our tears flowed as we hugged, but these were now tears of joy. My visit was a brief one, all of four weeks, but this was only the beginning. There will be more and longer visits to come. This is family, and the love of family and friends is what life is all about. Or as Jan Morris has written, there is a Fourth World, a diaspora without borders, an ageless nation of nowhere where "Kindness is what matters, all along, at any age—kindness, the ruling principle of nowhere."[116]

Burlington, Maine
February 2023

---

116 Jan Morris, *Trieste and the Meaning of Nowhere* (Simon and Schuster, 2001).

With Sultana and Natasha in December 2022

Acknowledgments

Remember old friends we made along the way
The gifts they gave that stay with us every day.[117]

This work has been over three years in the making since my retirement in September 2019 and the onset of the COVID-19 pandemic. It has also, in a sense, been the work of a lifetime.

I never could have succeeded on this path in life without the constant love and support of my sisters Gail, Irene, Chris, and Mary. I never could have walked this road without the acceptance of my son Matt, my most wonderful *Guy*.

Without Duane Butcher at the helm at Embassy Bucharest in 2011, my transition overseas could have been a fiasco. My friend Natalie Koza was scarcely a step behind him, and she also took on the Herculean task of rebuilding my State Department personnel folder to reflect my post-transition name and gender. Curtis Presson patiently guided our IT section and the local staff all through my transition. Most of all, I would not be writing these words if not for Kyna's support and encouragement when I first came out to her. Thanks also go to Peter Chordas, Kyna's successor, who kept close tabs on my medical condition all through my Thailand sojourn.

I owe a debt to my LGBT+ predecessors. If a few gay FSOs had not stood up and founded glifaa in the early 1990s, how much longer might it have taken for the Department of State to change its policies on gay and lesbian officers? Chloe Schwenke paved the road for me. She lost her job in 2008 so that I did not have to lose mine in 2011. It is thanks to her and the glifaa boards of that time that Secretary Clinton added gender identity to State Department non-discrimination policies. Shannon Doyle and her wife Mary became my role models on the path to a new life.

I express deep thanks to Chris Hoh, Jay Gilliam, Selim Ariturk, Regina Jun, and all members of the glifaa board of 2013–14; we achieved far more than we thought possible when we held our first retreat in September 2013. Thanks go to Ken Kero-Mentz, my predecessor as glifaa president who pushed me forward to take on the role.

---

117 McCaslin, Mary. "Old Friends." Lyrics Translate. Accessed September 10, 2023. https://lyricstranslate.com/en/mary-mccaslin-old-friends-lyrics.html.

Where would I be without friends who saw me through so many transitions in my life? Mike Korolenko, Chuck Taylor, Ron Enders, and Ellen Bouton—thank you for being there at key moments. Vika and Zhenya Izvarin, thank you for keeping me fed in the Leningrad winter of 1987–88 and for being a part of my life to this day. Alina Eremeeva, who is still going strong in her 90s and recently published a biography of Boris Gerasimovich, has been a guiding light of perseverance in the face of injustice.

To Mary Galloway and all our team on the Hubble PASS and MSRE projects, wasn't it a time? You taught me what we could accomplish using our imaginations and working as a team. To Allen Greenberg, thank you for keeping me sane during my year on the *Russia Desk*. If not for you, I would have gone running back to NASA.

Marzhan, Guzal, Bakhtiyor, Vera, Lynne, and Aron—without you I couldn't have been *Hubster* or an LGBT+ activist in Central Asia. What we accomplished, we accomplished together.

To Sasha, Patrick, Iulia Molnar, Irina Nita, and Tudor Kovacs, thank you for accepting me into the LGBT+ community in Romania and for continuing your activism to bring Romania closer to EU norms of acceptance. To Olympia, your mom will never forget you and is here for you.

To Sultana, Natasha, and Meruert—you are my family in Kazakhstan. I love you beyond words and will be coming back soon.

To John, the man in my life—you kept me lucid, smiling, and supplied with chocolate all through writing, re-writing, editing, and re-editing this manuscript.

To my independent editor Jay Blotcher and to Lisa Terry, Margery Thompson, and Mark Tauber at the Association for Diplomatic Studies and Training (ADST)—without your patient guidance and encouragement my story would have remained an unpublished manuscript. My thanks go also to Rahima Schwenkbeck and the entire crew at Westphalia Press for taking the manuscript through to this finished product. Finally, honors go to Intero, my artist friend in Astana, Kazakhstan, for the beautiful cover design.

Acronyms and Abbreviations

A/RSO	assistant regional security officer
AAAS	American Association for the Advancement of Science
ADST	Association for Diplomatic Studies and Training
ABC	annual bilateral consultations
AFSA	American Foreign Service Association
AFSPA	American Foreign Service Protective Association
BIPM	International Bureau of Weights and Measures
CAA	controlled access area
CDO	career development officer
COR	contracting officer's representative
CSC	Computer Sciences Corporation
DAS	deputy assistant secretary
DADT	Don't ask, don't tell
DCM	deputy chief of mission
DOE	Department of Energy
DOMA	Defense of Marriage Act
DRL/GP	Office of Global Programs in the Department of State Bureau of Democracy, Human Rights, and Labor
DS	Diplomatic Security
EEO	equal employment opportunity
EST	environment, science, and technology
ESTH	environment, science, technology, and health
EUR/RUS	Office of Russian Affairs in the Department of State Bureau of European and Eurasian Affairs, commonly referred to as The Russia Desk

FEHB	federal employee health benefits
FFS	facial feminization surgery
FHST	fixed head star tracker
FMLA	Family Medical Leave Act
FS	Foreign Service
FSBP	Foreign Service Benefit Plan
FSI	Foreign Service Institute
FSN	Foreign Service National
FSO	Foreign Service Officer
GCS	gender confirmation surgery
GIZ	German Agency for International Cooperation
GLIFAA	Gays and Lesbians in Foreign Affairs Agencies. This was the name of the foreign affairs LGBT+ association through 2014. Since 2014 the name has been "glifaa, lgbt+ pride in foreign affairs agencies," with glifaa in lower case to emphasize that it is not an acronym.
GPWG	Global Partnership Working Group
GSFC	Goddard Space Flight Center
GTC	gender transition committee
HEU	highly enriched uranium
HHE	household effects
HR	human resources
HRC	Human Rights Campaign
HRT	hormone replacement therapy
HST	Hubble Space Telescope
ICU	intensive care unit

IDAHOT	International Day Against Homophobia and Transphobia
IELTS	International English Language Testing System
IESH	Institute of Environmental and Social Health
IKI	Institut kosmicheskikh issledovanii (Space Research Institute)
IRCHAD	International Relations Committee of the Historical Astronomy Division of the American Astronomical Society
IREX	International Research and Exchanges Board
ISS	International Space Station
ISTC	International Science and Technology Center
IT	Information Technology
LES	locally employed staff
LEU	lowly enriched uranium
LGBT	lesbian, gay, bisexual, and transgender
MFA	Ministry of Foreign Affairs
MOH	member of household
NASA	National Aeronautics and Space Administration
NCTE	National Center for Transgender Equality
NEC	new embassy compound
NGO	non-governmental organization
NIST	National Institute of Standards and Technology
NIV	non-immigrant visa
NMI	national metrology institute
NRRC	Nuclear Risk Reduction Center in the State Department

	Bureau of Arms Control, Verification and Compliance
NTI	Nuclear Threat Initiative
OES	State Department Bureau of Oceans and International Environmental and Scientific Affairs
OIML	Organization of Legal Metrology
OPM	Office of Personnel Management
PASS	POCC Applications Software Support
PDAS	principal deputy assistant secretary
PIH	Phuket International Hospital
POCC	Payload Operations Control Center
Ps & Is	privileges and immunities
R&R	rest and relaxation
RSO	regional security officer
SAA	scientific affairs assistant
SAS	scientific affairs specialist
SCA	State Department Bureau of South and Central Asia
SFS	Senior Foreign Service
SI	International System of Units
SMART	State Department Messaging and Archive Retrieval Toolset
SSDP	same-sex domestic partners
SWO	senior watch officer
SWT	summer work and travel
TDOR	Transgender Day of Remembrance (November 20)
TIFA	Trade and Infrastructure Framework Agreement

U/S	undersecretary
UAB	unaccompanied air baggage
USGS	U.S. Geological Survey
UTC	Coordinated Universal Time
VBA	Visual Basic for Applications
WRS	work requirements statement

Appendix 1

Excerpt from September 2013 glifaa White Paper on Eliminating the Transgender Exclusion

All FEHB health policies include clauses that specifically exclude coverage of transgender-related health care. For example, the 2013 brochure for the Foreign Service Benefit Plan (FSBP) includes the following in *Section 6 — General exclusions — Things we don't cover:*

Services, drugs, or supplies related to impotency, gender reassignment, sex transformations, sexual dysfunction, or sexual inadequacy.

All FEHB health plans include similar exclusionary clauses. This exclusion denies medically necessary coverage of procedures and services to transgender employees who are going through gender transition. In many cases, the services being denied to transgender employees—such as estrogen or testosterone medications, hysterectomies, or mastectomies—are regularly being provided for non-transgender employees. Only a small percentage of glifaa's membership identifies as transgender, and a smaller fraction still will be prescribed medical treatments for gender transition. Thus, this transgender exclusion stands out by its harshness at a time when gender identity is included as a protected category in the Department of State's *Statement on Discriminatory and Sexual Harassment and EEO Policy.* Moreover, the Equal Employment Opportunity Commission has found that discrimination based on gender identity or presentation is, in fact, sex discrimination subject to all the remedies called for in Title VII of the Civil Rights Act of 1964.

APPENDIX 2

Excerpt from Secretary of State John Kerry's Pride Remarks[118]

SECRETARY KERRY: Robyn, thank you very, very much. Thank you to all of you. Welcome to this celebration of pride here at State, and I'm very, very honored to have a chance to be able to talk with everybody. And thank you especially for putting up with my tardiness, which is not my fault. Blame Iraq and—(laughter)—a few other places. But I'm really delighted to be here. Robyn's leadership is terrific, and Robyn works very, very closely with all of us on the Seventh floor. I could list any number of her accomplishments during her tenure, but let me just share two very quickly.

Her advocacy and partnership with OPM and with Under Secretary Kennedy—where is he? Somewhere here. Right in front of me. (Laughter.) Well, Pat, thank you very much. That advocacy made an enormous difference, and through it, she helped to lift the exclusionary ban that prevented insurance companies from providing coverage for medical needs to gender transition. And she's also made it her mission to ensure that our employees overseas can be accompanied by their families, and I think very few people have cared more, done more, or fought more to make that happen. So Robyn, thank you for your leadership. I really appreciate it. (Applause.)

I have to add something else. Robyn is the first transgender Foreign Service Officer to come out on the job, and believe me it wasn't easy. I think everybody here knows that. When she was posted in Bucharest, she faced a lot of prejudice, she had to deal with completely inappropriate judgments that people were making, questions about her abilities, but she didn't just persevere. In the end, she won the hearts of the Ambassador, her career Foreign Service colleagues, Civil Service colleagues, and the local staff, and she actually made Embassy Bucharest a model of acceptance. She even authored the first State Department report on transgender issues, and she didn't just get through a difficult period, she was determined

---

118 Secretary Kerry delivered his remarks on June 19, 2014, in the Ben Franklin Room at the Department of State to a standing room only crowd. Robyn McCutcheon served as moderator in her capacity as president of glifaa. Human rights activist Masha Gessen also participated and delivered remarks.

to turn it into a precedent-setting event, and as a result she made it a lot easier for those—or at least a little easier for those who follow. And I can't begin to tell you and I think everybody here knows what a difference that has made.

I also want to thank our guest of honor, Masha Gessen, for her own special perseverance and advocacy. When all the repressive anti-LGBT laws in Russia threatened literally to break apart her family, she put up a fight. Fearlessly, she spoke out on Russia's only independent television channel, and her Pink Triangle Campaign, which everybody became familiar with, unleashed a wave of grassroots activism. And the government in Moscow may look at Masha as a troublemaker to contend with, but here in the United States, we know that she is a wonderful person—a mother, a journalist, an extraordinary human rights defender—and we are honored by her presence here. Thank you for being here. (Applause.)

Now I know that all of us right now are more than aware of—we can palpably feel the wave of new, growing—the trend if you will, in some places for anti-LGBT laws that are metastasizing in various places. And for some it's, obviously, easy to get alarmed by that. But let me just share this with you: I don't think it's time to get alarmed. I think it's time to get active. Because your activism and your energy and your pushback—it won't be the first time you've pushed back—can make all the difference in the world for a lot of people. And if anybody doesn't believe that, just take a look at the recent history that we've all lived through here.

I came to the Senate in 1985. It was a time when AIDS was pilloried as a "gay disease." And somehow that may have been deemed to give some people the permission to ignore it. I remember just a few years later, I testified before Strom Thurmond's Armed Services Committee at an open hearing to speak out as a combat veteran about why gays ought to be allowed to serve openly in the military, and I ran into a world of misperceptions. Three years after that, I was the only United States Senator, as Robyn mentioned, to vote against DOMA.

Now—only one who was running for reelection—there were fourteen of us. Only fourteen who voted against it. Today, that would never pass. That is an amazing journey. That's a statement about how far we have come. Don't Ask, Don't Tell is repealed. LGBT Americans who are willing to die for their country are today allowed to fight for their country. And we've gone from a Senate that passed DOMA over my objections to one that recently welcomed its first openly lesbian United States Senator.

We've gone from a Senate where AIDS was a forbidden topic, to one where we were able to finally get Jesse Helms to join us in unanimously passing the first anti–AIDS legislation. And subsequently now, PEPFAR is in its eleventh year, and we stand on the brink of an AIDS-free generation. And I am proud to be the first sitting Secretary of State to support same-sex marriage working for the first President of the United States to support same-sex marriage.

So all of us in this room are pretty well aware of the debt that we owe to those who came before us, and whether it is those who stood up after Stonewall or incredible, inspiring visionaries like Harvey Milk. And I'm proud to follow in the footsteps of an extraordinary advocate for the cause. When Hillary Clinton gave that speech in front of the Human Rights Council in Geneva and said five simple words, "Gay rights are human rights," she transformed the debate. And standing here with Robyn, I want to build on that legacy, because LGBT rights are human rights, and human rights are LGBT rights.

The State Department, I'm proud to say, has always been at the forefront of equality in the federal government. And that's why I was proud to announce during my visit to London last year that we were tearing down an unjust and unfair barrier that for far too long stood in the way of same-sex families traveling together to the United States. And I was personally honored to hand over the first visa within two months of the Supreme Court's historic Windsor decision.

I am proud that we worked with glifaa and Pat Kennedy to press OPM to remove its exclusionary language from health insurance plans so that employees who have undergone a gender transition can get the health care that they need. And that's what it means to fight and that's what it means to win in a battle that we all know matters enormously, not as a matter of making these things a privilege, but to make sure that they are, in fact, a right.

So I am very proud of the progress that we are now making even in appointing LGBT ambassadors. I worked with the committee here at the State Department—with the D Committee, and I worked with the White House. And as a result, Ted Osius, sitting here, whom I've known a long time, and his family I know, will be the first openly LGBT officer nominated to serve as an ambassador in Asia. And on confirmation, he's going to join five openly gay ambassadors who are now serving their country. I'm working hard to ensure that by the end of my tenure, we will have lesbian, bisexual, and transgender ambassadors in our ranks as well.

Now, I see the possibilities for the simple reason that we now have hundreds of LGBT individuals in our bureaus at State, USAID, and at Posts all around the world. Foreign Service Officers like Lucia Piazza—where is Lucia? Somewhere—is she here? Not here right now. But she's here in Washington. Kerri Hannan in Buenos Aires. Michelle Schohn and her wife, Mary Glantz, in Tallinn. And the wonderful thing about this is nobody looks at these folks when they're out there and says, "Wow. That's a great LGBT diplomat." They look at them and say, "Those are great diplomats." And that's exactly how we make progress in this fight.

Now, we also know that none of this progress would have been possible without the courage and the creativity and innovation and effort of organizations like glifaa. And it's an amazing journey. I have to tell you, I have very, very good friends in the LGBT/gay community throughout the country, particularly. One of them, David Mixner, who I knew for a long time—I met him way back when we were—you may know him as a strong advocate, but we met years ago in the anti-war movement—well before he came out. And I remember him lamenting to me on the telephone once, years ago, how difficult it was and how he was going to funeral after funeral after funeral during a period when nobody was paying attention to AIDS.

So I know this journey and know it through friends, and I think back then there were a lot of meetings of people in secret rooms. People knew that if they opened up about who they were in glifaa, it would be shut down, their careers would be destroyed. But even then, there were people who stood up and fought, and people like AFSA, helpers like AFSA, and especially Sharon Papp—who has stood with our LGBT brothers and sisters since the beginning and who is standing with us today.

So we have come a long way at home, but everybody here knows there's a cloud hanging over this journey right now. We have a long, long way to go in the world. I won't go into the details of a couple of conversations I've had with presidents of countries trying to move them on their current laws.

From Uganda to Russia to Iran, LGBT communities face discriminatory laws and practices that attack dignity, undermine safety, and violate human rights. And we each have a responsibility to push back against a global trend of rising violence and discrimination against LGBT persons. Maybe all the success we've had here, we sort of felt, oh, gosh, it's got to be happening everywhere else. But it hasn't been. It'll come. It's going to take a while, and it's going to take courage and patience, stamina in order to continue the fight. Because we need to make certain that we make it clear to people everywhere that there is a fundamental truth—Anti-LGBT violence anywhere is a threat to peace and stability and prosperity everywhere.

That's why across the globe—Asia, Africa, Europe, and the Americas—our diplomats are supporting local LGBT organizations and human rights advocates. They're one and the same. And through the Global Equality Fund, the State Department has provided critical emergency and long-term assistance to promote and protect the human rights of LGBT persons in more than twenty-five countries. I'm proud that we've opened up the fund to corporate donations, and I want to urge our friends in the business community to step up their contributions to this cause. I was especially proud to speak at the first-ever ministerial on LGBT issues at the UN General Assembly last year, and I look forward to continuing to engage on this issue at the UN and other international fora.

So we are leading by example here. We are recognizing marriages for foreign diplomats who are assigned to the United States. Our Consular Affairs Bureau is implementing language on diplomatic passports to make sure we treat all spouses equally. Consular Affairs has also moved swiftly with other federal agencies to update our regulations after DOMA was struck down last year, and we're now considering all visa applications made by same-sex spouses in the same manner as those made by opposite-sex spouses.

So let me be clear: We oppose any effort by any country to deny visas for spouses of American staff. It's discriminatory, it's unacceptable, it has no place in the twenty-first century. And I understand how challenging this issue is for all of you, which is why I've sent instructions to ambassadors at Posts worldwide to engage at the highest levels on your behalf. Together we pay a price when these rights are trampled on, but together we win when these rights are protected.

One thing is clear: Making our shared vision a reality will require both the persistent protection of governments, as well as the active participation of citizens. I will never forget standing on the Capitol steps in October of 1998 when thousands gathered on a cool autumn evening, and we were there to remember Matthew Shepard two days after he'd been killed in Laramie, Wyoming. And as we gathered in the city of monuments, I posed a question: Is there a lesson that can become a monument to Matthew Shepard and to so many others who suffer because of the intolerance and prejudice of so few?

Matthew's mother, Judy, later provided us an answer. As she struggled to make sense of a question that only God can answer, she said loving one another doesn't mean that we have to compromise our beliefs. It simply means that we choose to be compassionate and respectful of others. In her life and in her work, Judy hasn't just spoken words about compassion and respect. She has lived them. And I'm proud that she's partnering with the State Department to speak out on these issues around the world. She is an example that reminds us, we each have a responsibility to speak out loudly and clearly, and we each have to choose – and it is a choice – to be compassionate and respectful of others. And as Secretary of State, I am very proud of the choice that our country has been making these past years.

We're here today to send a message: No matter where you are, no matter who you love, we stand with you. And that's what pride means, and that's what drives us today. The journey isn't complete, the march isn't over, the promise isn't perfected. But we will march on together. Thank you all. (Applause.)

ROBYN: Secretary Kerry, thank you for those words. I think I speak for many people in this room that I wanted to interrupt with applause a number of times. (Laughter.) If you can bear with us for just a few more minutes —

SECRETARY KERRY: So what the Hell's the matter with you? (Laughter.) I'm joking. (Laughter.)

ROBYN: I've got two questions that were submitted to us by glifaa members from around the world, and I'd like to pose them to you. The first question—I'll just read it out, and reading it, I'm realizing I think you answered much of it already. But let me read it to you, in any case:

"Mr. Secretary, we've seen so much progress here at home, but I have to tell you that for us in glifaa, in many ways we're feeling even more squeezed. All of us want to succeed, but the list of countries where we can serve is growing shorter and shorter. Countries that used to quietly give visas to our family members or our friends are now being asked for visas for our spouses, and that term is causing a knee-jerk reaction in many countries."

This one member writes, "I personally counted all the jobs on my bid list, and I had to cross off 68 percent of them just because I'm gay and that country will not give a visa to my partner. We need your support, and we need the Department to do something more. So as much as we all want to succeed, this is a serious obstacle that is hurting us in our careers and hurting our families. How does the Department plan to address this?"

SECRETARY KERRY: Well, thanks, Robyn. We are addressing it, I think you know. I think I spoke to that fairly—I made it pretty clear during the course of my comments. But look, we are instructing embassies to inform governments locally that this is our policy and that they need to honor our policy. It's that simple. And a lot of governments will respond positively; obviously, some won't. And where they don't, if they don't extend recognition and immunities, we're going to instruct them that we're also going to begin gathering information on the host government policies and practices on accreditation. And we will make this information that is relevant to assignments—make it easier for employees and all of you to sort of pick and choose and know what the lay of the land is.

But at some point in time, we may have to begin to make it clear to them that that can affect one program or another or the choices that we make. It's not going to be a normal relationship. This is who we are, this is what you have to respect, and that's the way it is. And we'll see how it goes as we collect this information and what the lay of the land is on that, but that 68 percent is daunting. And for—in one particular case, it doesn't mean it's across the board. But we've got to take a look at it, and we will push back. That's the bottom line. (Applause.)

ROBYN: Mr. Secretary, I know you've given great hope to our members with that statement. Our second question:

"Mr. Secretary, we hear so much about the difficulties

faced by transgender persons around the globe. In so many countries, transgender persons are denied documents that reflect the gender in which they live their daily lives. And as a result, they are denied basic services, jobs, access to medicine, and too often they feel forced into sex work because they see no other choice. What is the Department doing to support the human rights of transgender persons?"

SECRETARY KERRY: Well again, this part of what I said. It's really related to the first question also in many ways. It's part and parcel of the same response in places. We have instructed our posts to report on and perform outreach to transgender communities in countries. In addition, we have instructed our human rights and health officers to raise transgender issues in their host countries, and we have encouraged our public affairs officers to include the needs of transgender groups in their programming, so that we are showing that this is something that we're going to engage in. And we're supporting civil society organizations that increase the protection of transgender persons who face the potential of acute violence.

So we're taking steps specifically with respect to communities and with respect to the treatment of our folks. Again, it's going to be clear, and it is clear they need to make sure that they're not discriminated against, and that our people expect—we expect, our nation expects that all of our people will be afforded the full measure of human rights that we afford them here in our country. And as time goes on now, we'll accrue more and more information. We'll have a better sense of who's doing what, where the real trouble spots are and why. And we'll be able to begin to build a policy of response to that over a period of time as we get a better sense, and hopefully isolate those people for those policies —hopefully, first, actually, break through and get them to simply change without—just as a matter of a reasonable conversation and an understanding.

But if it's more entrenched and more broadly pervasive and damaging to our functioning in the way that we function, then we're going to have to consider what the options are with respect to actions that we'll take. And that's something that will evolve over the course of the next year or two, and we'll see where we are. But we're not going to sit around and permit what we have fought for so hard to be undone. And as I said earlier, LGBT rights are human rights and human rights are LGBT rights, so we will protect them, period. (Applause.)

I was just given my instructions. I was being told I have to go. (Laughter.) I'm sorry. Thank you all, and Happy Pride Day. Thanks. (Applause.)

ROBYN: Secretary Kerry, thank you.

APPENDIX 3

Moscow Diary Excerpts, 2005–07

Friday, November 11, 2005—On Wednesday I got out of the embassy for a few hours for a fishing conference and exhibition at VVTs,[119] the former VDNKh[120] for those who remember Soviet days. I first visited VDNKh in 1981 when I went to the neighboring Sputnik Hotel to meet up with astronomers from the U.S. Naval Observatory who were in the Soviet Union for that summer's total solar eclipse. I remember walking around VDNKh, the Soviet Union's equivalent of a permanent World's Fair, and spending hours going through the Cosmonautics and other science pavilions.

The VVTs of today is only the faintest shadow of VDNKh. Most of the pavilions—including the Cosmonautics pavilion—have been turned over to commercial firms, and some of them are now nothing more than warehouses. Only a handful of pavilions have retained their original function, and the fishing exhibit and conference are taking place in one of those few, Pavilion 69 in an isolated corner of the once grand VDNKh.

The sun already down, I took a good walk around this lonely relic of VDNKh at the end of the day. I felt as though I were in a Twilight Zone episode. The monuments to socialist labor still stand. They are dirty, uncared for, but they still stand. The fountains are dry, but I remember when they flowed, the polished statues reflecting in their waters. The Academy of Sciences pavilion that once housed the space exhibit is now a garden supply store. The loudspeakers that played patriotic Soviet music now play Russian top-10 hits punctuated by advertisements. At any moment I expected Rod Serling, or a Russian version of him, to step out of the shadows. At that point I thought yet again that despite my "Alice in Wonderland" feeling at the State Dept., what a wonderful time this is to watch what history has done—and is still doing—in Russia.

Sunday, November 13, 2005—Gray, gray, gray. There has been no rain these past two days, but neither has there been sun. With a cloud-filled sky and the sun being above the horizon for just over eight hours, even at mid-day all one sees is gray, gray, and gray.

---

119 All-Russian Exhibition Center

120 Exhibition of Achievements of the National Economy

Today I again took on the world on my own terms by heading out on the bike for almost exactly three hours. I made my way about ten miles through city streets to the *Krylatskaya trassa dlya velosipedistov*—i.e., bike path on Krylatskiye kholmy (Winged Hills). I had heard of this *bike path* from the driver who took me to VDNKh last Wednesday, and he had told me there was no way to get there other than by *car*. That was sufficient challenge for me to bike there. In fact, I hardly rode on the path itself. I got to it, rode perhaps a km on it, and then made my way back home through a different series of city streets. Overall, I rode for twenty-five miles. My frequent stops to consult my map kept the mileage down.

Tuesday, November 15, 2005—After two weeks I am finally not a total stranger in EST. I suppose I am able to adjust to anything even if it is getting harder to do so the older I get. As a song by Bruce Cockburn says, "I've had to prove who I am so many times that the magnetic stripe is wearing thin."

This is the week that Putin has chosen to shuffle his cabinet in a major way, probably the first step towards establishing the line of succession for the 2008 presidential elections. Putin's shuffle affected even my small, temporary realm, as Rumyantsev was removed as head of Rosatom and replaced by Kiriyenko. That was the subject of today's rush cable to D.C.

Much of the later afternoon was taken up by being control officer for a delegation led by Paul Simon, Deputy Assistant Secretary of State for Energy, Sanctions, and Commodities. They are in town for a diamond conference. It was nice to be out of our too quiet tower for a few hours.

Friday, November 18, 2005—I have survived the week and actually feel reasonably good to have done so. I just threw myself into today's task at hand—a cable on tuberculosis and a video conference on Iran that was suddenly scheduled for Monday—and managed to lose track of time. Before I knew it, it was 7:30 p.m. I headed downstairs with one of my EST colleagues and was happy to find that this was Papa John's pizza night at the embassy. I wouldn't say that three slices of pizza and a large Baltika beer made all my doubts disappear, but at least they moved onto the back burner for the night. I even overheard a couple of complimentary phrases during the day, so at least I feel reasonably confident that I will leave EST at the end of the month without letting anyone down. As I walked home,

I looked up at the sky . . . and actually saw the sky for the first time in two weeks. The stars were out, and Mars was shining brightly.

Tomorrow is Matt's seventeenth birthday. So for me it's early to bed tonight so that I can get up at 8:00 a.m., call home, and wish him happy birthday at midnight D.C. time. Such is life across the time zones.

Tuesday, November 22, 2005—Today was the forty-second anniversary of the assassination of President Kennedy. The thought crossed my mind in the morning, but I wasn't sure and it wasn't until late afternoon that I thought to check. When I confirmed the date and remarked on it, I realized that perhaps only half of the EST office had been born on that date in 1963. I was dimly aware of a place called the Soviet Union when I returned home early from fourth grade that day, but could I ever have imagined that I would live through the collapse of that country and would one day live and work in Moscow?

Saturday, December 3, 2005—The first day back in Consular was uneventful. I doubt that I will ever be fast with my interviews, however. If anything, my Russian works against me. I enjoy talking and get into long conversations. One of my colleagues, whose Russian is at a very basic level, goes through interviews at least three times faster for the reason that he can't move beyond simple questions and answers.

On Thursday night I went out with Tatyana and her friends to a performance of *Grezy (Грёзы) —Daydreams*—an eighty-minute concert-fantasy based on the songs of Robert Schumann and Franz Schubert. Once again Tatyana expanded my horizons by choosing a performance I never would have dreamed of going to on my own. It was a wonderful performance and a wonderful evening.

And now, Saturday, the moment of truth has come: Ambartsumian. Today I roll up my sleeves and start, finally, to work on my biography of Viktor Ambartsumian for the *Dictionary of Scientific Biography*.

And did I ever mention the table of contents that I am working on for Alina? Alina has written a book on the history of meteoritics. The book is in Russian but is to include an English language table of contents for non-Russians who at least want to know what is in the book. Alina asked that I check her English, and several weeks ago I agreed. Unfortunately, the table of contents is sixteen pages long, and in my copious spare time I have only managed to work through eight pages. One way or another, I need to complete that project in the next week in addition to getting a good draft of the Ambartsumian biography under way.

Wednesday, December 14, 2005—The biography is written, Alina's table of contents has been edited, and I am still here. Last weekend was the biggest marathon of writing I have had in a number of years. From the time I came home Friday night until I headed to work on Monday morning, I did not step out of my apartment even once. Neither did I get on my bike for more than a few minutes. The living room is still a mess with piles of paper everywhere. But despite my state of exhaustion Sunday night, I felt a great weight off my shoulders knowing that I had finished what I had set out to do. I'm sure I will need to make some changes before I head to the U.S. for the holidays, but the overwhelming lion's share of the work is done. I celebrated Monday afternoon by declaring myself sick and coming home early and getting a good night's sleep.

The only other event of note over the past week was last Wednesday's concert by *Mashina vremeni* (*Time Machine*), Russia's version of the Beatles that has been singing for at least 30 years now. The timing for this concert was not the best given all I had to do, but I had purchased the tickets a month in advance. Also, although theater in Moscow is quite inexpensive by U.S. standards, popular music concerts are not. A balcony (bel'etazh) ticket cost a full 2000 rubles—about $70. At that price, this was one concert I was not going to miss.

I had good company for the *Mashina vremeni* concert. Inna from our customer service unit joined me for the evening, and we had a wonderful time talking as we walked from the embassy to MXAT Gor'kogo for the concert and then again on the walk back. And so now, in addition to my theater group with Tatyana and her Foreign Service National (FSN) friends, I have another wonderful social contact in Inna.[121] Talking with both Tatyana and Inna, I gather that I am an exception to the rule among Foreign Service Officers. I had already noticed that the Consular Foreign Service Officers eat lunch and socialize together, but our Russian FSNs are hardly ever part of the group. It seems that I broke through a barrier when

---

121 FSN is the old name for what are now called locally employed staff (LES). The name changed during my time as an FSO.

I reached out to the FSNs in my search for theater partners at the end of October.

Saturday, December 17, 2005—To my own surprise, this Saturday has turned out to be one of the best, most memorable days since my arrival in Moscow last September. With marathon writing weekends behind me, I went out today to do Christmas shopping. With some amount of dread, I headed to Izmailovskii Park, where artists and hucksters mix in Moscow's largest outdoor crafts fair. I say *dread* because bargaining for a price is the name of the game, and as a good NE liberal American Democrat, bargaining for price is not one of my strong suits. Thus, I headed to Izmailovskii in near certainty that I was about to be taken for all I am worth. Indeed, when I stopped there after the Intl. Flight Dynamics Seminar in 2003, I overpaid dearly for a fur hat that turned out not to be of the best quality.

I arrived at Izmailovskii with 10,000 rubles (~$400) in my pocket and kept repeating to myself that at least I could not be robbed of more money than I had with me. To my own delight, however, I was able to ignore the hucksters who congregate near the entrance and who do all they can to separate Western tourists from their money. For over three hours on this cold Saturday (~-5 deg C), I wandered through the aisles of stalls where craftsmen and artists have their works on display in great variety. I quickly filled the bicycle pannier that I had brought with me and found myself with a half dozen other plastic bags in my hands by the time I finished. I purchased mainly touristy type items such as matryoshkas, carved Christmas figures, shawls, and lacquer boxes, but I now have enough to take care of most everyone on my Christmas list.

I got into a long conversation with two artists from whom I bought painted wooden eggs with scenes of Russian churches. It turned out that one of them is a physicist who had worked many years at the Kurchatov Institute and at Izmiran, and the other is a cartographer who in Soviet days had worked at the Shternberg Inst. (GAISh). From that point onward I found myself in interesting conversations with almost every craftsman from whom I purchased something, and even though I had some success with bargaining, I found the afternoon so wonderful that I hardly cared that I might not always have managed to get the lowest price.

A women's choir was singing somewhere, and the snow, which was falling lightly when I arrived, became heavier. I was in the midst of a Russian winter scene, and I could feel Christmas and New Years in the air. I was smiling and humming Christmas carols to myself as I made my way to the metro with my load of purchases. I was reminded of the *Christmas feeling* of New York City in my teenage years, a time at which I never could have imagined I would one day live and work in Moscow.

Wednesday, January 18, 2006—Unlike my previous trip in October, last Friday I did not miss the Avrora, the 4:30 p.m. train to Petersburg. In October, I made a mistake I will not repeat—I took a taxi instead of the metro to the Leningradskii Vokzal. What would have been a 30–40 minute trip by metro took me over an hour by taxi, as a result of which I missed the train and had to go through the *cultural experience* of exchanging my ticket for a later train with an accompanying 50% penalty. This past Friday I did not repeat October's mistake. I took the metro.

Zhenya and Sid met me at the Moskovskii Vokzal in Petersburg, and within minutes we were at Zhenya's and Vika's apartment near St. Isaacs' Cathedral. Their Christmas / New Year's tree was fully up and decorated, easily touching their fifteen-foot ceiling. The table was set with Vika's usual wonderful cooking, and we watched the Kremlin clock strike the midnight hour as we toasted the coming of 2006 in the Julian calendar.

The big news of this week is the *Kreshchenskie morozy*—the *peasant frosts*. The temperatures have ranged from a daytime high of -20°C (-4°F) to a nighttime low of -35°C (-31°F). This is the first time in a decade that Moscow has experienced such frosts, and it is the first time in my life that I have seen such extreme cold. My twenty-five-minute walk to the embassy this morning was even painful. By the time I had arrived my face mask was a frozen sheet of ice.

Thursday, February 9, 2006—I have not gotten off to a good start in the New Year insofar as these notes are concerned, but this time I feel no guilt. I was so overwhelmed with work from the time I returned from St. Petersburg through last Friday that I truly had no time to write. When I think about it, I realize that outside of going home for the holidays, I have been very overworked since the start of November when I started my month in EST. I need to slow the pace, and I even have the hope now that this may be possible.

Vika came down from St. Petersburg for the weekend, and it was fun and restful to hear another human voice in this apartment. Vika's brother Slava is in Moscow. I met them both, and on Saturday evening Slava and his wife Mariana brought dinner. On Sunday Vika, Mariana, and I strolled down the Stary Arbat in the -25°C *morozy* and had lunch at a Georgian restaurant. All in all, it was the most restful couple of days I have had in a long time. I need to continue the trend.

Sunday, February 26, 2006—At last I have had a break. For the past five days I have finally been able to live life at a slower pace. Last Wednesday, in particular, stands out in my memory as a day in which I was able to sleep late and occupy myself with nothing more intense than baking a fruitcake. I kept myself away from the computer except to put on carols for one last goodbye to the Christmas season. It may seem strange to listen to Christmas music in February, but somehow that became a tradition with me a decade or so ago when I first noticed the holidays fly past at rocket speed. Presidents' Day, not Epiphany, came to seem like the true end to the holidays as well as a day on which to switch focus from the long winter to the coming of spring. On Wednesday evening I even watched *White Christmas*, and over the next few days I followed that up with *A Christmas Carol* and *It's a Wonderful Life*.

On Friday evening I had Slava (Vika's brother) and Marina over for dinner. As part of saying goodbye to the holidays, I cooked one last turkey with all the trimmings.

Saturday, February 25, marked the second anniversary of *the call* and my acceptance of the offer to join the State Dept. Can it be that two years have passed since I sat in my office in Laurel and said, "Yes?"

I got back to cultural activities. On Thursday night I went to the puppet theater with Tanya and her friends to see *Beri shinel', poshli domoi (Take your greatcoat, let's go home)*, a patriotic salute to Russia's suffering and triumph in the Great Patriotic War (i.e., WW II), and I was with them again on Saturday evening to see a performance of *Antigone*. During the day on Saturday, I went with Masha from our embassy *okhrana* (i.e., guard) to see an art exhibit by a woman who lives in a Russian village and paints in a primitive style, and on Sunday I was with Inna and Masha at the Pushkin Museum for a guided tour about Pushkin's life and principal works.

From this description, it sounds as though I did not really spend too much time sitting around and doing nothing. OK, I suppose I was increasingly on the go as the five days went on. But for all of Wednesday and for those moments on the other days when I was not running around, I successfully resisted *making work*. I took a long bath on Tuesday evening, and I managed to take a few naps. While lying on the couch with my eyes closed, I imagined for a few moments that I was in Little Orleans. Overall, these were the most relaxing days I have had in Russia since last October.

The trick will be to make this last as I return to the world of work. I am now in the last third of my career. As I make my way through the 50s, I must at last learn not to do *work outside of work*. I must finally convince myself that slowing down is not just not a bad thing but is, in fact, imperative. Whatever career success I am going to have, I have, in fact, had already. There is no career ladder for me to climb at State. The next real career step for me is to retirement and hiking the Appalachian Trail.

Saturday, March 25, 2006—The news of the weekend is that I am the embassy *Duty Officer*. I have to carry a cell phone, log book, and a huge instruction manual. My job is to field any phone calls that happen to come in. So far there has been just one call from an American citizen living in Moscow who is receiving unwanted phone calls.

As part of my *Duty Officer* role, I am not supposed to go to the movies, travel in the metro, or otherwise be out of touch. In fact, I am supposed to call Post 5 — i.e., the Marines — if I take a shower. Thus, my motto for the weekend is, "If you want to be clean, call a marine!"

I am using my enforced stay-at-home *Duty Officer* status as an excuse to continue installing Debian Linux on this computer. If that works, I hope to use it as a means not to forget the little bit of Unix I managed to learn during my final 2–3 years at CSC. I might even do some programming. Those skills could yet be important in my life if this Foreign Service venture proves to be temporary in nature.

Sunday, March 26, 2006—Yesterday evening I received a *Duty Officer* phone call from an American woman married to a Russian in Kursk. Apparently, there is a long story of abuse here. The point of her call was that her husband would be driving her to Moscow through the night in order for her to catch a train to Tallinn and, thereby, leave Russia once and for all.

She was worried about driving through the night with her husband. There wasn't much I could do other than talk with both her and the husband and to tell the husband that I would expect a phone call in the morning telling me of their safe arrival. (I also got his cell phone number and called it back to verify.) The good news is that I received a call from the woman this morning telling me she had arrived safely and is waiting for her train.

Saturday, April 1, 2006—It is April 1, Brazil has a man in space, and that's no April Fool's joke.

It has been a long and eventful week in Moscow, my (current) hometown. The week's saga begins with Monday night. Having survived a relatively uneventful weekend as *Duty Officer*, I was certain the hard part was behind me. I was wrong. I went to bed at 11:00 p.m. Monday evening. After what felt like hours but in fact was only forty-five minutes, I was awakened out of a deep sleep by the ringing of the *Duty Officer* phone. Two American businessmen with GE had flown into Moscow around 11:00 p.m. on an Aeroflot flight from Paris, and Russian passport control would not let one of them into the country because his passport had become worn to such a degree that the pages were loose and getting ready to fall out. For the full story, I am appending a slightly edited version of my report. The good news for the GE executive was that after being forced to spend the night sitting up in the transit lounge at Sheremetyevo Airport, Russian immigration's day crew arrived and agreed to let him into the country if an embassy representative went to the airport, vouched for the worn passport, and then took the American straight to the embassy to print a new one.

It was after 3:00 a.m. when I finished with the GE executive. I was just about to go back to bed when the phone rang again. This time Russian border guards at the Russia-Ukraine border had removed the husband of an embassy USAID employee from a train bound for Kyiv. This should not have happened, but it was not the first incident of this kind.

The background is that U.S. personnel with diplomatic passports are permitted to enter and leave Russia only at specific border crossings. The same applies to Russian diplomats in the U.S. Last autumn the U.S. and Russian governments agreed to add one border crossing. Russians in the U.S. had Atlanta added to their list so that they could take advantage of Delta's new Moscow-Atlanta flight. In exchange the U.S. diplomatic community got a town whose name no one can remember that happens to be the border crossing for the overnight train from Moscow to Kyiv. Several times now the Russian border guards have removed Americans from the train at that border crossing. The guards say emphatically that since the visas do not specifically list that town in the middle of nowhere (i.e., the visas were issued before the U.S. and Russia added the new entry/exit points), they don't care what the U.S. State Department and the Russian Ministry of Foreign Affairs have agreed to. The border guards have their own bosses in the Ministry of Internal Affairs. Monday morning was no exception. The guards refused to have anything to do with me over the phone, and the American was put on the next slow train back to Moscow.

To the best of anyone's knowledge, no Russian trying to enter the U.S. in Atlanta has been similarly turned around. The embassy will be protesting Monday morning's incident, and sooner or later I am certain the border guards in that town in the middle of nowhere will receive corresponding instructions.

By the time I was finished with the border incident, it was 5:00 a.m. I realized there was little point in going to bed. I got dressed, walked to the embassy, and did a couple of hours' work before the start of the official workday. I would have considered calling in sick if it were not for the fact that 670 Russian college students were scheduled for visa interviews that morning as part of the *Summer Work and Travel* program (SWT). If you have ever vacationed in Ocean City, MD, and wondered how all those Russian, Ukrainian, and Polish students ended up working for the summer at Dumsers or Thrashers, you now have the answer: SWT.

With 670 SWT hopefuls about to show up in the Consular section, all hands were needed. One of the little gems of working in the fraud protection unit is that the rotating junior officer—in this case yours truly—gets the fun of helping with fingerprinting in the morning. For 1–2 hours I stand there with one other officer and keep repeating the same phrases over and over again in Russian. "Please put your left index finger on the red glass. Press harder please. Now the right index finger. Wonderful!"

I thought this Tuesday that I would survive my 1–2 hours and then go home, but I had no such luck. The person who takes over for me after those 1–2 hours had herself called in sick! And thus I had the joy of doing fingerprints for over four hours. That's about 350 sets of fingerprints. After that I did not ask but rather informed the fraud chief that I was leaving.

Once home, I collapsed on the couch for four hours. And then, come 8:00 p.m., the duty phone started ringing again. This time it was the Russian Ministry of Defense needing information on arrangements for the next day's planned phone call between Rumsfeld and Sergei Ivanov, the Russian Minister of Defense. The hard part for me was simply trying to find the right person at the embassy who could answer those questions.

At 11:00 p.m. I headed to bed, but I did not sleep for long. At 12:30 a.m. a Russian woman called to say that she and her seven-year-old American citizen son were surrounded by an aggressive group of young Russians who, she was afraid, were getting ready to attack them. I was able to get nothing more than her name and cell phone number before she said she had to hang up. All I could do was call the Russian police and report what little information I had. Their first question was, "What is the child's skin color?" There have been several bad race incidents recently in St. Petersburg, but so far Moscow has been immune. I couldn't help with an answer to this. I will say, however, that the Russian militsia was helpful and thorough. Over the next two hours the Russian police called me several times with progress reports. Two different units were dispatched to the vicinity, but no one matching the description of "woman and child surrounded by aggressive crowd" could be found. Neither the police nor I were able to reach the woman at the cell phone number she had given. Could this have been a prank call? I suppose so, but in my position I had to treat it as a very real threat to an American citizen—i.e., the seven-year-old child. I was relieved the next day to find no reports in the Russian news about a woman and child being attacked.

And so there I was, going to bed somewhere around 2:30 a.m. When morning came, I returned my duty phone and log book. The *Duty Officer* week that seemed it would never end has now done just that. No longer will I have to worry about the phone ringing in the middle of the night. . . .

That brings me back, finally, to Marcos Pontes, the first Brazilian in space. The Russian and Brazilian press have dubbed him the *Brazilian Gagarin*. He was launched into space from Baikonur last Wednesday as part of the Soyuz crew heading to the International Space Station (ISS). The NASA representative at the embassy put me on the access list to go along to the VIP balcony at the Russian Flight Control Center (TsUP) this morning to view the docking. It felt strange and rather sad to be in such an operations area and not to be doing operations myself.

I will say, however, that I was infected by the excitement of the Brazilians. There were at least as many Brazilians who had come to see the docking as there were Americans. When the hatch opened between the Soyuz and ISS and Marcos Pontes entered ISS with the Brazilian flag unfurled, I found myself applauding and saying "Parabens!" Green and yellow, the Brazilian colors, were very much in evidence throughout the viewing area. I managed to get one small banner issued in honor of the Brazilian cosmonaut. In its way the banner is a good analog for my life: Russia, Brazil, and space. Who could have ever known that those three elements would all come together on an April 1 morning in Moscow?

Wednesday, May 3, 2006—Last weekend I went on a long, tiring, but wonderful tour to Suzdal. It truly is a *museum city* that has changed little since the train line passed it by in the nineteenth century. Walking through the town, one begins to have a feeling of what it might have been like to live in a Russian town before the revolutions of 1917. Suzdal is filled with churches and monasteries that pre-date the founding of the U.S., but it is the Rozhdestvenskiy sobor in Suzdal's ancient kremlin that leaves one most in awe. Founded in the 1220s, it pre-dates Moscow and even the Mongol invasion that destroyed Kievan Rus.

The bus ride each way to and from Suzdal took four hours, and that gave me time to talk with my seat-neighbor, a young woman from Dagestan who lives on the edge of Moscow. With a kandidat degree in linguistics, she now teaches English and French at a private language school and earns only a minimal salary. I felt uncomfortable telling her that I have an apartment on *Kutuzovskiy prospekt*, Moscow's equivalent of New York's Park Avenue.

I celebrated Monday, May Day, by taking my first bike ride that took me beyond the MKAD, Moscow's Ring Road that now rivals the Washington Beltway for traffic density. I found a quiet crossing that let me avoid negotiating the major interchanges, and once on the other side I found myself in suburbs that made me feel as though I might be back in the D.C. area. My one problem on the ride was learning that not all the secondary roads indicated on my *Atlas of Roads of the Moscow Oblast'* necessarily exist. Some seem to be roads that once were there but that have reverted to dirt tracks. On the other hand there were others, most likely products of Moscow's building boom, that are not in the atlas at all.

Today marks my second anniversary in the Foreign Service. It was two years ago today that I walked into the A-100 class at the FSI in Ballston. The question is, where will I be two years from now?

Tuesday, May 9, 2006 —Victory Day. How many people in the U.S. recall that today is the sixty-first anniversary of VE Day, the end of World War II in Europe? Okay, we can quibble. The U.S. celebrates VE Day on May 8, but I doubt that even yesterday the anniversary crossed the minds of any but those old enough to have lived through the war. Even then, the thoughts were most likely fleeting.

Not so in Russia. Even sixty-one years after the end of World War II, this is one holiday that unites the entire country. The old Soviet holidays have faded away, yet to be replaced by *new* national holidays that capture the imagination, but Victory Day unites liberal democrats and hard-line communists, Putin supporters and the heads of increasingly hard-pressed NGOs. Everyone has a grandfather or two who died in the war, and the stories of how individual families suffered are passed down from parent to child. The posters around Moscow with pictures of a young child and an elderly veteran proclaim, "Thank Granddad for the Victory!"

This is the first time I have been in Russia on Victory Day, and I will mark it by walking to Victory Park. I have no plans in mind. I just want a sense of how it feels to walk the streets of Moscow on this day. I am reminded of George Kennan's story of how a large crowd gathered spontaneously in front of the U.S. Embassy on this day in 1945—an exceedingly rare event in those years of Stalinist control—and how he climbed out a window to greet them.

On Saturday, the first day of this four-day weekend, I repeated my bicycle ride of last week out to Peredelkino. This time I knew where I was going and did not repeat my mistakes of the previous week—thus, I was able to go much further. I stopped by the Peredelkino cemetery and was reminded of the day in 1978 when a group of us from my first tour of the USSR departed from Intourist plans and searched out Pasternak's grave. Tomorrow Russian TV will begin showing the first-ever serialization of *Doctor Zhivago* in Russian. Who could have ever imagined that this day would come?

On Sunday I took another all-day tour out to Rostov Velikii, the first pre-Muscovite capital of Kievan Rus' Northeast territories. Rostov's kremlin looked immediately familiar, and I soon found out why. Rostov is where the 1970's comedy *Ivan Vasil'evich Changes Professions* was filmed. On the way to and from Rostov I sat next to Tonya, a young Russian woman who will be receiving a *kandidat* degree in economics this spring. Born in 1982, she was only nine years old when the Soviet Union collapsed.

Alina Eremeeva and her brother Volodya came for dinner yesterday. Between beans and rice, pirozhki, and brownies, we had a Brazilian-Russian-U.S. international dinner.

Sunday, May 14, 2006 —Yesterday was one of those work Saturdays for which I had no expectations but that in its way will turn into a day that will stand out from my life in Moscow in the years to come.

The day began early with my alarm clock going off at 7:15 a.m. I had done some Internet research and discovered that a new rapid transit service out to Sheremetevo 2 Airport had begun last winter, and it occurred to me that this might be a nice alternative to a $40 taxi drive when I fly home in two weeks. I wasn't about to trust my flight home to a few newspaper articles on the Internet, however, and thus I decided I would use Saturday as a trial run to find out if what I had read is really true. I walked out my door at 8:15 a.m. and took the metro to Savelovskii vokzal just in time to get the nearly empty 9:00 a.m. express elektrichka (suburban train) to Lobnya, the station nearest to Sheremetevo. Just as advertised, there was a large, modern shuttle bus waiting at the station to take passengers to the terminals at Sheremetevo. By 10:00 a.m. I was walking into the international terminal. Total cost? This entire trip cost 75 rubles—a little less than $3.00 even with the ever-falling dollar. Getting a cup of coffee and danish in the terminal cost much more at 200 rubles. At 10:45 I was sitting in a marshrutka (jitney cab) on my way to the nearest metro station at rechnoy vokzal and was on my way back into the city. As a byproduct of the trip, I now know where to catch the free shuttle bus that runs from rechnoy vokzal to the Ikea mega-mall.

Around noon I was at the embassy, a place I usually try to avoid on my days off. My reason for stopping this weekend was an embassy-wide yard sale. The summer transfer season is upon us, and many departing families are emptying their closets. Surprisingly, I found nothing worthwhile to buy other than a single Christine Lavin CD.

Leaving the embassy, I stopped at *Novinskii pasazh* to pick up film I had left for developing, and from there I started heading in the general direction of *Ploshchad' Mayakovskogo* because of an announcement I had noticed regarding a special event in connection with Bulgakov's 115th birthday. Instead of taking the usual route along the Garden Ring, I decided to experiment by taking Bol'shaya gruzinskaya. At a certain point I came to a large square with a building on one side where I noticed an observatory on the roof. I came closer and discovered that the building belonged to the Moscow Center for Child and Teenager Development.

Turning around, I found the Konovalov Ophthalmology Center across the street. I thought to myself, "Why not?" I went in and asked how long it would take to schedule an appointment. To my surprise, I found they could take me right away. For 1,100 rubles ($40-45) I had a 2–3 hour exam that included full refraction, pressure measurement, retina photograph (or whatever that is called), dilation, and diagnosis. In other words, for $40–45 out-of-pocket I had just about everything I normally have in the U.S. for $25 after insurance. The equipment appeared state-of-the-art, and the attention I got was first-rate. It turned out that my eye pressure is normal and that my current eyeglass prescription is fine, but for the first time I gave in and accepted the recommendation that I get a second pair of glasses for reading. I headed next to the optometrist suggested to me by the folks at Konovalov and placed an order for reading glasses that will cost 2,400 rubles. For a total cost of 3,500 rubles ($130) without insurance of any kind, I have had a full eye exam and will be getting a new pair of glasses.

It now being sometime after 5:00 p.m., I sat in the warm sunlight on a marble bench and enjoyed a molochnyi kokteil' (milk shake). From there I set out for Dom knigi where I purchased a few books and DVDs, including *Doctor Zhivago* that surprisingly is for sale on DVD even as it is being shown on Russian television. I finally make my way back home around 7 or 7:30 p.m., took a shower, ate dinner, watched an episode of *Doctor Zhivago*, and collapsed into bed. I slept for ten hours ....

Why was it that Saturday will stick out in my mind? The answer is that this was a day on which I felt I was living my life as a Muscovite, not a pampered FSO representative of the U.S. government. Despite the fact that I spend the vast majority of my time at work on the embassy compound, there come moments such as those I had yesterday when I feel I have blended in and even my accent gets barely a notice. On days such as yesterday I have to pinch myself and ask whether I am really here. On days such as yesterday I feel that the sacrifices have been worthwhile.

Alas, I am bone-tired exhausted, as witnessed by my ten hours in bed. I need not a week but at least a month lying in the hammock in Little Orleans to get beyond this and the neck and shoulder aches that follow me all through the week. I joke that I joined the Foreign Service to feel as though I was twenty-five again, but the truth is that a midlife career change is exhausting beyond words. I have described and will continue to describe the culture shock problems of working in the State Department. These are at the root of my exhaustion and even the depression that I experience through the work week. (Keep in mind that I slept ten hours last night after a work week that consisted of only three days.)

The flip side is that I try to keep myself sane by working on Debian Linux to maintain some degree of technical ability and that I try to get out and about as much as possible during my days off. I feel forever frustrated that I don't get out and about as much as I would like at the same time that I am thirsty and downright greedy for a few hours of solitude. Sunday evenings always come too soon. After such a memorable day yesterday, this Sunday (Mother's Day) I will be doing laundry and paying bills. It's unlikely that I will get out of my apartment at all. If I could, I would and should spend the day sitting on my balcony with a book.

What will I decide when I am presented this fall with my next list of possible postings? Where will the State Dept. want to send me? What will I do? Will I find some way of staying in Russia? It's hard to believe that my time here is nearly half over.

Saturday, June 24, 2006—It's been a busy week in Moscow, my hometown. This was my first full week of interviews in the non-immigrant visa (NIV) section, where 4–6 officers averaged 350–400 interviews per morning. Once again State planning showed itself in all its glory. Of those 4–6 officers, two of us are new to NIV. The experienced head of NIV left post a month ago, and his experienced but temporary replacement left post last week. Finally, the temporary replacement's replacement went on vacation the same day that the temporary replacement left. Am I beginning to paint a picture? This was not quite a week of the blind leading the blind, but it was pretty close. Our morning interviews begin at 9:00 a.m., and on a couple of days we did not complete the *morning* interviews until around 1:30 in the afternoon. An experienced interviewer can do an NIV interview in a minute from start to visa approval or refusal. It took me at least 3–4 times longer as I was still trying to figure out which buttons to push on the computer screen and trying to understand what I should be looking at in visa application packets. Even at this lackluster pace, the speed of these interviews left me giddy. I felt as though I was on launch support with the added problems of almost no advance training and no contingency plans.

But I feel quite pleased that I refused outright only a handful of applicants. I have my own way of looking at 214b, the provision of U.S. immigration law that defines all visa applicants as intending illegal immigrants unless they can prove otherwise to the satisfaction of the interviewing officer. I found myself approving many applicants who had been refused by my colleagues in the past. It does not take much to convince me that an applicant has a firm tie to Russia. I approved university students —applicants who normally are refused because of no salary, wife, and children—as long as they were enrolled in a good degree program at a well-known university. I approved pensioners going to visit children, in one case simply because the widowed applicant before me showed me pictures of her well-tended rose garden. The only applicants I refused outright were those who came to the window with almost no papers and not even a good verbal story.

My NIV psychology could get me into trouble, and in this regard it is good that I will be in NIV for just two and a half months. I am hoping that my high approval rate will go unnoticed during such a short period at a time when we are going through the turmoil of summer personnel turnovers and vacations. The worst that can happen is that I will be taken aside for a discussion on my *poor judgment*. Even if a note goes into my performance appraisal, it is more important to me that I be able to live with myself. One of the good aspects of starting a new career at age 50+ is that unlike my young colleagues, I have no illusions of climbing any career ladder and therefore do not stand in fear of the annual performance appraisal.

In light of my approach to work in NIV, perhaps it is good that I have been pulled to work next week as a liaison officer for the Secretary of State's visit to Moscow. My duties are not yet clear to me, but I do know I will be involved in twelve-hour shifts once the Secretary lands on Wednesday evening.

The weather in Moscow has finally turned hot with temperatures in the mid-80s. I have closed my windows and turned on the two room air conditioners. I am riding my Rivendell through the streets of Moscow for an hour every morning before rolling through the embassy gates. Last evening, I rode up to the viewing platform on Vorob'evy Gory by Moscow State University and looked out at one of the best views of Moscow. During this, the week of the solstice, the sun is setting around 10:00 p.m., and there was still enough light to read a newspaper as I stood on my balcony after 11:00 p.m. last night. Summer has arrived, and outside the embassy gates, at least, the living has become easy.

Saturday, July 1, 2006—The weather has suddenly and unexpectedly turned autumnal. Overnight the temperature dropped to the upper 40s, and it was only in the low 50s as I headed out to the Krylatskoe bike track this morning. The sky was overcast and looked threatening, but weather forecasts on two radio stations gave assurance that there was no chance of precipitation. I knew better and should have believed my own eyes rather than the weather forecast. I had not gone even a mile before a light rain began that continued with only a few breaks throughout my ride. When I got back to my apartment, I spent an hour in the parking lot doing my best to wash the bike with a bucket of soapy water and two 3-liter soda bottles with rinse water. I was not about to repeat last fall's experience of washing the bike in my bathtub. What I wouldn't give for a hose ....

All last week the temperatures were in the upper 80s, which is very unusual for Moscow. Since it is so unusual, very few buildings have the heavy-duty air conditioning that we are used to in the U.S. This is true even of U.S.-owned and operated hotels such as the Marriott Grand, a hotel that I got to know very well this week since this was where Secretary Rice and her team stayed.

I went to the Marriott on Wednesday afternoon. The Secretary's plane touched down at 5:00 p.m., and I was in the lobby as she entered at 6:45. As one of two liaison officers, I took up residence in the suite assigned to the Executive Secretariat. I took the night shift from 7 p.m. to 7 a.m. and Dave Paradise, my partner in crime, took the days. As we quickly found out, our function had little to do with liaison. When Dave arrived for the day shift on Thursday, I told him we were little more than glorified go-fors. When I took over from him again in the evening, Dave said I had exaggerated when I used the word *glorified*.

Being liaison officer did have a few bright moments, the most exciting of which involved serving as an interpreter between U.S. Diplomatic Security personnel and their counterparts in the Russian FSB (i.e., the modern-day KGB). Those moments came early in the first evening when Diplomatic Security noticed suspicious-looking vehicles in the vicinity of the hotel. Through the first night I was also responsible for handling the classified correspondence that was funneled to and from the hotel via the embassy. Believe it or not, all classified materials are kept within a portable tent that is set up within one of the Secretariat rooms. The tent is large enough for two small tables, a chair, and a folder rack. This may sound strangely low-tech, but surprisingly it works. The tent shields the paper from any optical devices, and it provides a centralized reading room that keeps the classified materials under control. With the tent in place, classified papers are not going to wander off on their own.

So what else did I do as liaison officer? I ran errands, wrote a few thank you letters, and manned the telephones. At midnight on the second night, I was tasked with making a name tent for Assistant Secretary Dan Fried, who at the last minute was added to the U.S.-Japanese bilateral meeting scheduled for the next morning and for whom no name tent had been made. I was instructed that Dan Fried's name tent should look as good as that belonging to Steve Beecroft, one of the Secretary's advisers, in order not to add fuel to an apparent rivalry between the two. (I kid you not!) I worked with two office management specialists (OMS—i.e., secretaries), and after somewhat more than an hour the three of us had contrived to coax PowerPoint into producing an acceptable looking name tent. I shudder to think how much this one name tent cost the American taxpayer.

The hardest part of being liaison officer was staying awake between the hours of 2:00 a.m. and 6:00 a.m. Those were the hours when the Executive Secretariat staff had gone to bed, and I was left in charge of the phones. This is where the lack of effective air conditioning came into play. Our rooms were downright hot, and we had all the windows open to get what cooler air we could. It took calisthenics and lots of coffee to keep from nodding off.

The most distasteful part of being liaison officer was breaking down the command center after the Secretary's departure late Friday morning. I stayed on after my night shift in order to help David with this fun activity, which involved doing a sweep of all the rooms used by the Secretary, her advisers, and her staff. In each room we went through the trash cans and looked in each nook and cranny for any papers that inadvertently might have been left behind. We looked in and under the recently occupied beds for anything that might be hiding there. And yes, we did find a few things that in haste had been left, albeit nothing that would shake the pillars of U.S. foreign policy.

Being at the hub of the Executive Secretariat during the Secretary's visit to Moscow was, nevertheless, quite interesting. It was educational to see how high-level trips of this kind are run from minute to minute even if my own role was a menial one. For excitement and a feeling of accomplishment, however, I will take launch support over trip support any day. Unfortunately, the educational component of supporting the Secretary's visit included the negative reinforcement of my view that the State Department makes woefully inefficient use of its resources. Although I enjoyed the experience, my participation was entirely unnecessary. I believe the same can be said of a good portion of the rest of the support staff. Our roles were superfluous and expensive.

I finally walked through my apartment door mid-afternoon on Friday. After a shower to wash off the traces of the high and mighty trash cans and beds I had searched by hand, I threw a pizza in the oven and collapsed on the couch. I had been up for twenty-four hours and could scarcely stay awake as I ate my pizza. I fell into bed at 6:00 p.m. ... and did not wake up until 6:00 a.m. the next morning.

Sunday, July 9, 2006—This was my weekend for a long-distance bicycle tour from Moscow to Borodino and back. I had had this idea in mind ever since returning to Moscow after Matthew's high school graduation. I brought most of my camping gear with me from the U.S. last year, but it sat unused in my closet. With the warm weather and long sunlit days of the Russian summer, I knew that I had come to the point of *now or never*.

I set out Friday evening. Heading westward on *Kutuzovskiy prospekt*, I soon discovered that getting out of Moscow on a Friday evening in summer makes the trip from D.C. to Ocean City look easy. It took me a full hour to make it to the MKAD, a trip that normally should take half that time. I thought the traffic would ease once I crossed the MKAD, but I was quickly disabused of that notion. The main westbound highway out of Moscow, M1, is a good road with two travel lanes and shoulders in each direction, and I had found it an easy road to ride on when I first tried it on a Sunday a month ago. On Friday evening, however, I discovered that Russian drivers consider the shoulder to be an extra travel lane. More than that, motorists were driving on the dirt next to the shoulder, thereby raising a large dust cloud that hung over the highway and that quickly coated me with dirt. After three hours I had managed to travel only twenty-four miles.

At 9:00 p.m. I stopped for dinner at a McDonald's, and after another 2-3 miles I turned off the road and headed into the woods. I found an acceptable camping spot, leaned the bicycle against a tree, and started doing a jig as a swarm of large, vicious mosquitoes descended on me. Almost tearing open my bags, I grabbed a long-sleeve shirt and long pants, meanwhile swatting the mosquitoes that were biting me on my nose and ears. Under these conditions, setting up the tent was not an easy proposition. Once inside the tent, I spent a quarter hour killing every mosquito that had followed me inside. I sponged off the grime as best I could, got myself ready to climb into my sleeping bag, and only then realized that I had to take care of a call of nature. Thus, I had the pleasure of repeating my tent-entry, mosquito search and destroy procedure all over again. After that I lay awake, listening to the traffic on highway M1. It must have been 2:00 a.m. before I finally fell into a fitful sleep.

When I awoke Saturday morning, I thought I might abort this entire adventure. I took down the tent, packed everything on the bike, and headed out to the highway. Standing on the shoulder, I saw that the unbelievable Friday night traffic had disappeared, and thus after a moment's hesitation, I got on the bike and continued in a westward direction. Temperatures were in the low 80s, and the sun was shining brightly. At first the terrain was as flat as the American Midwest, but it became more rolling the further I got from Moscow. After three hours I was starting to have the definite impression that I was going uphill far more often than downhill, although I must allow that after nearly a year in Moscow, my legs are no longer used to long-distance, loaded touring. I finally reached the Borodino turnoff not a moment too soon after about four hours of almost non-stop pedaling.

I was puzzled, however, that I saw no sign for Borodino at the turnoff. I had plotted my route using a road atlas that I had bought in Moscow. According to this atlas, the distance from the turnoff to Borodino was only about five miles, so why was there no sign for Borodino?

I quickly found out why. Rounding a bend after 2-3 miles, I was confronted by a fence, a gate, and armed military guards. The guards seemed nearly as confounded to see a bicyclist as I was to see them. Flustered, I dismounted and started to ask how to get to Borodino. In their turn, the guards asked for my ID. I showed them the *diplomaticheskaya kartochka* identifying me as a third secretary at the U.S. Embassy and the diplomatic note from the Ministry of Foreign Affairs giving me permission to travel by bicycle from Moscow to Borodino. (According to Cold War agreements that neither side has pushed hard to rescind, U.S. diplomats in Moscow and Russian diplomats in Washington are required to obtain travel notes for any travel beyond a certain distance—I believe 40km— from the city center.) The guards told me that I had stumbled on a *zasekrechennyi ob'ekt* – a secret military site. No wonder there had been no sign for Borodino at the turn-off. Although the road I was on did go to Borodino, it ran right through this military base and therefore was not a through road.

After several uncomfortable moments, a guard who apparently was going off duty offered to lead me on a detour around the base that would take me to Borodino. He got into his car, and I proceeded to follow on my bike as we headed down a dirt track. After 5-10 minutes the guard stopped his car, got out, and pointed to two monuments on a hill, one to the 1812 Battle of Borodino and the other to the disastrous 1941 battle in which the juggernaut German advance surrounded and destroyed several Soviet divisions. The guard told me that we were standing on sacred land that was saturated with Russian blood ... and then he told me that he hates Americans.

That's when I realized he was drunk. He told me his name was Andrei, and he told me that as an American diplomat, I had to accept his invitation to find out what real Russian life is like by going with him to his home and bathing in his private banya (Russian bath house). I tried to deflect the invitation but realized I was in the middle of nowhere with a tipsy, muscle-packed Russian soldier who would take it as an insult if I did not accept. Then I noticed that he had several children in the back of his car. Thus Andrei's invitation, as tipsy as it was, probably would not end badly. I gave in and followed slowly as Andrei turned onto another dirt track. After several minutes we pulled into a small village of dachas (Russian vacation camps). Andrei pulled up in front of one of the dachas, and the children jumped out and ran toward the house yelling, "Granddad, we have an American!"

What started out ominously ended as perhaps the most memorable experience of my bicycle adventure. Andrei lives with cousin Anton, also a soldier, and with his uncle, a high school history teacher from Moscow. They sat me down under their outdoor canopy and proceeded to give me food and beer (thank goodness no vodka!) and pump me with questions about life in the U.S. I felt I had gone back in time. This was the sort of experience I remember having frequently in the Soviet Union in the 1970s and 1980s. Foreigners, Americans in particular, have become commonplace in Moscow and are no longer the object of fascination that they once were. As I discovered on Saturday, this is not the case in the countryside, where Americans are still a rarity.

Andrei's uncle and cousin apologized profusely for Andrei's somewhat drunken state and for his repeated assertions that someday Russian tanks would be on the streets of Washington. We exchanged addresses and telephone numbers, after which they walked me to the train station in Borodino. It turned out I had been only a 10-15 minute walk from Borodino when I first pulled up to the military base gate. At 5:12 p.m. I was sitting on the elektrichka back to Moscow. At 8:00 p.m. I walked through my apartment door. A smelly, grimy mess, I headed straight to the shower.

My total distance on the bicycle was 85 miles. That pales in comparison with the century rides I used to do around Washington, but I was fully loaded with tent, sleeping bag, and other camping gear. Although tired from the road, I found that I had not overly exerted myself. The main ill effects were mosquito bites everywhere and a bad case of sunburn. I need to remind myself to buy sunblock.

Ironically, I did not get to see much of anything of the Borodino battlefield. That was the price of my stumbling upon a military installation. By way of compensation, I put the 1970s Soviet version of War and Peace in the DVD player as I went to bed Saturday night.

I nearly forgot to mention that the Fourth of July in Moscow turned out to be something of a workday. Coming off my duties as liaison officer for the Secretary of State visit, I found out last Monday that I had been assigned to be a working guest at the Ambassador's July Fourth reception at Spaso House, the ambassadorial residence. Being a working guest mainly involved escorting and mixing with invited, non-working guests. As such the experience was a pleasant one, but it did mean that I had to report to

Spaso House at 4:00 p.m. and did not get home until nearly 11:00 p.m. The Fourth was not a day of rest.

Thursday, August 24, 2006—I am down to my final week in the consular section. Next week I move to the nuclear portfolio in EST. I never did manage to *rest up* as I should have in preparation for this move. The staffing was so thin in consular this summer that the hours were long and exhausting. Surprisingly, however, I actually enjoyed my time in NIV. I enjoyed the brief conversations that gave a glimpse into the lives of the hundreds of people who passed by my window. Only this week, with the arrival of new staff, has the pace slackened to the point that I feel justified in doing my best to take it easy in preparation for the new whirlwind that will be my life starting next week.

On Tuesday, I went for a long evening of meteoritics and history of astronomy with Alina and did not get home until nearly 1:00 a.m. Feeling a cold fed by exhaustion coming on, I called in sick for Wednesday and spent the day trying to catch up on the domestic chores that I had not gotten to over the weekend.

Saturday, September 30, 2006—Over a month has passed since my last entry. Summer is over, and on this last day of September, autumn is very much in evidence. The air is brisk, the sun is setting before 7:00 p.m., and there is almost a taste in the air announcing that winter is not far around the corner. The leaves are changing, and I would estimate that they will be at their maximum color in just another week. The end of September in Moscow is like the end of October or even early November in Washington.

I have had many weighty reasons for not writing for so long. The short list includes:

- The visit by Gail, Pat, and Irene
- My transfer to EST
- Ma's illness

It has been a busy month.

It was wonderful to have my sisters Gail and Irene and my brother-in-law Pat visit. This is the first time I have had visitors, and I had fun showing them life in a country they probably never thought they would see. We took a tour boat down the Moscow River on a Friday evening, I showed them the *rynok* (market), and walked them all over town. We went to see *Madame Butterfly* at the Bolshoi and *The Merry Widow* at the Operetta Theater, but I also took them to see a Russian-language version of the French comedy *Boeing-Boeing*. I had fun sitting between Irene and Gail and interpreting at a whisper into their ears.

We also went to St. Petersburg for a three-day weekend, going up on Aeroflot and returning on the Avrora fast train. Zhenya and Vika had taken everything into their hands, choreographing our tours around the city and to the Hermitage, Petrodvorets, and Tsarskoe selo. We went to an evening of ballet at the Mariinskiy Theater, and of course we ate enough food in three days to last for a week. Vika was in usual good form in her kitchen, and we finished the weekend by going to brunch at the Evropeiskaya Hotel.

Gail, Irene, and Pat's visit was spoiled only by the news that Ma had gone to the emergency room. Helena called us in St. Petersburg with the news. In fact, Ma went to the emergency room three times in almost as many days. Knowing that Ma is one never to complain about anything, we knew this must be serious. It was Gail and Irene who usually keep an eye on Ma, but here they were in Moscow. Helena, my nephew Kevin, and my niece Kathi took turns being with Ma, but even after the emergency room doctors recommended gallbladder surgery, Ma did not want to go through with it unless Gail and Irene were present. Our holiday atmosphere evaporated, replaced by anxiety during Gail, Irene, and Pat's last 3–4 days in Russia.

The good news about Ma is that she had the surgery earlier this week and seems to be recovering well. The main concern now is that her blood pressure is much too high. The doctors do not want to release her until that is under control.

My transfer to EST also kept me from spending as much time with Gail, Irene, and Pat as I would have liked. Just as I expected, the pace in EST is grueling. This past week I worked fifty-four hours, and even at that I did not come anywhere near to completing everything I should have. I finally walked out Friday at 7:30 p.m. leaving many things at loose ends.

My predecessor Susan, as it turns out, had at least a decade working on nuclear policy issues, including a stint at the Department of Energy (DOE).

Unlike Susan, I have no nuclear background. It's a case of sink or swim. I feel like Sisyphus pushing the boulder up the hill.

This is not the worst of it. The EST deputy Peg had to rush home on emergency travel. In her place, I spent a day visiting a nature preserve that breeds bison.

Despite the pace, I get goosebumps to think that I am here in Moscow— in Moscow!—handling nuclear issues. Some of the more exciting tasks included:

- Shepherding a protocol on Plutonium Disposition Liability through final edits. Much of this was a matter of commas and quotation marks, but I was the one sitting in the Ministry of Foreign Affairs getting those commas in the right place before the protocol was signed in Washington two weeks ago.

- Sitting in on U.S.-Russian negotiations at Rosatom on the Mayak Transparency Agreement that will give U.S. observers access to the Russian Mayak nuclear weapon destruction facility.

- Sitting in on another negotiating session in which Dept. of Commerce Assistant Secretary Spooner presented a plan to Rosatom head Sergey Kiriyenko (a Putin associate) by which Russia would gradually be permitted freer access to U.S. nuclear fuel markets when current restrictions expire in 2013. Spooner himself seemed to know from the start that limits in the plan would not please the Russians, and Kiriyenko did not disappoint him. As the two-hour session ended, Kiriyenko said he doubted the plan could serve even as a starting point for negotiations. Russia and the U.S. may be headed towards confrontation on this issue.

- Slipping a question to Rosatom's director for international relations Kuchinov in which I got him to confirm press reports that Iran's Russian-built reactor will be operational in a year.

- Accompanying a delegation from the General Accounting Office to Dubna, the home of the Joint International Nuclear Research center on the banks of the Volga.

I know I cannot continue to work 50+ hour weeks every week and maintain my health, but today was a beautiful autumn Saturday in Moscow. I spent the day having lunch with Bill Barry from the NASA International Office and going with him to an engineering museum I didn't even know existed. From there I took a long walk and trolley ride home. Tonight, I will disconnect the phone and sleep as long as I can, and on Sunday I will do as little as possible. Monday and a new week will be here in the blink of an eye.

Friday, October 6, 2006—Thank goodness this week has not been as overwhelming as last. All in all, I worked only forty-nine hours, which after fifty-four hours the previous week seemed almost relaxing. There were fewer delegations in town. The only group that took any real time from me was an interesting trio from the Nuclear Threat Initiative (NTI), an NGO founded by former Senator Sam Nunn and Ted Turner, that was in town to advance the concept of a uranium fuel bank that NTI proposed at last month's International Atomic Energy Agency meeting in Vienna. The group met with the Ambassador on Tuesday and gave a general briefing to the embassy today.

Another interesting person in town was Peter Westwick, a historian from UC Santa Barbara who came my way today through a colleague at the U.S. Naval Observatory. Peter is working on a history of the Strategic Defense Initiative (SDI, aka *Star Wars*) and was in Moscow to interview a number of Russian scientists and retired military officers to understand the Soviet reaction to SDI in the 1980s.

I managed to send out my first substantive cable this week. The subject was last week's Spooner-Kiriyenko negotiating session.

I also had my first solo meeting at the MFA. It was with Mikhail Kondratenkov, a former nuclear physicist who moved to the Foreign Ministry six years ago and spent his first overseas posting in Africa. It was a nice surprise to find someone in Russian diplomacy whose life story has parallels with my own.

On Wednesday I had lunch with Sari Rautio, a second secretary from the Finnish Embassy who follows nuclear issues. Prior to coming to Moscow, she had served in Ethiopia doing anything but nuclear issues. I gather the Finnish foreign service must have the same *generalist* model for its diplomats that we have in the State Department.

Ah, a three-day weekend impends! I find it strange to have Columbus Day as a holiday for the first time since high school, but in the Foreign Service I need and will take all the holidays I can get. In fact, it will not be a completely work-free weekend. On Friday I must submit my bids for my next, post-Moscow Foreign Service posting. The final list of open posts has been out for a week, but I have not had a chance to do more than take a quick look. Out of 350+ open posts on the bid list, I must choose twenty where I would be willing to serve. I will never have time to do the necessary research and compile the list during the workday, and so it is that I will need to do most of the work this weekend.

Monday, October 9, 2006 —Today, Columbus Day, I will finally get to looking at the bid list. Saturday and Sunday were both beautiful autumn days with temperatures in the upper 50s, and it would have been almost sinful not to be out and about. On Saturday morning I took care of normal weekend chores and then got together with Inna in the afternoon. We went for dinner at a good Hungarian restaurant in Kitai gorod and then went to see a one-act play, *Litsa*, based on Chekhov short stories at the beautiful, new Et Cetera theater. On Sunday I got the bike out on the road for what could be one of my last rides this year. My ride was not particularly inventive—just the usual route to and around Krylatskoe—but it felt good to get a workout on the road and enjoy the autumn leaves. (Afterward I had the *fun* of washing the bike in my parking lot using a bucket of soapy water and several bottles of clean rinse water. What I would not give for a hose.)

My decision to enjoy myself on Saturday and Sunday was the right one. Today, Monday, is dark and rainy. Temperatures are still relatively warm for Moscow in October (i.e., 50s), but I was just listening to a recording of the WAMU *Computer Guys* broadcast from last week and heard the forecast for D.C. temperatures in the mid-80s. Despite the long and frigid winters, I am starting to think of the Moscow climate as more normal. One has all four seasons here, and the hazy, hot, and humid 90s of D.C. in July just do not happen. Perhaps I really do prefer higher latitudes?

If there is a negative side to this weekend—in fact to the past two weekends—it is that I am not sleeping well. Even on the weekends I am not entirely able to put aside the stresses of the week. At night I am troubled by dreams about work, the uncertainties of bidding, Ma's health, and the future in general.

Saturday, October 14, 2006—It has been a good learning week for me in EST even as I despair that I will not be in my position long enough to become truly effective. Robert Einhorn, Assistant Secretary for Disarmament in the Clinton administration, was in town to gauge Russian attitudes towards a U.S.-Russian *123 Agreement* on cooperation in the civilian nuclear sector. The U.S. has such agreements with many countries, and a U.S.-Russian *123* was first talked about in the 1990s. For various reasons this did not move beyond talk until Presidents Bush and Putin unexpectedly announced plans for such an agreement during the G8 meeting in St. Petersburg last summer. Surprisingly, Bob Einhorn found during his meetings in Moscow this week that in fact Russia does not seem to have much interest in this agreement. I sat in the audience at the Carnegie Center as Einhorn asked what advantages Russia saw for itself in concluding such an agreement. The audience, which included many influential engineers, scientists, and political figures from the nuclear industry, responded with a silence. No one could respond to Bob Einhorn's question with anything more than platitudes and mumbles. Based on this, I will be surprised if a *123 Agreement* moves beyond talk anytime during my tenure in EST.

My main activity this weekend is to host a dinner on Sunday. Dale Cruikshank, an astrophysicist from NASA Ames, is arriving for a conference at the *Institut kosmicheskikh issledovanii* (Space Research Institute [IKI]), and I will be hosting a reunion dinner for him and Alina Eremeeva. Alina had known Dale in the early 1980s when he spent several months at the Shternberg Institute, but they lost contact many years ago. I put them back in touch when I sent Dale a copy of Alina's book on the history of meteoritics. Dale then contacted me by email with the news that he would be coming to Moscow for the IKI conference, and I offered my apartment as the venue for a reunion dinner. I will be cooking and cleaning for the remainder of today.

Friday, October 20, 2006—I'm sitting in the Avrora at the Moscow Station in St. Petersburg waiting for the train to leave. We won't pull into Moscow until six hours from now, and thus I have time on my hands. I thought I would use it to do some writing longhand (fancy that!) and transcribe it later.

This has been the easiest and most pleasant week I have had since moving to EST. On Tuesday afternoon I boarded the train to St. Petersburg together with my FSN adviser Aleksey Davydov. A group of DOE engineers and scientists accompanied by an admiral and an undersecretary were to conduct a joint training exercise with a similar group from Rosatom and other Russian agencies. This event had been on the calendar since before my arrival in EST, but the truth is I had been too busy to pay attention to the details until Aleksey and I were on our way. Our purpose of travel was to observe the exercise and to *show the flag* as State's representatives.

In St. Petersburg we were housed in the Renaissance Baltic just off St. Isaac's Square and around the corner from Zhenya and Vika. On Wednesday morning we boarded a bus that took us to the Rosatom Emergency Response Center north of the city. The first day was a simple one in which both sides presented short papers followed by the start of the exercise itself in which a radiological source was reported to have gone missing. On the first day the DOE and Rosatom teams gathered data on the source and its possible location, and additional support centers in Moscow and the U.S. were alerted and brought into the picture.

On day 2 everyone moved to the site where data gathered the first day indicated the source should be located. The site was an abandoned dump, and for the next several hours the U.S. and Russian teams combed the area with their detectors in search of the missing low-intensity source, which had been hidden in an undisclosed location. The exercise concluded when the teams located and identified the principle source and two smaller sources.

The second day concluded, of course, with the obligatory *torzhestvennyi obed* (banquet) that consisted of shashlyk and endless vodka toasts. Given that we were still in the open air at the search site with temperatures in the low 40s, both the shashlyk and vodka were much appreciated.

It was during the *torzhestvennyi obed* that it finally got through to me that the whole purpose of my being there was exactly that: being there. As staged as it was, this was the first such U.S.-Russian joint search for a missing nuclear source that has ever taken place. DOE implements policy while State makes it. Thus, when my turn came to propose a toast (third on the U.S. side after only the admiral and undersecretary), I asked that all raise their glasses and drink to the policy of cooperation in the nuclear field that had been implemented so brilliantly that day. In fact, I really did represent the Ambassador and the U.S. Government. Even I got goosebumps at this thought.

Due to a mistake or a quirk in the scheduling, my ticket back to Moscow was not until Friday afternoon. I used the time to visit Zhenya and Vika on Thursday evening, and today I made my way to the Consulate for lunch with Allen Greenberg, Mike Flores, and Mike's wife Rebecca. This was the first time I set foot in the Consulate since I was on my IREX grant in 1987–88, a full nineteen years ago. Although chilly, the day was bright and sunny, and I walked all the way from the Consulate to the Moscow Station. For once the Foreign Service had given me a *gift day* at the end of an interesting and non-exhausting week. I enjoyed every moment.

Monday, October 30, 2006 —"I'm Dreaming of a White Halloween, Just Like the Ones I Never Knew." Yes, folks, it's a White Halloween in Moscow. Even I was surprised to wake this morning to find that 2-4 inches of snow had fallen during the night. With temperatures in the 20s, Moscow remained white through the day. Last year I do not recall snow until sometime in November.

Last week was so busy and overfilled that by Thursday night I had worked a full fifty-six hours. I called in sick on Friday, not fully sure myself if I was sick or just exhausted beyond the limit. The main event of the week was a meeting of the G8 Non-Proliferation Directors' Group. DAS Andrew Semmel and his two assistants came from Washington, and I was the control officer. That took up most of Mon-Wed with long hours that included the meeting itself and a long dinner with the Japanese delegation with yours truly invited along as notetaker.

Sunday, November 12, 2006—Hurrah, we have a Democratic Congress, and Rumsfeld has resigned as Secretary of Defense! I got up at 4:30 a.m. on Wednesday morning, cooked myself a full American breakfast, and settled in to watch the election returns roll in. For the first time in a dozen years, I had something to celebrate. When I got to the embassy, I could tell that many others were quietly celebrating as well. Perhaps now some sanity will start to return to U.S. foreign policy.

This has been the closest to an easy week that I am likely to have for quite some time. With National Unity Day on Monday and U.S. Veterans' Day on Friday, it was only a 3-day week for us embassy types. I would rather have those days around Christmas and New Year's, but I will take whatever off-time this organization can give me. The three workdays were as over-full as ever. "Hell week" is about to start with not one but two delegations coming to down with me as control officer for both. The first group started arriving yesterday for Monday-Tuesday talks on a *123 Agreement* for U.S.-Russian cooperation in the civilian nuclear sector. The second group will arrive on Wednesday for the Thursday-Friday meeting of the Global Partnership Working Group (GPWG), another G8 initiative. I have been phoning and emailing over the weekend with both groups. Even though it is going to be fascinating to participate in both events, I am doing my best not to think how many hours I will be working between now and Friday night.

But this weekend has been relaxing. Today I have been cooking in preparation for Thanksgiving. It is snowing again, and it is pleasant to look out the window at a white Moscow as Thanksgiving smells fill my apartment.

Sunday, November 19, 2006—Matthew turns eighteen today. Could I have imagined, the day he was born, that this day would come so soon? On that warm November day in 1988, eighteen years seemed an enormous length of time. Diapers and money seemed nearly insurmountable obstacles, and in my head the day Matthew would turn eighteen was a point on a curve that was asymptotically approaching the retirement axis. Now eighteen years feels as though they have passed with impossible speed at the same time that retirement continues to feel impossibly distant even though I know it is closer than I think.

As I expected, it was a long, grueling, but fascinating week. In answer to my own question from a week ago, I managed to put in a day and a half of overtime in a five-day week. It was truly impressive to watch Dick Stratford lead the U.S. delegation negotiating the *123 Agreement*, and it was equally impressive to watch Nikolay Spasskiy, his Russian counterpart from Rosatom. This was just their second negotiating round (the first had been in D.C. a month ago), but after two days of talks and a working dinner, they had agreed on almost every point. As he left, Dick Stratford said that in all his years, never had he been so close to concluding a *123 Agreement* after only two rounds of talks.

The GPWG was only slightly less interesting. This initiative, first announced at the Kananaskis G-8 Summit in 2002, is now in its fourth year. Through it the G-8 and other partner countries contribute to chemical weapons destruction, nuclear submarine dismantlement, and non-proliferation efforts in Russia and other countries of the former Soviet Union.

My role in both the *123* talks and the GPWG was that of master of logistics and notetaker. By week's end I had sent both groups safely on their way back to the U.S. and had written and dispatched the reporting cables for both events. Together with Alexey I also somehow managed to complete the draft of our analytical cable on "Kiriyenko's First Year at Rosatom." Finally, on Friday I unexpectedly found myself having to deliver talking points and a non-paper (yes, that's what it's called!) to the MFA asking for Russian government support on several issues to be voted on at next week's meeting of the IAEA.

When I finally left on Friday evening, I had scarcely an ounce of mental energy left. I hardly paused as I walked through *Thai Night* in the embassy's cafeteria area, where I ran into Masha and her artist friend Lyusya Morozova who was displaying a number portraits, including the one she had painted of me and Tamara last summer. I had not eaten all day. When I got home, I threw a frozen pizza in the oven, put *One Flew Over the Cuckoo's Nest* in the computer, and can hardly remember how I got myself into bed. I do remember how I woke up around 4:00 a.m., however, with my stomach in knots. I paced the floor, read a book, but only got back to a fitful sleep around 7:00 a.m. It was as though I had managed to hold myself together through the week by working flat out and *acting on instinct* to hit back all the balls that were flying at me. Now, with the pressure suddenly off, my body reacted to what I had put it through.

I recovered on Saturday by running errands, visiting the new shopping mall that has opened by *Kievskiy vokzal*, taking a long bath, watching a DVD, going to bed early, and finally sleeping ten hours. Today I have stuck my nose outside only long enough to shake out my welcome mat.

Sunday, November 26, 2006—My second annual Thanksgiving Dinner in Moscow came off beautifully. I baked my turkey on Thursday (i.e., Thanksgiving Day) and made final preparations. For once in my life, I had begun preparing so far in advance that I was able to go to bed early Friday evening and sleep nine hours. All that was left for me to do on Saturday was to make the gravy and then manage to get and keep everything warm. Inna came over early to help with any last-minute setup disasters, and I think she was shocked to find that I had been lying on the couch reading a book!

Overall, twenty-one people came through my door between 4:00 and 10:00 p.m. Although I have done a number of dinner parties over the past year, this was my first and perhaps only attempt to have an open house for which I had cast my net widely. I feared I had invited too many people and that the food would disappear in minutes, but in the end I had so much food left that I might not have to cook another thing between now and the time I fly home on December 16. My guests included a pretty equal mix of Americans, Russians, and one Austrian. Almost all of my good Russian friends came. At the last minute I had found the piece of paper on which I had written the phone number of the Russian family that took me in last July when my bicycle route to Borodino brought me to a military base. The father and one of his sons were among my guests. Also present was my Austrian neighbor from upstairs. We first met two weeks ago at 9:00 a.m. on a Sunday morning when I pounded on his door. The sound of his electric drill that morning had launched me out of bed.

Celebrating Thanksgiving overseas is special. More so even than July Fourth, Thanksgiving is a holiday that symbolizes the things that are good about America in a way that non-Americans can understand and appreciate. Russian faces begin to light up as one explains to them about the Pilgrims, Lincoln and the Civil War, and the need to give thanks for the things we have. If there ever was an American holiday that could become international without any political overtones, it is Thanksgiving.

Saturday, January 20, 2007—I have a bad cold (temperature of 101°F), and some fireworks continue at home in the U.S. On the other hand, a light snow is falling, and Moscow is finally turning white. Sitting inside my apartment and looking out on the winter scene is not a bad place to be. Let it snow!

Work in the EST office continues to be light compared with the fall, but that is likely to change the week after next when Undersecretary Bob Joseph comes to town. A fun change this past week was my participation in a Fulbright Scholarship selection panel on Friday morning. My only prior experience with such an event was on the other side of the table when I interviewed for my IREX grant back in 1986. I enjoyed talking with Russian scholars about their hopes for research programs they would like to undertake in the U.S.

As I sat in those Fulbright interviews on Friday, I became increasingly aware that I was catching something. By mid-afternoon I was feeling quite miserable. I had a ticket to go see Пролетая над гнездом кукушки (a Russian production of *One Flew Over the Cuckoo's Nest*) at the Lenkom Theater on Friday evening. Feeling the way I did, I tried to find someone who would buy or even take my ticket from me, but there were no takers. Unlike most other dramatic theaters in Moscow, the Lenkom charges real prices. I had paid 1,400 rubles (about $53) for my ticket, and at that price I decided to force myself to go no matter how awful I was feeling. I was happy I did. The production was excellent, and it was fascinating to see a Russian interpretation of an American classic. (When McMurphy bribes the ward guard to let in his prostitute friends, he turns to the audience and comments, "Corruption will destroy the State.") Today, however, I am paying the price for going out when I should have been eating chicken soup.

The fireworks going on at home are one of the greatest inducements I have to stay in the State Department and move on to Tashkent when my Moscow time is over. Despite several attempts, I have never been able to bring myself to go through a divorce. I'm like a character from a Graham Greene story whose Catholic roots are just deep enough to lead to an emotional and spiritual short circuit whenever the question of divorce enters the picture. For over twenty years I have realized that Helena and I are and will continue to drive each other crazy no matter how much we care for each other and for Matthew, but I have not been able to carry through on two abortive attempts to separate. My career in the Foreign Service has, in effect, given me this separation without legal proceedings of any kind. Helena is in Maryland and will never come to Moscow. When I sit in my apartment on a Saturday afternoon and look at the falling snow, I am surrounded by peace and calm.

Saturday, January 27, 2007—Life in the Foreign Service fast lane has returned to normal. A delegation led by U/S Bob Joseph began to arrive on Thursday. I had dinner with Dick Stratford, last here for *123* negotiations in November, on Thursday evening. On Friday we shifted to high gear as I accompanied Stratford, Assistant Secretary John Rood, and a cast of others to a meeting with Oleg Rozhkov and an equally large Russian cast in the Office of Security and Disarmament at the MFA. The meeting began at 2:30 p.m. It ended at 6:15. Both DOE's Michele Dash and I took notes, and it was hard to keep up through those four hours as the two sides discussed a new initiative to make nuclear technology available to countries that make long-term commitments not to pursue the full nuclear fuel cycle.

When the meeting was over, I asked Jim Timbie, U/S Joseph's senior adviser, what kind of reporting cable he wanted. His response was sufficient to send me straight back to the embassy, where I finished a draft somewhere after 11:00 p.m. Michele had to accompany DOE's Assistant Secretary Will Tobey, and so it was that I was on my own. I probably could have gotten away waiting until today, but I knew I wouldn't sleep with this cable on my mind. Michele will have the easier job of correcting my mistakes and filling gaps.

On Monday the show begins again as U/S Joseph and Deputy Foreign Minister Sergey Kislyak sit down for their *Strategic Dialog*. Fortunately for me, I am responsible for taking notes only during the first hour, much of which is likely to be devoted to a recap of Friday's meeting. Thank goodness.

Although I felt not too awful last Saturday, on Sunday my cold took a turn for the worse, and I decided to stay home on Monday. Given the extra hours I put in on Friday, I'm glad I did.

I learned that I am enrolled in Uzbek language training starting the day after Labor Day. Based on that, I now expect that I will be leaving Moscow on or about August 4. Time is moving quickly.

Tuesday, February 6, 2007—I'm sitting in Sheremetyevo 1 with over two hours to wait before my flight to St. Petersburg. I'm so early that I can't even check in yet. If I had my druthers, I would be going by train, but perhaps I should give thanks for the few hours' enforced inactivity on a Tuesday. The irony of flying to St. Petersburg is that between travel to and from airports and all the waiting at airports, flying takes as long as taking the train—on the order of 5-6 hours. The fast train, however, doesn't leave until 4:30 p.m., whereas going by plane, I should be in my hotel by 6:00 p.m. or so. That isn't such a bad deal.

I am going to St. Petersburg to sit in on public hearings for new reactors that are to be built at the Leningrad (yes, it's still called that) Nuclear Power Plant. I will also visit a facility that reprocesses nuclear waste. That will all be on Wednesday. On Thursday I will visit Bellona, one of the grass-roots *green* organizations, before getting the 4:00 p.m. train back to Moscow. I will be accompanied in all this by at least two people from the Petersburg Consulate, but the bad news is that my adviser Aleksey, who set this up and knows the full history of the Leningrad plant, caught a bad case of the flu yesterday. I am traveling blind without the most knowledgeable person at my side.

Last weekend was one of my busy weekends, so busy in fact that I was hardly home at all. On Saturday I went with Inna to the Whistler exhibit at the Tretyakov, after which we had dinner at a restaurant called Propaganda and went to Rob Doughton's farewell party. (Rob was my work sponsor when I arrived in Moscow not quite a year and a half ago.) On Sunday, physicist and historian Vladimir Temnyi carried out his threat to put me on cross country skis. It was fun, but I spent a good amount of time in the snows of Bitevskiy Park rather than on them.

· · · · · · · · · · · · · · · ·

Having finally checked my one bag, I'm sitting in the passenger lounge, looking out the window at a very wintry scene. It is snowing, and the visibility doesn't look particularly good. I wonder if this flight will depart on time?

Helena finally spoke with me Sunday evening, but I think it was by mistake. I used my Russian calling card rather than the embassy's IVG line to place the call, thereby confusing the caller ID. At least Helena sounded surprised to hear my voice. Helena was businesslike but frosty. Even with an ocean between us, my stomach and mood have not exactly been in the best shape these past two weeks. Why, why, why can't we just get along or let each other go? Why can't we resolve this mutually inflicted torment one way or the other?

On Friday evening I watched *The Shipping News*, a movie that takes place mainly in Newfoundland. Given my liking for the Russian climate, I started to think that this is another possible retirement location. Checking property prices via the Internet, I see that some very nice homes can be had for $100-150K Canadian.

Thursday, February 8, 2007—Sitting on the Avrora bound for Moscow, I look out on the beauty of a winter sunset. All is white, and the sun shines brightly on the horizon. I feel I am in a scene out of Dr. Zhivago. What beauty.

Saturday, February 10, 2007—Once again I write by hand as I sit in Sheremetyevo. Only four days ago I sat in Sheremetyevo 1, waiting for my short flight to St. Petersburg. Today I sit inside Delta 31 at Sheremetyevo 2, waiting to pull back from the terminal to fly to New York and then Baltimore. I can't believe this is happening ....

I am going because Ma is in the hospital, apparently with a stroke, and Irene said, "Come home." She called yesterday just before 6:00 p.m. I did everything I could do to arrange emergency travel home before everyone disappeared from the embassy for the weekend. I slept only one or two hours. I am exhausted and numb. My departure is so rushed that only at the airport did I see that my ticket was for August 10, not February 10. I had to have it changed on the spot. I am so much in shock that I have yet to feel. I can't believe this is happening ....

Sunday, March 4, 2007—Ma is gone. After over three weeks at home, I am on my way back to Moscow. Everything around me seems unreal.

I can't yet put into words how I feel. To *exhausted and numb* from February 10, I can add *drained and stunned*. When I arrived home on February 10 and for much of the next week, I thought there had been a mistake. Despite the doctors, I thought Ma's condition was not that serious. On Valentine's Day, February 14, she was awake, alert, and in almost full control of her faculties. That evening we began to think she would be released from the hospital and would return to her apartment or the assisted living facility. I thought I would be flying back to Moscow on the weekend. The next day was a shock. Irene, Gail, Helena, Matthew, and I surrounded Ma, held her hands, and stroked her head as her breathing became ever shallower. At 6:25 p.m., Ma took her last breath.

Funeral arrangements, resurrection mass, the cemetery, burial, packing Ma's possessions and moving them to a storage facility, closing the door of Ma and Dad's home for the last time—these are the heart-wrenching events that dominated my life these past two weeks.

I do not plan to return to the embassy for a full week. I need the time simply to stop and collect myself. What a difficult time this has been.

Saturday, March 10, 2007—I don't know if this week was such a good idea after all. I am very down and have little energy for anything. Only through long walks and hot baths have I kept my spirits from hitting rock bottom. I haven't wanted to talk with anyone. With the exception of Thursday, the weather has been warm (40s F) and as gray as my mood. Except for a few days in January and early February, winter has somehow missed Moscow this year. It is colder in D.C. than it is here.

Other than the walks and baths, my main activity has been to write letters to Ma's friends and relatives. I also need to get to bills and taxes, but I have not gotten there yet.

To add to the joys of my return, upon entering my apartment I discovered that the circuit breaker for the refrigerator and freezer had tripped. All my food had spoiled, and my first task was to carry everything to the dumpster. Judging from the smell and look, the electricity must have been off for most of the time I was in the U.S. Over the next two days I had to do more food shopping than I have at any time since my arrival in 2005.

I am not looking forward to my return to the embassy on Monday. I have no motivation, no interest in work.

Sunday, March 18, 2007—On Friday, a short fuse tasker to produce snake oil for the embassy's Mission Strategic Plan finally woke me out of my lethargy. I am not out of the grieving woods, but with the snake oil written, I left the office on Friday evening in a mood not as low as the one I have been in these past many weeks.

Since returning to Moscow, I have in my own strange way relived all holidays starting from Halloween onward. Somehow, after all the suffering and death, I felt I needed to feel as though I had lived through Halloween, Thanksgiving, Christmas, New Years, and even Valentine's Day. I still have the calendar for February on my wall. At some level I needed to build a bridge from the before time to the present. I re-watched *The War of the Worlds*, listened to Christmas music and watched holiday movies, and even found a French turkey in one of the Russian stores. I know this sounds strange, in its own way a sign of depression, but I felt comforted by going through a minor noting of the normality I had missed. By this weekend I felt ready to acknowledge that it's mid-March. Friday evening, I watched *The Gangs of New York* on DVD, thereby catching myself up to St. Patrick's Day.

Inna came for pancakes and sausage on Saturday morning, after which we went to the Borodino Panorama Museum a short distance up *Kutuzovskiy prospekt* from where I live. I have started a list of things I want to see and do in Moscow before I leave at the end of July. Most of these are things I have not taken time for until now because I had consigned them to the category of things I could do whenever I wanted. The Borodino Panorama, a 360-deg in-the-round painting of the 1812 battle dating from early in the twentieth century, fell in that category. Now I must recognize that my time is growing short. In fact, the time remaining is less than the time I spent in the Soviet Union for my IREX grant in 1987-88 and just over twice the time I spent in the USSR during my driving and camping trips in 1978 and 1981.

Sunday, March 25, 2007—This has been a quiet weekend, lonely in a nice way. I have eighteen weeks left in Russia, and as I walk about the city, I have a heightened awareness that my time is limited. Despite my doubts and concerns about working in the Foreign Service, the past year and a half have been a dream come true. It seems impossible that this time has gone by so quickly. When I leave, will I ever come back?

Last year I spent a small sum on framing posters and photos, but I stopped short of framing one poster that I purchased on my first trip to the Soviet Union in 1978. The poster does not have much artistic or historic merit on its own – it's just a Komsomol poster from the Brezhnev period—and it has suffered from moving with me from one CSC office to another. Finally, however, I decided that it's a historic document from my own life, and yesterday I took it to the framing shop. I will be paying nearly $100 to frame a poster that cost me 10 kopecks in 1978.

After this I spent 2-3 hours walking through the Museum of Modern Russian History, another must-do stop on my list of things to do before my Moscow time comes to an end. I can't begin to count how many times I have passed this museum on Tverskaya without going in. I may even have been in it in 1978, when it was the Museum of the Revolution. If I was there in 1978, I know the portrait of Alexander Kerenskiy and the room devoted to the 1917 February Revolution were not. Overall, the museum does a good job of presenting twentieth century Russian history, both good and bad, in an objective way. In one room there are photos of Yeltsin standing up to the attempted hard-line Communist coup in 1991 by mounting a tank in front of the Russian White House. A few steps away hang photos of the same White House blackened by tanks after Yeltsin ordered them to open fire in 1993 to put down his opponents in the Supreme Soviet.

Today I took my first bike ride since October. Looking back at my journal from last year, I see that I did not return to the road until April 24. That shows just how mild this winter has been. The snow is gone, and temperatures are now firmly in the 40s. My ride was a local one, about 18-19 miles along the Moscow River embankment and up and around Moscow State University, but it felt very good to be in the saddle again.

Now, finally, I must get to work on taxes. One can leave the U.S. and live overseas, but the IRS is never far behind.

Monday, April 2, 2007—I am back to living the Moscow work and personal life to the hilt. The past week has been both exhausting and exciting.

The *Uranium Suspension Agreement* took over my life. The background here is that in the early 1990s, Russia flooded the U.S. market with cheap uranium, as a consequence of which Russia was barred from the U.S. market through anti-dumping legislation. Shortly thereafter an agreement was reached to dismantle Soviet warheads and down blend their highly enriched uranium (HEU) to lowly enriched uranium (LEU) for use in U.S. civilian nuclear power plants. This required suspending the anti-dumping legislation under what became known as the *Uranium Suspension Agreement*. The HEU-LEU agreement ends in 2013, and Russia wants a transition period leading to open access to the U.S. market by 2020. A team came to Moscow last September for a first round of negotiations, and other meetings have been held in Washington and Vienna since then. Secretary of Commerce Gutierrez is coming to Moscow this week, arriving today for that matter, and it was decided that this would be a good time for Gutierrez and Rosatom Director Sergey Kiriyenko to sign an amendment to the *Suspension Agreement* that would lay the groundwork for the transition period.

A signing ceremony in Moscow is a wonderful idea, but it does require one key element: an agreement. To hammer this out, Deputy Assistant Secretary of Commerce Joseph Spetrini and his team arrived last Wednesday. They had meetings at Rosatom on Thursday and Friday in which it turned out that agreement is not as close as everyone had believed. In fact, so much is up in the air that it is not at all clear an agreement can be signed this week. The next two days will tell.

Prior to the arrival of Spetrini et al., I served as notetaker for Ambassador Burns' meeting with Kiriyenko. It was fascinating to watch Kiriyenko speak in Russian, and the Ambassador reply in English.

On Sunday I went with our intern Dylan, Inna, and Inna's son Nikita for a whole day hike at the Borodino Battlefield. Yes, I finally got to see Borodino after failing to see it last July when I accidentally ended up on my bicycle at a military base. We left Moscow by electrichka at 9:30 a.m., and we did not arrive back in Moscow until 10:00 p.m. We hiked a good 15+ miles. Nikita was our personal guide the whole way. He has been to Borodino several times and knows his 1812 history well.

Sunday, April 8, 2007—Suspension talks failed to give an agreement that could be signed by Gutierrez. The Russian side would not back down from their position that the agreement should cover not just separative work units but all enriched uranium products and even natural uranium. Such an expanded agreement would provoke strong opposition from mining companies and labor in the U.S., enough possibly to keep the agreement from coming into force. (Ironically, most U.S. uranium mines are owned by a Canadian company.) The two sides will continue to talk and there will be an agreement in a few months, but it did not happen in Moscow.

I was so worn out by the end of the week that instead of getting a good night's sleep on Friday, I had the opposite experience of a long night of insomnia and a churning stomach. I wish that did not happen with me, but that is how I react sometimes to days and weeks of overwork. I had been invited to visit Aleksey Lepko and his family at Zvezdny gorodok, and I probably should have called and canceled. Instead, I looked at the calendar, decided that time is precious, and went to Yaroslavskiy vokzal and got on the electrichka. This was the first time I had seen Aleksey, Lena, Dima, and Katya since I had them over for dinner last July. It was a pleasant afternoon, but at 6:00 p.m. I was almost asleep on my feet. I had to excuse myself and make an early departure. I got home, took a bath, crashed to bed, and slept ten hours.

Today is Easter Sunday in both the Orthodox and Roman Catholic churches, but I'm afraid it's not much of a holiday for me. I have so much paperwork piled up at home that I will be working hard all day. I feel as though I am in one of those dreams in which I am running through water. No matter how hard I try to run, I can't get anywhere. The paperwork continues to mount up. Most of the blame for my failure to make progress lies squarely with me. I am trying to be out and about as much as I can, and that means I am not at home to take care of chores and paperwork. Thus, it is that for me Easter Sunday is a day of work this year.

I fear that Helena and I are positioning ourselves as two locomotives heading for each other on a single track and picking up speed. This week Helena announced that she would not permit Matthew's college fund to be used to pay for a dormitory next fall. I am beginning to understand that I will not be returning to a happy home in August. Tashkent as a follow-on posting is starting to look like not such a bad fate after all.

Wednesday, April 18, 2007—I have been so busy that I did not have time to write even over the weekend.

The arrival of Ambassador Michael Guhin and his Pu disposition team dominated last week. The plutonium disposition talks took place only on Thursday and Friday, but the preparation and the talks themselves seemed endless. Russia and the U.S. agreed to destroy thirty-four tons of weapons grade plutonium way back in 2001, but for various reasons, neither side has made much progress. Some things have happened recently, however, that bode well for moving beyond words to action. That's why Amb. Guhin was here, and that's why I did not leave the embassy until 10:30 p.m. on Thursday night and 8:30 p.m. on Friday. Last week's talks were just the beginning. I expect another round of Pu talks sometime in early or mid-May.

On Friday evening I rushed as fast as I could to Leningradskiy vokzal, but I was still a few minutes late to meet the Avrora from St. Petersburg. I found Vika standing on the platform with Slava and Marina. Vika stayed with me Friday night, and the next day we went to Slava's. I left Vika there in the late afternoon and made my way home to get ready for my next event, a Sunday dinner with David Wilson from the Museum of Jurassic Technology.

David contacted me last summer about his interest in making a documentary film about the 1936–37 purges of Soviet astronomers. We corresponded briefly, and then I fell out of touch because of all the events taking place in my own life. I heard from David again about two weeks ago and was surprised to find that he and his two assistants were already filming at Pulkovo. From there they were headed to Tashkent to film at the Tashkent Astronomical Observatory as I had suggested last year. They were passing through Moscow on Sunday on their way home, and thus I suggested they come to my apartment for dinner.

This was my first dinner party since Thanksgiving. The main course was just black beans and rice, but the conversation is what made the afternoon. I had invited Alina Eremeeva and Elena Mirskaya, and thus the conversation centered around Soviet astronomy and science in the 1930s. I'm afraid we got into the subject so deeply that I finally wore out Inna's patience. Inna left around 7:00 p.m., and the rest of my guests didn't leave until after 9:00 p.m. It was a wonderful evening.

Monday and Tuesday of this week were dominated by the visit of Assistant Secretary John Rood. I spent two and half hours as one of two notetakers during his Tuesday meeting with Russian Deputy Foreign Minister Sergey Kislyak. I learned more about missile defense during those two and a half hours than I had during my entire time in the EST office.

So is it any wonder that I am exhausted on Wednesday evening? The five and a half weeks since I returned to work have been grueling. I have lost track of my overtime hours, but they must add up to several days. Yesterday I put in a request to take off Monday, April 30, so that I will have a four-day weekend when I combine the day off with the May 1 holiday.

I feel my time in Moscow is slipping through my fingers no matter how hard I try to slow it down. I am reminded of the movie *Eternal Sunshine of the Spotless Mind* in which the protagonist watches helplessly as his memories, his reality disappear ....

Monday, April 23, 2007—Boris Nikolayevich Yeltsin is dead. A man of many faults, he was a great man for two reasons. In 1991, he stood up to the attempted hard-line Communist coup by standing on a tank in front of the Russian White House. Without his action, the coup likely would have succeeded. Then, in 2000, he voluntarily gave up power, the first leader in

Russian history to leave office alive and not under duress. For these two actions, in particular the second, he deserves to be remembered well by the people of Russia and the world. A great man has passed.

Saturday, April 28, 2007—It has been another long, exhausting, but in its way exciting week. Former Presidents Bush and Clinton came to Moscow to attend the Yeltsin funeral. I was pulled in as site officer for Christ the Saviour Cathedral and Novodevichy Cemetery.

What does a site officer do? In my case it meant a long Tuesday evening trying—and succeeding—in finding the right person within the external relations office of the Moscow Patriarchate who could give me precise information on how the funeral service would proceed and what our ex-presidents should expect.

Why would such precise information be needed? Well, think of this: the last Russian head of state to have a funeral service in an Orthodox cathedral was for Alexander III. That was in 1894, 113 years ago! Moreover, American heads of state are used to funerals, but not to Orthodox funerals. At 10:30 p.m. on Tuesday I was writing a *scene setter* that was given to the presidential teams when they landed late Wednesday morning. Even then it was uncertain whether VIP guests should expect to pay their last respects (i.e., approach the coffin and silently bow) before or after the church service. My contact in the Moscow Patriarchate told me this would be decided only on the morning of the funeral. I had to stay on my cell phone early Wednesday afternoon to learn the final decision (it was "before") and relay the information on to Spaso House so it could be passed on to the Presidents as they were getting into their limousine to go to the cathedral.

At another point in the run-up to the funeral, I found myself pulled into a Russian language conference call with the Protocol Office at the MFA to learn and pass on the details of when the Presidents should arrive at the Cathedral, how they would be met, and how they would be conducted to the cemetery afterward. I still grimace over my linguistic inadequacies, but I must accept the fact that it is now common knowledge at the embassy that I am one of a select few who can be trusted with conducting a telephone conversation in Russian when there is important information to be passed.

The funeral itself was anticlimactic in that my colleague David Paradise and I simply stood in front of the cathedral, waiting to call the overall control officer with the news that "they're coming out, and the motorcade is ready to move." That was it. As mundane as that sounds, we were overcome by the feeling that we were witnessing an important moment: for the first time in its history, Russia was saying goodbye to a popularly elected president who voluntarily turned over the reins of power.

On Friday the cellist and conductor Mstislav Rostropovich passed away. In 1991, he appeared side by side with Yeltsin in defiance of those who would turn back history. Now he will be buried side by side with Yeltsin at Novodevichy.

The feeling that an age, if not passing, at least is entering a new phase extended to my personal life. I have been back at work for seven full, long, hard weeks since returning in early March. That accounts for one third of the time until I leave Moscow for good, exactly three months from today. Next Tuesday is May 1, and I am taking off Monday so as to have a four-day weekend. From this point on, my focus will be changing towards preparing to leave.

I purposely made no plans for this long weekend. I need a rest. Last night I went out to see a good performance of *Much Ado about Nothing* at the Theater on Malaya Bronnaya, but that's as adventurous as I plan to get. I have no dinner parties to host or to attend. This is a weekend to recharge.

With the end of this past week, I mark my third anniversary in the Foreign Service. If, three years ago today, I had been granted a glimpse of my life in the Foreign Service, what would I have done? I venture I would have run for the proverbial hills and then signed on for another fifteen years at CSC.

My opinions of Foreign Service life have not changed much since my first jolting introduction to work in EUR/RUS (the *Russia Desk*) in 2004. For someone with a technical background, the culture shock is intense. With its large bureaucracy and constantly changing, *I need it yesterday* deadlines, work in the Foreign Service is a never-ending ride on a rodeo bronco. One never knows what the next day or even the next hour will bring. Praise lavished for work done in support of one or another important goal is forgotten within days or upon receipt of the next *action cable* from Washington. The hours are long and grueling, one is never in control of one's fate, and it is hard to sleep at night as one's mind replays the previous and coming days to see if something important has fallen between the cracks.

If I had known three years ago what I know today, I never would have joined the Foreign Service. For that reason, I am thankful I was not given the gift of foresight. I have learned more about myself these three years than I could have in my entire life had I remained at CSC. Most importantly, I have learned that I can cope with constant change. After twenty-five years of doing more or less that same thing, I have now had three radically different jobs in three years. I now know that even if my preference is to lie in a hammock and contemplate the clouds, I have in me whatever it takes to handle the at present unknown crisis that is going to land squarely on my desk tomorrow. In the Foreign Service I have tested my limits and found that I am capable of more than I ever imagined.

Wednesday, May 23, 2007—It has been three weeks since my last entry. My time in Russia is fast coming to a close even as I try to hold on. The days of keeping an even semi-regular journal are behind me as the walls close in, time and space compress.

I am sitting in a train at the Kharkiv station, waiting to pull out for my overnight journey back to Moscow. This is the first time I have been in Ukraine since 1981, my first time ever in Kharkiv other than for an evening in a campground on the edge of town when I passed by on my first trip to the Soviet Union in 1978.

I arrived last Sunday. I came to participate in a conference celebrating the 110th anniversary of Otto Ludvigovich Struve, one of the leading American astrophysicists of the twentieth century who was born and educated in Kharkiv. An officer in Anton Denikin's Volunteer Army during the Civil War, he made his way to the U.S. via a refugee camp in Turkey. The rest, as they say, is history as Struve went on to head first Yerkes Observatory, then McDonald Observatory, and then the National Radio Astronomy Observatory.

Throughout the years of Soviet power, Struve was a non-person in his hometown. The name of a White Army officer could only be mentioned in hushed whispers. If someone had told me in 1978 that I would one day attend a conference in his honor in Kharkiv, I would have thought that person quite mad. For the past four days I have had the constant feeling of needing to pinch myself.

The moving force behind the conference was Marat Balyshev, a local historian of astronomy who took it upon himself to restore Struve's memory in his home city. Marat first contacted me 4-5 years ago for help in his research. I helped with what I could, but it was Kevin Krisciunas (Texas A&M) who did the most. That's how Kevin and I found ourselves honorary members of the organizing committee. My good NASA buddy Rob Landis and Stanislav Juznic, a professor from the University of Oklahoma, rounded out the U.S. presence.

The conference papers were good, and I had my own small, contributed talk. The main events, however, were Marat's keynote talk, the dedication of a plaque in Struve's honor, and the opening of a museum exhibit. Throughout these days I was deeply aware that I was representing the U.S. government. Never before in my three years in the Foreign Service had I felt so honored to carry the flag.

The icing on the cake came today, when Marat opened the archives and found there what Rob Landis had been searching for at least two years: letters written in the 1840s by America's first astronomer, Ormsby Mitchel, to Wilhelm Struve, Otto's great-grandfather and founder of Pulkovo Observatory. The excitement was great as Marat handed the folder to Rob, and the scene was caught by cameras from a local TV station there to film the museum. Overall, Kevin, Marat, Rob, and I were on the local TV news several times over these past three days, and we shared a feeling of embarrassed honor as students asked to have their pictures taken with us.

It was good to see Rob again after more than a year, but it was also special being able to see Kevin. I corresponded with Kevin in the 1980s when I was doing my Russian astronomy research, but I had only actually ever seen him once before this—I believe in 1994. I wish I had seen more of him. If I had, I probably would have loosened up a long time ago!

The sun now hangs low over the rolling green Ukrainian hills. In another half hour, we cross the border back into Russia. In the morning I will be in Moscow.

My entries are likely to become ever fewer and further between, but I needed to note these exciting and important days. On Sunday, Matthew and his second cousin Meghan arrive from the U.S. For the following two weeks I will be on vacation as I try to show Matthew what it is that has attracted me to this land for so long.

Saturday, July 7, 2007—And this is it, my final journal entry from Moscow. The movers arrive a week from Thursday, and today I begin the process of getting ready to move out. There is so much to do that it's hard to comprehend how I will be ready in time.

Matthew flew back to the U.S. on Thursday. The nearly six weeks he was here were the best weeks I have ever spent in this country. Matthew was supposed to be here for only three weeks, but he extended first for two weeks and then for another week. I think he would have stayed even longer if it were not for the fact that my time here is at an end.

Matthew saw and did things in six weeks that I have not managed to do in two years. It was wonderful to have two weeks off when he first arrived and to travel with him around Moscow and St. Petersburg, but Matthew truly blossomed when I went back to work and he had to get around town on his own. He quickly figured out the metro system and started acquiring words and phrases with which to navigate. Although I introduced him to many people, he started meeting people and making friends on his own. He even ended up doing volunteer work for a group that is providing aid to Chechen refugees. He came to love Moscow at night and made many a midnight (or 3–5 a.m.!) stroll through Red Square—so in addition to experiencing a new city and culture, Matthew for the first time found his independence. After a year in college, he said it took coming to Moscow to find out what the first steps of independence that go with college life are about. By the time he left, he said he knew Moscow better than Washington and that he now wants to explore Washington the way he explored Moscow.

The apartment feels quite empty now that Matthew is gone. It will feel even more empty as I begin the serious business of packing. My final visitors will be Ron Enders and Ellen Bouton, who in fact arrived last Saturday but who are now on a tour of the Golden Ring on their tandem bicycle. They will stay with me again next weekend before heading up to St. Petersburg. After that the movers will be here to take everything away. For my final week I will live out of a departure kit that will consist of little more than a set of sheets, a towel, and something in which to heat water for instant coffee.

This brings my Moscow Diary to an end. I fly out on Saturday, July 28. I will have five weeks of home leave, two weeks of which I plan to spend traveling around Maine, Nova Scotia, and Newfoundland and another week of which I plan to spend at the PATC cabin in Little Orleans. My goal is to stay out of cell phone and Internet range as much as possible. I then report for Uzbek training at FSI the day after Labor Day.

A chapter in my life is closing; a new one is about to begin. Will I ever live in Russia again?

Goodbye, до свидания, до встречи. . . .

Related Titles from Westphalia Press

The Limits of Moderation: Jimmy Carter and the Ironies of American Liberalism

The Limits of Moderation: Jimmy Carter and the Ironies of American Liberalism is not a finished product. And yet, even in this unfinished stage, this book is a close and careful history of a short yet transformative period in American political history, when big changes were afoot.

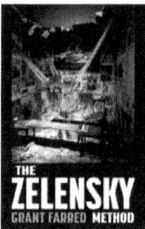

The Zelensky Method
by Grant Farred

Locating Russian's war within a global context, The Zelensky Method is unsparing in its critique of those nations, who have refused to condemn Russia's invasion and are doing everything they can to prevent economic sanctions from being imposed on the Kremlin.

Sinking into the Honey Trap: The Case of the Israeli-Palestinian Conflict
by Daniel Bar-Tal, Barbara Doron, Translator

Sinking into the Honey Trap by Daniel Bar-Tal discusses how politics led Israel to advancing the occupation, and of the deterioration of democracy and morality that accelerates the growth of an authoritarian regime with nationalism and religiosity.

Essay on The Mysteries and the True Object of The Brotherhood of Freemasons
by Jason Williams

The third edition of Essai sur les mystères discusses Freemasonry's role as a society of symbolic philosophers who cultivate their minds, practice virtues, and engage in charity, and underscores the importance of brotherhood, morality, and goodwill.

Bunker Diplomacy: An Arab-American in the U.S. Foreign Service
by Nabeel Khoury

After twenty-five years in the Foreign Service, Dr. Nabeel A. Khoury retired from the U.S. Department of State in 2013 with the rank of Minister Counselor. In his last overseas posting, Khoury served as deputy chief of mission at the U.S. embassy in Yemen (2004-2007).

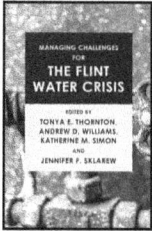

Managing Challenges for the Flint Water Crisis
Edited by Toyna E. Thornton, Andrew D. Williams, Katherine M. Simon, Jennifer F. Sklarew

This edited volume examines several public management and intergovernmental failures, with particular attention on social, political, and financial impacts. Understanding disaster meaning, even causality, is essential to the problem-solving process.

User-Centric Design
by Dr. Diane Stottlemyer

User-centric strategy can improve by using tools to manage performance using specific techniques. User-centric design is based on and centered around the users. They are an essential part of the design process and should have a say in what they want and need from the application based on behavior and performance.

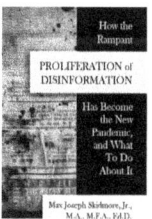

How the Rampant Proliferation of Disinformation Has Become the New Pandemic, and What To Do About It by Max Joseph Skidmore Jr.

This work examines the causes of the overwhelming tidal wave of fake news, misinformation, disinformation, and propaganda, and the increase in information illiteracy and mistrust in higher education and traditional, vetted news outlets that make fact-checking a priority.

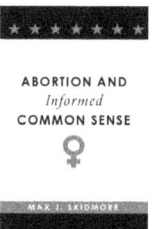

Abortion and Informed Common Sense
by Max J. Skidmore

The controversy over a woman's "right to choose," as opposed to the numerous "rights" that abortion opponents decide should be assumed to exist for "unborn children," has always struck me as incomplete. Two missing elements of the argument seems obvious, yet they remain almost completely overlooked.

The Athenian Year Primer: Attic Time-Reckoning and the Julian Calendar
by Christopher Planeaux

The ability to translate ancient Athenian calendar references into precise Julian-Gregorian dates will not only assist Ancient Historians and Classicists to date numerous historical events with much greater accuracy but also aid epigraphists in the restorations of numerous Attic inscriptions.

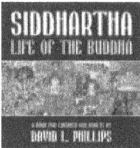

Siddhartha: Life of the Buddha
by David L. Phillips,
contributions by Venerable Sitagu Sayadaw

Siddhartha: Life of the Buddha is an illustrated story for adults and children about the Buddha's birth, enlightenment and work for social justice. It includes illustrations from Pagan, Burma which are provided by Rev. Sitagu Sayadaw.

Growing Inequality: Bridging Complex Systems, Population Health, and Health Disparities
Editors: George A. Kaplan, Ana V. Diez Roux, Carl P. Simon, and Sandro Galea

Why is America's health is poorer than the health of other wealthy countries and why health inequities persist despite our efforts? In this book, researchers report on groundbreaking insights to simulate how these determinants come together to produce levels of population health and disparities and test new solutions.

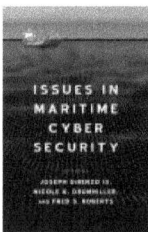

Issues in Maritime Cyber Security
Edited by Dr. Joe DiRenzo III, Dr. Nicole K. Drumhiller, and Dr. Fred S. Roberts

The complexity of making MTS safe from cyber attack is daunting and the need for all stakeholders in both government (at all levels) and private industry to be involved in cyber security is more significant than ever as the use of the MTS continues to grow.

Female Emancipation and Masonic Membership:
An Essential Collection
By Guillermo De Los Reyes Heredia

Female Emancipation and Masonic Membership: An Essential Combination is a collection of essays on Freemasonry and gender that promotes a transatlantic discussion of the study of the history of women and Freemasonry and their contribution in different countries.

Anti-Poverty Measures in America: Scientism and Other Obstacles
Editors, Max J. Skidmore and Biko Koenig

Anti-Poverty Measures in America brings together a remarkable collection of essays dealing with the inhibiting effects of scientism, an over-dependence on scientific methodology that is prevalent in the social sciences, and other obstacles to anti-poverty legislation.

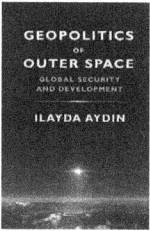

Geopolitics of Outer Space: Global Security and Development
by Ilayda Aydin

A desire for increased security and rapid development is driving nation-states to engage in an intensifying competition for the unique assets of space. This book analyses the Chinese-American space discourse from the lenses of international relations theory, history and political psychology to explore these questions.

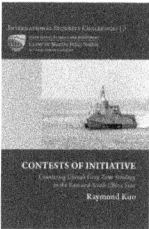

Contests of Initiative: Countering China's Gray Zone Strategy in the East and South China Seas
by Dr. Raymond Kuo

China is engaged in a widespread assertion of sovereignty in the South and East China Seas. It employs a "gray zone" strategy: using coercive but sub-conventional military power to drive off challengers and prevent escalation, while simultaneously seizing territory and asserting maritime control.

Discourse of the Inquisitive
Editors: Jaclyn Maria Fowler and Bjorn Mercer

Good communication skills are necessary for articulating learning, especially in online classrooms. It is often through writing that learners demonstrate their ability to analyze and synthesize the new concepts presented in the classroom.

westphaliapress.org

www.ingramcontent.com/pod-product-compliance
Lightning Source LLC
Chambersburg PA
CBHW071314090426

42738CB00012B/2699